A BEGINNER'S SPANISH GRAMMAR

BY

ALBERT A. SHAPIRO, Ph. D.
ASSOCIATE PROFESSOR OF SPANISH IN THE UNIVERSITY OF
NORTH CAROLINA

CHAPEL HILL, N. C.
THE UNIVERSITY OF NORTH CAROLINA PRESS
LONDON: HUMPHREY MILFORD
OXFORD UNIVERSITY PRESS

COPYRIGHT, 1924, BY
THE UNIVERSITY OF NORTH CAROLINA PRESS

PRINTED BY THE J. H. FURST COMPANY
BALTIMORE, MD.
THIS BOOK WAS DIGITALLY PRINTED.

PREFACE

In presenting a new Spanish grammar, the author feels that, as so many American students are not intimately acquainted with the ordinary facts of general or even English grammar, special emphasis and drill on syntax is the most important feature of foreign language study, whether one inclines to the direct or the grammar method. It seems important, therefore, to explain many elementary and seemingly obvious facts of language structure, avoiding, so far as possible, technical terms.

Pronunciation has been incorporated within the body of the text, to make the student feel that it is an essential feature of language work. At the beginning of the grammar, it is taken up in its broad aspects, to give the student a working acquaintance with it; at the end of the book, when the student has already a certain intimacy with the language, it is considered in some finer details. The lessons, which are short on the average so that an ordinary class can cover each assignment in an hour, are designed to be progressive. Idiomatic structure is emphasized throughout, both in special idioms and in general construction. Thus the subjunctive, which presents such difficulty to American students, is given special attention. It has a general introduction, explaining its peculiar function; and the ten lessons on it are not put in one group, but are separated, so that the student may acquire the use of the mood more at leisure and with the feeling that it works all through the language. There is an appendix with a complete summary of the subjunctive, so that the student may at all times have a bird's-eye view of the subject. Similarly, the irregular verbs are made the topics of special lessons, with exercises based directly upon them, with the idea of having the students learn their verbs by using them, exactly as they make use of nouns and pronouns, gender and number.

A high school course in Spanish might well occupy three years; but owing to the demands made on students by other work, two years are usually the maximum given. This grammar is designed to be covered in two years of high school or one year of college. It is strongly recommended that each lesson of the grammar should be done completely, the pupils being thoroughly quizzed on subject matter and vocabulary. The drill work, usually in A and AA, may be done orally, as also B; but BB should always be written out at home in exercise books and gone over in class with board work. It is suggested also that review tests should be held about every five lessons, the results to determine whether the students are prepared to go ahead or should spend further time on the work. This grammar work should be accompanied by reading as soon as the progress and ability of the class warrant, oral work to start the first week and to continue in increasing proportion.

In concluding, the author wishes to express his obligations to Miss G. E. Simonds, one time teacher of modern languages at Haverhill High School, whose sympathetic assistance has done much to make this book possible; Dr. S. E. Leavitt, head of the Spanish department at the University of North Carolina, whose careful and intelligent reading of manuscript and proof has been of very material help in clearing the text of errors; to Dr. L. R. Wilson, head of the University Press, who has encouraged and aided the author in the many difficulties arising in connection with the printing. Much of the merit of this text is due to their helpful interest.

A. A. SHAPIRO.

CHAPEL HILL, N. C., 1924.

CONTENTS

		PAGE
Lesson I	Consonants	1
II	Vowels	3
III	Accentuation; Punctuation	4
IV	Present Indicative of *hablar*	6
V	Gender; Definite Article	7
VI	Gender of Nouns	9
VII	Position of Adjectives. Possession	11
VIII	Preterite Indicative. Negation	13
IX	Number and Agreement of Nouns and Adjectives	14
X	Present and Preterite Indicative of Second Conjugation	16
XI	Present and Preterite Indicative of Third Conjugation	18
XII	Plural of Nouns and Adjectives Ending in a Consonant	19
XIII	Subject Pronouns	21
XIV	*ser*, to be	24
XV	*estar*, to be	26
XVI	The Passive	28
XVII	Possessive Adjectives	30
XVIII	Interrogative Pronouns and Adjectives	32
XIX	*un* for *una*; *el* for *la*. Apocopation	34
XX	Cardinal Numbers to 99	36
XXI	Conjunctive Pronouns	39
XXII	Cardinals (concluded). Adjective as Noun	41
XXIII	Comparison	44
XXIV	Relative Pronouns	47
XXV	Relative Pronouns (concluded)	50
XXVI	Imperfect (Past Descriptive) Tense	52
XXVII	*tener*, to have	55
XXVIII	*haber*, to have	58
XXIX	Idioms with *tener* and *haber*	61
XXX	Demonstrative Adjectives and Pronouns	63
XXXI	Demonstratives (concluded)	66
XXXII	Future (Indicative) and Conditional	68
XXXIII	Nouns and Adjectives—Gender and Position	72
XXXIV	Plural	75
XXXV	Radical-Changing Verbs (Classes I and II)	78
XXXVI	Radical-Changing Verbs (Class III, Classes II and III)	81
XXXVII	Formation of Present Participle	83
XXXVIII	Conjunctive Pronouns	86
XXXIX	Radical-Changing Verbs (continued). Summary of Indicative	90
XL	Possessive Pronouns	93
XLI	Negation. *pero, mas, sino*	96
XLII	Disjunctive Pronouns	98
XLIII	Present Subjunctive	101
XLIV	Past Subjunctive	104
XLV	Conditional Sentences	108

CONTENTS

		PAGE
XLVI	SUBJUNCTIVE (cont'd.). IMPERSONAL EXPRESSIONS	110
XLVII	DATIVE OF TAKING AWAY. PAST ANTERIOR	112
XLVIII	REFLEXIVES AND RECIPROCALS	114
XLIX	REFLEXIVES AND RECIPROCALS (concluded)	117
L	CONJUNCTIONS WITH INDICATIVE. CONJUNCTIONS WITH INFINITIVE. INFINITIVE AS NOUN	120
LI	ORTHOGRAPHIC CHANGES	123
LII	SUBJUNCTIVE OF RADICAL-CHANGING VERBS	127
LIII	SUBJUNCTIVE IN ADVERBIAL CLAUSES	130
LIV	SUBJUNCTIVE IN MAIN CLAUSES. SUBJUNCTIVE IN ADJECTIVE CLAUSES	132
LV	SUBJUNCTIVE IN NOUN CLAUSES	135
LVI	THE INFINITIVE	139
LVII	PRESENT PARTICIPLE AND INFINITIVE (summary)	142
LVIII	ORTHOGRAPHIC CHANGES (concluded)	145
LIX	INDEFINITE AND DEFINITE ARTICLES (summary)	149
LX	DATES; WEATHER	151
LXI	USES OF DEFINITE ARTICLE	155
LXII	IMPERATIVE	158
LXIII	IMPERATIVE WITH PRONOUN OBJECTS	161
LXIV	SPANISH PRESENT FOR ENGLISH PERFECT. $e = y$; $u = o$. por AND para	164
LXV	IRREGULAR PAST PARTICIPLES	168
LXVI	PRINCIPAL PARTS OF VERBS. salir, traer, valer	170
LXVII	ORDINALS	174
LXVIII	andar, estar, caer, huir, oir, reir	177
LXIX	EXCLAMATIONS AND INTERJECTIONS	182
LXX	haber, saber, ser, caber, ir	184
LXXI	VOWELS	189
LXXII	dar, ver, poder, querer	191
LXXIII	CONSONANTS	195
LXXIV	decir, venir, hacer, poner, tener	197
LXXV	STRESS AND ACCENT; DIVISION INTO SYLLABLES	202
LXXVI	antojarse, constar, placer, asir, soler, yacer, SUPERLATIVE ABSOLUTE. INTENSIVE (EMPHATIC) PREFIXES	203
LXXVII	AUGMENTATIVES AND DIMINUTIVES; FUTURE SUBJUNCTIVE	206

Appendices

A	PERSON AND NUMBER	208
B	IDIOMS	208
C	SUBJUNCTIVE (preliminary)	210
D	SUBJUNCTIVE (summary)	212
E	ORTHOGRAPHIC CHANGES	215
F	ABSTRACT AND GENERIC NOUNS	216
G	ORDINALS	217
H	IDIOMS AND TRANSLATION	217
	LIST OF IRREGULAR VERBS	220
	GENERAL VOCABULARY—SPANISH-ENGLISH	223
	GENERAL VOCABULARY—ENGLISH-SPANISH	242
	INDEX	261

A BEGINNER'S SPANISH GRAMMAR

ABBREVIATIONS

adj.	adjective	*irreg.*	irregular
adv.	adverb	*part.*	participle
art.	article	*pers.*	personal
cf.	consult, compare	*pl.*	plural
conj.	conjunction, conjunctive	*pluperf.*	pluperfect
cst.	construction	*pos.*	possessive
def.	definite	*pp.*	past participle
demonstr.	demonstrative	*prep.*	preposition
disj.	disjunctive	*pres.*	present
indecl.	indeclinable	*pro.*	pronoun
indef.	indefinite	*R-ch.*	radical-changing
int.	interrogative	*rel.*	relative
interjec.	interjection	*sent.*	sentence
intrans.	intransitive	*sing.*	singular
		subjunct.	subjunctive

LESSON I
CONSONANTS

1. The letters of the Spanish alphabet are:

a(a), b(be larga), c(ce), ch(che), d(de), e(e), f(efe), g(ge), h(hache), i(i), j(jota), k(ka), l(ele), ll(elle), m(eme), n(ene), ñ(eñe), o(o), p(pe), q(cu), r(ere), rr(erre), s(ese), t(te), u(u), v(ve corta), x(equis), y(i griega), z(zeta or zeda).

w (doble u) is found only in foreign words: **Washington**.

2. f, k, l, m, n, p, t, and x are pronounced about as they are in English. So y, if followed by a vowel.

The other consonants differ in **sound** from the corresponding English **written** consonants.[1]

3. b and v are pronounced exactly the same. The sound is a cross between that of English w(wet) and b(bet), and is produced by resting the upper lip and teeth on the lower lip.

burro, burro   vaca, cow   lavar, to wash

4. c before e or i, and z generally, have the same sound, that is, **th** in English through.

cero, zero   cilindro, cylinder
zorra, fox   azahar, orange flower
zumbar, to buzz   luz, light

5. c before a, o, u, or a consonant, or at the end of a word; and qu generally, have the same sound, that is, **k** in English kin.

cama, bed   cura, priest
con, with   frac, dress coat
occidente, occident   querer, to wish
quiero, I wish

---

[1] These indications are merely approximate, not rigorously exact from a scientific standpoint—but only as close as is consistent with a beginner's ability to grasp the essentials. The important thing for the young student is to hear the teacher pronounce the sounds associated with the letters.
A detailed description of some of the more difficult sounds is given in Lessons LXXI and LXXIII.

Note that c *with the pronunciation of English* k *is found only before* a, o, u, *or a consonant, and at the end of a word; and that* c *with the pronunciation of* th *in* through *is found only before* e *or* i.

6. **d** is usually pronounced like **th** in English **this**.

    duro, dollar   **medida**, measure   **ciudad**, city

7. **g** before **e** or **i**, and **j** generally, have the same sound, that is, a sound like a clearing of the throat, or much like that heard in gargling except that it is not prolonged.

    jaguar, jaguar   **jugar**, to play   **reloj**, watch
    conjugar, to conjugate   **jota**, iota
    general, general   **giro**, bank draft

8. **g** before **a**, **o**, or **u**; and **gu** before **e** or **i**, have the same sound, that is, **g** in English **good**.

    agosto, August   **garboso**, graceful   **gustar**, to please
    guisar, to cook   **guerra**, war

Note that g *with the pronunciation of English* good *is found only before* a, o, *or* u; *and that* g *with the throaty, gargling pronunciation, is found only before* e *or* i.

9. Compare, above, the similarity of principle governing the pronunciation of **z**, **c** on the one hand with that of **j**, **g**, on the other; of **qu**, **c** on the one hand with that of **gu**, **g**, on the other.

10. **h** is never pronounced in Spanish.

    hallar, to find (*be sure not to pronounce the* h)

11. **ll** is pronounced as **lli** in English William.

    hallar

12. **ñ** is pronounced as **ni** in English onion. The mark over the **ñ** is called the **tilde**.

    año, year

13. **r** is trilled, with a single tap of the tongue (in English, the **r** is not trilled).

    pero, but

14. rr is trilled about twice as long as single **r**.

perro, dog

15. s is pronounced as in English sit. (Never give Spanish **s** the **z** sound of English has).

A. Pronounce the consonants below:

"Grito postrero

"La pálida Nereida americana
la reina de los mares de occidente,
sacude su melena refulgente
como un rayo de sol en la sabana.

"Radiante y luchadora, la mañana
acarició su ensangrentada frente,
y su selva escuchó cual mar rugiente
el tropel de la carga soberana.

"Hoy, si el que ayer se declaraba hermano
nos quiere avasallar, ¡guerra al tirano!
brille el acero en nuestro puño fuerte

"y resuenen de nuevo los clarines
llamando a los heroicos paladines
al último combate de la muerte."

LESSON II
VOWELS

Review Lesson I.

Only the accented vowels need be considered here, as those unaccented are the same, in general, but for the difference produced by stress (cf. Eng. **the** alone and in the phrase **the man**).

1. **a** has the sound of English **a** in harm.

vaca[1]   papel, paper

2. **e** has the sound of English **e** in there.

cero   ver, to see

---

[1] Meanings already given are not repeated.

3. **i** has the sound of English i in machine.

    giro   cilindro

4. **o** has the sound of English o in bought.

    zorra   loro, parrot   dos, two

5. **u** has the sound of English oo in hoof.

    burro   ninguno, none

(The Spanish sound is somewhere between **oo** in English **hoof** and **boot**.)

6. In diphthongs or triphthongs (two or three vowels coming together), pronounce each vowel as it is pronounced when standing alone, but run the two (or three) together. **y** at the end of a word takes the place of **i**.

hay, there is	ley, law	hoy, today	aun, even
tibio, warm	cuando, when	miedo, fear	buey, ox
Cousiño, Cousiño (*proper name*)		agua, water	

A. Pronounce the following words, putting the stress on the next to the last syllable.

cuando agua tibio toro burro ojo hinchado medida mejilla González cuidado azahares zorra chubasco centro

B. Pronounce the following words, putting the stress on the last syllable.

llorar ciudad frac general querer temblar huracán alemán papel vaivén sillón descubridor

C. Pronounce the passage at the end of Lesson I.

LESSON III

ACCENTUATION; PUNCTUATION

Review Lessons I and II.

1. There is only one written accent in Spanish, the acute, as in **sillón**.

2. A word with an accent mark is always stressed on

the syllable with that mark. The accent mark indicates usually that the word is irregular in stress.

   atlético, athletic   González   vaivén, fluctuation   orín, rust

An **i** with an accent mark is not dotted: í.

3. Where no accent mark is written, the word is regular, that is, it is stressed according to one of the two rules below.

(a) A word ending in a consonant, except **n** or **s**, stresses the **last** syllable.

   general   azul, blue   jugar, to play   tomar, to take

(b) A word ending in either consonant **n** or **s**, or in any vowel, stresses the **next to the last** syllable.

   quieren   quieres   cama

4. In general, two vowels coming together are pronounced as a diphthong; that is, they count as a single syllable.

   hay, there is   miedo, fear   tibio, warm   muy, very

However, if an accent is written over either **i** or **u**, the two vowels are pronounced separately, forming two syllables.

   aún (a ún), yet   acentúo (acentú o), I stress

5. Punctuation marks are the same in Spanish as in English, except at the beginning of an exclamation or question, where another exclamation point or question mark, **inverted,** is placed.

   ¡ajá! Aha!   ¿Quién? Who?

Paragraphs in quotation are not enclosed in quotation marks, but are begun with a dash. But a quotation within a quotation is enclosed in quotation marks.

   Y así dijo: And thus he said:
   — Señoras y señores . . . "Ladies and Gentlemen . . ."

6. Capitals are used as in English, with the following exceptions:

(a) Adjectives of nationality begin with a small letter.

inglés, English

(b) **yo, I,** has a small letter; but **Vd.**, the abbreviation for **usted,** *you,* has a capital.

A. Read aloud the passage in I, A, paying attention to pronunciation of consonants and vowels, and noting the accent marks.

LESSON IV
PRESENT INDICATIVE OF hablar

Study Appendix A.

1. **hablar,** to speak (stem **habl-**)

Singular	Plural
hablo, I speak	hablamos, we speak
hablas, you speak	habláis, you speak
habla, he, she, it speaks	hablan, they speak

2. Note that (a) no pronouns need be used in Spanish; (b) the third person singular may mean **he, she, it,** the context usually determining which is meant; (c) the second persons singular and plural are different in Spanish.

3. In English, there are three forms for the present of a verb, as **I speak, I am speaking, I do speak.** In Spanish, there is usually one form (given above), which is equivalent to any of the three English forms according to the sense: **hablo,** *I speak, am speaking, do speak;* **hablas,** *you speak, are speaking, do speak;* etc.

VOCABULARY [1]

América, America
dólar, dollar
el, the
en, in, on
hablar, to speak
hallar, to find

hoy, today
por, for
sombrero, hat
trabajar, to work
pagar, to pay, to pay for

---

[1] Words in sections on grammar should be learned as well as those in formal vocabularies.

A. 1. Pagamos por el sombrero. 2. Pagamos el dólar.
3. Trabajáis en América. 4. Trabajo. 5. Halla el dólar.
6. Trabajan en América. 7. Habla hoy. 8. Pagan.
9. Hallo el dólar. 10. Pago el dólar hoy.

B. 1. I work. 2. I do work. 3. They work in America.
4. I am paying for the hat. 5. We are speaking today.
6. Today we speak. 7. They are paying for the hat.
8. She pays for the hat. 9. You work. 10. You do work
(*singular*). 11. You are working (*plural*). 12. They are
working in America.

LESSON V

1. **Gender.** In Spanish, there are only two genders, masculine and feminine. Objects which in English are masculine or feminine are usually the same in Spanish; but objects which in English are common or neuter, are either masculine or feminine in Spanish.

    hombre, man (*masculine*)   **mujer,** woman (*feminine*)
    casa, house (*feminine—but neuter in English*)
    niño, child (*masculine—but common in English*)

In Spanish, therefore, the gender of nouns is largely a matter of grammar.

2. In English, adjectives have no gender; thus, the definite article **the** may be used with a noun of any gender; **the man, the woman, the house, the child.** In Spanish, however, the adjectives, like the nouns, have gender, taking the gender of the noun they modify.

If the masculine form of an adjective ends in **-o**, the feminine ends in **-a**.

    pequeño, small (*masculine*)   **pequeña,** small (*feminine*)
    pequeño niño, small child   **pequeña casa,** small house

Other adjectives have but one form for both genders.

    fácil, easy (*masculine and feminine*)

SPANISH GRAMMAR

3. Definite Article. The definite article in Spanish is **el,** masculine singular; **la,** feminine singular.

el verbo, the verb **la mujer,** the woman

The preposition **a,** *to,* and **el** contract to **al.**
The preposition **de,** *of,* and **el** contract to **del.**
There are no other written contractions in Spanish.

4. Always repeat an article or a preposition in Spanish referring to different objects.

el libro y la tiza, the book and chalk

5. Interrogation. A verb is made interrogative by putting the subject **after** the verb. If the subject is not expressed, the tone of voice indicates the question.

¿Trabaja el hombre? Is the man working?
¿Trabaja? Is he working?

VOCABULARY

alumno, -a, pupil, student	para, for,
amigo, -a, friend	la pizarra, slate
con, with	la pluma, pen
el hombre, man [1]	sin, without
el lápiz, pencil	la tiza, chalk
la mujer, woman	y, and

A. 1. con la pizarra 2. para el hombre 3. de la mujer 4. al hombre 5. del libro 6. con la pluma 7. el hombre y la mujer 8. el amigo del alumno 9. sin tiza 10. la pluma del hombre 11. el papel y el lápiz del hombre

AA. 1. the woman 2. a pencil 3. with chalk 4. without the slate 5. the friend of the pupil 6. for the pupil 7. the pencil and (the)[2] pen of the student 8. to the friend of the pupil 9. without paper 10. with the paper of the student 11. Is the man working? 12. Does the man work? 13. Is he working?

B. 1. Trabajo con el lápiz del alumno. 2. El amigo del hombre habla. 3. ¿Hallan el sombrero del alumno? 4. Trabajamos en América. 5. Hoy hablamos con el alumno.

---
[1] The definite article is put before nouns in the vocabularies to indicate gender.
[2] ( ) means supply or substitute the expression so enclosed;
[ ] means omit the expression so enclosed.

6. El alumno halla el sombrero. 7. El alumno conjuga el verbo. 8. La mujer lava el sombrero. 9. Toman lápiz y papel y estudian. 10. Tomo el lápiz del amigo del hombre. 11. Toma el libro y la pluma del alumno. 12. ¿Toma el libro del alumno?

BB. 1. We wash the pen. 2. They conjugate the verb "to take." 3. They are speaking with the pupil. 4. We are speaking with the friend of the student. 5. The woman takes the hat. 6. They are working with chalk. 7. Is the student working with chalk? 8. I am taking the pencil. 9. Are you taking the pen and (the) pencil? 10. They are speaking with the friend of the student. 11. Are they speaking with the friend of the student?

LESSON VI
GENDER OF NOUNS

Review Lesson V.

1. Nouns ending in unstressed -o are regularly masculine.

el piano, piano **el tío**, uncle **el hermano**, brother
el libro, book **el verbo**, verb **el trabajo**, work

2. Nouns ending in unstressed -a are regularly feminine.

la tía, aunt **la hermana**, sister

3. If, however, a noun ends in a consonant, or in a vowel other than -o or -a, its gender must be learned at the same time as its meaning.

el papel, paper **el hombre**, man **la madre**, mother

But nouns ending in **-ión**, **-ad**, or **-ud** are always feminine.

la virtud, virtue

4. Nouns ending in -o in the masculine change the -o to -a to form a corresponding feminine.

el tío, uncle **la tía**, aunt

VOCABULARY

blanco, -a, white
es, (he, she, it) is
fácil, easy
grande, large
el hermano, brother; la hermana, sister
la lección, lesson
la madre, mother
el mozo, boy, waiter; la moza, girl
negro, -a, black
el niño, boy, child; la niña, girl, child
el padre, father
el piano, piano
el primo, cousin; la prima, cousin (*fem.*)
la salud, health
la tinta, ink
el tío, uncle; la tía, aunt
tocar, to play (*an instrument*)
el trabajo, work
la verdad, truth
la virtud, virtue

A. *Put the correct form of the definite article before the following words, and translate:*

1. amigo 2. hombre 3. lápiz 4. tío 5. tiza 6. lápiz 7. lápiz y papel 8. tía y hermana 9. hermano y tía 10. salud y virtud 11. lección y trabajo 12. padre y madre 13. verbo y lección 14. tía 15. primo 16. prima

AA. *Give the Spanish word for each of the following, prefixing the correct form of the definite article:*

1. brother 2. uncle 3. health 4. pupil (*feminine*) and slate 5. cousin (*feminine*) and uncle 6. woman with book 7. brother with sister 8. brother and sister 9. slate without chalk 10. white (*masculine*), black (*masculine*). 11. friend (*masculine*) 12. pupil (*masculine*) 13. pencil and paper

B. 1. El verbo es fácil. 2. El piano es negro. 3. La alumna habla con el padre. 4. El tío del niño es grande. 5. ¿Es negra la tinta?[1] 6. La tiza es blanca. 7. El trabajo del hombre es fácil. 8. La lección de la alumna es muy grande. 9. La pizarra es negra y la tiza es blanca. 10. El trabajo del hermano es grande, pero el trabajo de la niña es fácil.

BB. 1. Is the chalk white? 2. The chalk is white, and the pencil is black. 3. The lesson of the pupil is easy.

---

[1] If the verb means *to be*, this is the common order in a question with one noun and one predicate adjective. With more than one predicate adjective, the order is usually the same as in English.

4. The uncle is large. 5. The book is white and the pen is black. 6. The lesson of the boy is easy. 7. Is the man large? (Is large the man?) 8. Is he conjugating the verb "to speak"? 9. Is the man playing the piano? 10. Is the chalk white? 11. The waiter is large.

LESSON VII

1. Possession. Possession, as **John's book, Mary's lesson,** is in Spanish expressed by **the book of John (el libro de Juan); the lesson of Mary (la lección de María).**

    el padre del primo, the cousin's father (*lit.*, the father of the cousin)

The apostrophe, used in English to denote possession, does not exist in Spanish.

2. Position of Adjectives. (a) Limiting adjectives are placed before the nouns they modify; (b) descriptive adjectives, however, follow.

    el hombre, the man   *But* **alumno diligente,** industrious student
    mucho trabajo, much work   **hombre feliz,** happy man

A limiting adjective is one which refers to quantity or existence: **a, the, one, thirteen, first, such, this, that, which,** etc. Associate the verb **is** with these: **A man is . . . ; that man is . . . .**

A descriptive adjective is one which refers to quality, to a characteristic of a noun, to that which marks it off from all other nouns of the same class. Thus, **apple** may be any apple whatsoever; but **red** apple refers to the quality of redness, marks off apples with the quality of redness from all others. Associate the verb **has** with these; **red apple** = an apple **has** redness. Note, too, that it is only descriptive adjectives which are readily used as predicate nominatives: **apples are red.** (But we could not say: **apples are the.**)

VOCABULARY

contento, -a, contented, satisfied, glad
diligente, diligent, industrious
feliz, happy
grande, large, great
la mesa, table, desk
ni, nor
o, or
pequeño, -a, small, little
perezoso, -a, lazy, idle
poco, little (*adverb*)
también, also
tomar, to take

A. 1. la mesa del hombre 2. la hermana del primo 3. el lápiz negro 4. el libro bonito 5. el hombre contento 6. el trabajo del alumno perezoso 7. el mozo feliz 8. el libro negro 9. la tiza blanca

AA. 1. the man's book 2. the mother's piano 3. much work 4. the chalk 5. great work 6. the white chalk 7. the large man's brother 8. the diligent student 9. easy lesson 10. black pencil 11. satisfied man

B. 1. El alumno toca el piano. 2. El hombre toma el libro del niño. 3. La lección es fácil. 4. El trabajo es grande. 5. El hombre diligente es feliz. 6. Tomo la mesa pequeña. 7. Toman el libro de la hermana y el (**libro** *is understood but not expressed*) del hermano también. 8. Tomo la pluma del primo y la de la prima. (*See Sent. 7*) 9. Conjugan el verbo muy difícil "ser." 10. El tío toma los libros de los primos. 11. Lavan la pizarra de la alumna y también la del alumno.

BB. 1. They are taking the student's book. 2. They are speaking to the uncle and also to the aunt. 3. They play the piano. 4. The pupil's work and the cousin's (*see B, 7*) is difficult. 5. They are taking the student's book. 6. I am speaking to the cousin and to the uncle. 7. She is washing the black slate. 8. The father is large, but the uncle is small. 9. The large student is conjugating the verb. 10. The student is diligent, and the sister is also diligent. 11. Is the student diligent?

LESSON VIII

Review Lesson IV.

1. Preterite Indicative of hablar (*stem* habl-)

Singular	Plural
hablé, I spoke	hablamos, we spoke
hablaste, you spoke	hablasteis, you spoke
habló, he, she, it spoke	hablaron, they spoke

2. The ordinary past tense of Spanish is known as the preterite. It denotes a simple action, completed in the past.

3. The endings of the preterite, like those of the present, are added directly to the stem.

4. **Negation.** Negation in Spanish is expressed by putting **no** before the verb.

No hablo, I do not speak.
No hablé, I did not speak.

5. In a negative question, also, **no** precedes the verb.

¿No habló el tío? Didn't the uncle speak?

VOCABULARY

la cara, face
cocinar, to cook
la comida, dinner, meal
comprar, to buy, to purchase
el diente, tooth
flaco, -a, thin, lean
limpiar, to clean
el muchacho, boy; la muchacha, girl
no, not; no
preparar, to prepare
un, a (*masculine*); una, a (*feminine*)

A. 1. conjuga 2. tomé 3. lavaron 4. ¿no lavaron? 5. ¿no tocaste el piano? 6. ¿tocó el tío el piano? 7. no toco el piano 8. hablaron 9. el tío grande habló 10. no conjugamos el verbo, pero tocamos el piano

AA. 1. we do not conjugate 2. they did not play the piano 3. didn't he play the piano? 4. we spoke the truth 5. you conjugated the verb 6. didn't you take the large table? 7. I did not clean 8. didn't they speak? 9. we did not buy the table 10. didn't you play the piano?

B. 1. ¿Es fácil preparar una comida? 2. La madre preparó la comida para el niño. 3. El niño no es diligente, es perezoso. 4. No prepararon la lección. 5. El primo es muy feliz; halló el lápiz y la pluma también. 6. El primo no habló con el alumno perezoso. 7. El hombre halló poco trabajo. 8. ¿No limpiaron la mesa del alumno? 9. No; no lavaron la mesa del alumno, ni la del padre. 10. El niño perezoso no conjugó el verbo "ser". 11. ¿Es fácil la lección? 12. No; no es fácil. 13. ¿No compraron la mesa? 14. El niño es muy flaco.

BB. 1. The child is not very thin. 2. He worked little, but he conjugated the verb well. 3. He did not clean the table, he cooked the dinner. 4. I cleaned the teeth of the child. 5. He plays the piano [but] little. 6. Did they conjugate the verb "to be"? 7. No, they did not conjugate the verb. 8. Did you prepare the dinner? 9. I did not take the pupil's pen. 10. Don't you play the piano? 11. It isn't easy to prepare a meal well. 12. They also played the piano. 13. They did not clean the table. 14. They did not tell (**dijeron**) the truth to the father or (**ni**) to the mother. 15. They did not prepare the lesson.

LESSON IX

NUMBER AND AGREEMENT OF NOUNS AND ADJECTIVES

1. Nouns and adjectives ending in an unstressed vowel form the plural by adding -s.

hombre, man	**hombres,** men
pluma, pen	**plumas,** pens
bueno, good (*masc. sing.*)	**buenos,** good (*masc. pl.*)
buena, good (*fem. sing.*)	**buenas,** good (*fem. pl.*)

2. The plural of the indefinite article is **unos** for the masculine and **unas** for the feminine. These forms mean **some**.

The plural of the definite article is **los**, masculine, and **las**, feminine.

unos hombres, some men	**unas plumas,** some pens
los hombres, the men	**las plumas,** the pens

NUMBER AND AGREEMENT OF NOUNS AND ADJECTIVES 15

3. When an adjective modifies more than one noun, the adjective is feminine only when all the nouns are feminine; if at least one noun is masculine, the adjective is masculine plural.

>**pizarra y pluma negras,** black slate and pen
>**papel y lápiz blancos,** white paper and pencil
>**tiza y papel blancos,** white chalk and paper

The same rule applies to nouns which have a masculine or a feminine form.

>**hermanos,** brothers   **hermanas,** sisters
>**hermanos,** brother and sister, *or* brothers and sister, *or* brothers and sisters, *or* brother and sisters
>**padres,** fathers, *or* fathers and mothers, *or* parents

A. *Give the plural of* **el, la, una, un.**

AA. *Give the plural, with the definite article, of:*

1. alumno 2. pluma 3. pizarra 4. hombre 5. piano
6. hermano 7. padre 8. grande 9. flaco 10. niño
11. grande 12. contento 13. alumno 14. hermana
15. pequeña 16. hombre flaco 17. libro blanco 18. alumno perezoso 19. niña flaca

AAA. 1. the men 2. a diligent student 3. the lean men 4. the large students 5. the white chalk 6. the black slates 7. the satisfied students 8. the lazy men 9. the large pianos 10. the industrious children 11. the black books

B. 1. Los alumnos diligentes hablan la verdad. 2. Las alumnas conjugan los verbos en el libro blanco. 3. Limpian las mesas. 4. Compran una comida muy grande. 5. Tomamos los libros y las plumas grandes. 6. ¿Limpiaste muchas pizarras? 7. Los alumnos diligentes prepararon el trabajo. 8. Cocinan siempre las comidas. 9. Tomaron los libros blancos y negros. 10. ¿No preparasteis los verbos?

BB. 1. The pupils prepared the meal. 2. We spoke a good deal (*much*) with the brother and sister (**los hermanos;** *or for greater clearness,* **el hermano y la hermana**).

3. Did you clean the large table? 4. Did the cousin prepare the dinner? 5. The slates are (son) black. 6. We cleaned the teeth of the children. 7. They got (prepared) their dinner. 8. Are the books and pencils large or small? 9. The lazy pupils did not prepare the verbs. 10. They took a book. 11. Are the chalk and pencil white or black?

LESSON X
SECOND CONJUGATION

1. **Present Indicative** of **beber,** to drink (*stem* **beb-**)

Singular	Plural
bebo, I drink, *etc.*	bebemos, we drink
bebes, you drink	bebéis, you drink
bebe, he, she, it drinks	beben, they drink

Preterite Indicative (*stem* **beb-**)

bebí, I drank	bebimos, we drank
bebiste, you drank	bebisteis, you drank
bebió, he, she, it drank	bebieron, they drank

2. Comparing the above tense endings of the present tense with those of the first conjugation, it is seen that the only difference is the vowel e for a in all persons but the first singular, where both conjugations have -o.

3. In the preterite tense, i is the vowel throughout the second conjugation, with the diphthong -ió in the third singular and -ie- in the third plural.

VOCABULARY

beber, to drink
bueno, -a, good
la casa, house
comer, to eat
la cosa, thing
difícil, difficult
mucho, much, a great deal
   (*adverb*)
mucho, -a, much (*adjective*);
   (*plural*) many
muy, very
que, which, that, who, whom
   (*relative pronoun*)
satisfecho, -a, satisfied
tampoco, either (*negative*)
temer, to fear, to be afraid
vender, to sell

A. *On the above models, conjugate in the present and preterite:* vender (*stem* vend-) comer (*stem* com-) temer (*stem* tem-)

SECOND CONJUGATION

AA. *Locate the forms:*
1. bebí 2. comieron 3. comimos 4. vivió 5. bebemos
6. ¿bebiste? 7. comes 8. comer 9. no temen 10. temieron
11. comemos 12. bebimos 13. coméis 14. vendo 15. vendió 16. vendí 17. temió 18. teme 19. bebió 20. ¿no bebieron? 21. bebisteis 22. temieron

AAA. *Give the Spanish:*
1. I sold 2. they drink 3. did-he-eat? 4. we fear
5. you-are-selling 6. does he eat? 7. we eat 8. we ate
9. we sell 10. does she fear? 11. they did not sell 12. don't you drink? 13. I am eating 14. I ate 15. they ate
16. they sold 17. did they sell? 18. they did not sell
19. she is selling

B. 1. Vende las plumas y los papeles. 2. El tío no comió la comida. 3. Vendieron las plumas que hallaron.
4. Beben, comen, y tocan el piano—pero no trabajan.
5. ¿Preparaste la comida que comimos? 6. No vendió la mesa que halló en la casa. 7. Cocina bien (well), pero no come las comidas que prepara. 8. Los alumnos perezosos no limpiaron los dientes de los niños. 9. Vende pizarras, plumas y libros grandes y pequeños. 10. ¿No comes la comida que preparó? 11. No, no como la comida. 12. Bebieron, y comieron mucho también.

BB. 1. They sold the slates which they found. 2. Did you drink much? 3. No, we ate, but we did not drink.
4. The mother prepared a large meal, which they ate very [much][1] satisfied. 5. The diligent students do not fear the exercises, but the lazy ones fear the lessons (**lecciones**).
6. It is difficult to sell a piano which is not good. 7. Did you eat a good meal? 8. No, we did not eat, and we did not drink, either. 9. Were you afraid? 10. He doesn't sell desks—he sells pianos. 11. Did the men eat the meal you prepared? 12. The brothers sold the things they found.

[1] In Spanish, one says muy for English very much before a past participle.

LESSON XI
THIRD CONJUGATION

Review Lesson X.

1. **Present Indicative of escribir,** to write (*stem* **escrib-**)

Singular	Plural
escribo, I write, *etc.*	escribimos, we write
escribes, you write	escribís, you write
escribe, he, she, it writes	escriben, they write

Preterite Indicative (*stem* **escrib-**)

escribí, I wrote	escribimos, we wrote
escribiste, you wrote	escribisteis, you wrote
escribió, he, she, it wrote	escribieron, they wrote

2. The endings of the present tense of the third conjugation are the same as those of the second except in the first and second persons plural.

3. The preterite endings of the third conjugation are exactly the same as those of the second.

VOCABULARY

aburrir, to bore, to weary, to tire
acudir, to hasten; to come (to)
allí, there
aquí, here
ayer, yesterday
mañana, tomorrow
rojo, -a, red
salir, to go out
sí, yes
tiene, (he, she, it) has
tienen, (they) have
vivir, to live

A. *Conjugate in the present and preterite:*

vivir (*stem* **viv-**)   aburrir (*stem* **aburr-**)

AA. 1. escribió 2. escribimos 3. salieron 4. aburre
5. acudimos 6. vivimos 7. vivo 8. vivió 9. viven 10. bebieron 11. acude 12. aburrió 13. sale 14. escribió
15. escribieron 16. ¿no acudes? 17. no escribí 18. ¿no salisteis? 19. viven 20. ¿escribiste? 21. tienen

AAA. 1. he has 2. they are living 3. did he live?
4. she is not going out 5. they hastened 6. did she hasten?
7. I lived 8. did you hasten? 9. are you writing? 10. are you going out? 11. you wrote. 12. did she go out?
13. she did not go out 14. we hastened 15. is he hasten-

ing? 16. he lived 17. he bores 18. they are boring 19. they bored. 20. I am drinking

B. 1. ¿Tiene un trabajo difícil? 2. No, tiene un trabajo fácil, y no tiene verbos para mañana. 3. ¿Vivió aquí? 4. El alumno vive en la casa blanca, y la alumna en la casa de la tía del alumno. 5. ¿Teméis un trabajo difícil? 6. Los alumnos perezosos aburren mucho. 7. La mujer que vive en la casa blanca preparó la comida para los niños. 8. Escriben la lección en el libro negro. 9. Tiene todo el trabajo de hoy en un libro muy pequeño. 10. Los alumnos viven en la casa roja, y las alumnas en la de la tía. 11. Los niños acuden al padre.

BB. 1. Did they live in the white house? 2. Do the lazy pupils write a great deal? 3. The little children hastened [over] to the uncle. 4. She is going out. 5. He has much difficult work today. 6. Is she preparing the meals? 7. The child who found the slate is writing. 8. Did you go out yesterday? 9. They live neither (They do not live) in the red house nor in the white [one]; they live in the large house which the uncle has (which has the uncle). 10. He sold the house in which he is living. 11. Has he a piano?—Yes. 12. I don't live in the white house either.

LESSON XII

Review Lesson IX.

1. Plural of Nouns and Adjectives Ending in a Consonant.

Nouns and adjectives ending in a consonant form the plural by adding -es.

mujer, woman	mujeres, women
nación, nation	naciones, nations
lápiz, pencil	lápices, pencils
fácil, easy (*sing.*)	fáciles, easy (*pl.*)

Words like **nación**, which are stressed according to rule when forming the plural, automatically lose the written accent.

Words ending in z change the -z to -c- when adding -es for the plural.

2. a, with a Direct Object. The preposition **a** is used before a direct object when that object is a specific person or a proper noun.

> Busco al hombre, I am looking for the man.
> Busco a Juan, I am looking for John.

In the sentence, "I am looking for someone to write the exercise," **a** would not be used because "someone," though a person, is not specific; and in the sentence, "I am looking for the book," the preposition **a** would not be used either, because "book," though specific, is not a person.

3. Neuter lo. The pronoun **lo** is used in referring to a predicate adjective previously mentioned. **Lo** is classed as neuter because it refers to an adjective, which in itself does not determine grammatical gender.

> ¿Es feliz?—Sí, lo es. Is he happy?—Yes, he is (*it*).

Note the position of **lo**.

VOCABULARY

buscar, to look-for, to seek
la calle, street
Elena, Helen
Enrique, Henry
Gabriel, Gabriel
hay, there is, there are
Juan, John
María, Mary
la pieza, room
el reloj, watch, clock
la vez, time (*used in series, as:* eight times, eighth time)

A. *Give the plural of:*

1. mujer 2. salud 3. nación 4. virtud 5. reloj 6. verdad 7. pieza 8. casa 9. papel 10. lápiz 11. fácil 12. feliz 13. difícil

Give the singular of:

1. verdades 2. fáciles 3. lápices 4. hombres 5. niños 6. mujeres 7. lápices 8. naciones 9. casas 10. difíciles 11. naciones 12. veces

AA. *Give in Spanish the plural of:*

1. easy 2. house 3. nation 4. paper 5. happy 6. room

7. truth 8. pencil 9. woman 10. nation 11. virtue 12. difficult 13. watch

B. 1. Hay muchos relojes en la casa. 2. Tiene lecciones fáciles y difíciles también. 3. Hallé muchos papeles en la calle. 4. ¿Tiene lápices para los alumnos? 5. Sí, tengo muchos, y plumas y pizarras también. 6. ¿Buscáis a Juan o a Elena? 7. Las mujeres compraron los relojes ayer. 8. No es fácil preparar una comida buena. 9. Los alumnos diligentes no son siempre felices, ni los perezosos lo son tampoco. 10. La verdad es muchas veces difícil. 11. Compré el reloj en la casa de Enrique. 12. No buscamos los lápices.

BB. 1. The lazy pupils do not have easy lessons and they are not happy either. 2. Are the diligent pupils happy? 3. They do not come (*use correct form of* **acudir**) to (the) class with good lessons. 4. In the street we found many things—papers, slates, pencils, and pens, some good and some not (**no**). 5. I am looking-for John. 6. Did you look for the pencils?—Yes, but we found the pens, not the pencils. 7. Are the industrious pupils good (Are good the industrious pupils)? 8. The ladies whom we are looking-for are Gabriel's and Mary's aunts. 9. They are (**Son**) always happy. 10. We have many pencils and pens for the students. 11. Are you preparing the dinner? 12. No, I eat and drink, but I do not cook. 13. It isn't very easy to cook. 14. It is the truth.

LESSON XIII
SUBJECT PRONOUNS

Review Lesson IV, 2.

1. **yo**, I
   tú, you (thou)
   { **él**, he; it
   { **ella**, she; it
   usted, you

   { **nosotros**, we (*masc.*)
   { **nosotras**, we (*fem.*)
   { **vosotros**, you (ye) (*masc.*)
   { **vosotras**, you (ye) (*fem.*)
   { **ellos**, they (*masc.*)
   { **ellas**, they (*fem.*)
   ustedes, you

2. **Usted** and **ustedes** take the verb in the third person singular and plural respectively.

Usted escribe, You are writing.

3. The formal pronoun subject of address is **usted, ustedes**. This is used in all cases of politeness or formality, as in speaking to older persons, persons of position or rank, and persons whom one meets casually, including servants, waiters, clerks.

Note. Unless otherwise informed, the student should always use the **usted** forms.

4. In speaking to people with whom one is intimate—close friends or near relatives, young children—or to animals such as pets, one uses **tú** and **vosotros**.

5. Note that there are special forms for the feminine in all but the first and second singular, and in the **usted** forms.

6. Always use the pronoun **usted** or **ustedes** once in a sentence. The other pronouns are generally omitted, though they may be kept for clearness or emphasis: He is writing, but I am studying.

7. In writing, **usted** may be contracted to **Ud., Vd.,** or **V.**; and **ustedes** to **Uds., Vds.,** or **VV.**

8. Never change from an **usted** to a **tú** form, or vice versa.

VOCABULARY

el cielo, sky, heaven
estudiar, to study
la Moneda, the Mint
otro, -a, other, another
perder, to lose
el piso, floor, story (*of a house*)
por consiguiente, consequently, therefore
la puerta, door
el señor, Mr.; gentleman
la señora, Mrs.; lady, madam
la señorita, Miss; young lady
el suelo, ground; floor (*of a room*)
la ventana, window
ya, already; ya no, no longer

A. 1. usted 2. tú 3. Ud. 4. yo 5. él 6. nosotras 7. ellas 8. ella 9. Vd. 10. VV. 11. vosotros 12. ellos 13. vosotras 14. él habla 15. ¿habla él? 16. yo hablo 17. ¿cocino yo? 18. ¡No, señor!

AA. 1. he 2. she 3. they (*masculine*) 4. you (*polite singular*) 5. you (*polite plural*) 6. they (*fem.*) 7. you (*int. pl.*) 8. they speak 9. I 10. you (*int. sing.*) 11. you (*int. pl. masc.*) 12. they (*masc.*) 13. they (*fem.*) 14. he 15. you (*polite pl.*) 16. **they** speak 17. no, **we** speak 18. **we** are eating 19. you speak, but he works.

B. 1. ¿Vendió usted las casas, Señor X.? 2. No, Juan, tú no acudes al trabajo, por consiguiente, no tocas el piano muy bien. 3. Nosotros estudiamos las lecciones difíciles y las fáciles también. 4. ¿No limpiáis vosotras la cara del niño? 5. Hay muchas ventanas y puertas en la casa blanca. 6. Nosotras vivimos en el piso en que ellas viven. 7. La señorita no tiene buena salud. 8. Nosotros aburrimos al señor. 9. Él no vive en la calle en que vivimos nosotros (*pronouns used for contrast*). 10. En el cielo no hay lecciones ni trabajo. 11. El otro señor no busca a la señora; busca al padre. 12. Ellas (*emphatic*) ya no viven aquí; viven en la Calle de la Moneda.

BB. 1. Do you live in Moneda Street, Mr. X.? 2. The young ladies are studying the lesson. 3. They are studying with the other students. 4. **They** speak the truth; **you** do not speak the truth. 5. They study the easy lessons, but they do not study the difficult [ones]. 6. John and Mary are brother-and-sister; she is small, but he is large. 7. Again (**Otra vez**) you lost your book, Mary and Helen. 8. Are you buying others today? 9. They are drinking; we are eating. 10. She is studying, and he is writing. 11. They prepared the dinner, but they did not eat. 12. Is she happy? Yes. 13. There are good students and bad [ones]; she is [a] good [one]. 14. I bought a pencil, but he bought pens. 15. He has two pencils, but he is buying [an] other.

LESSON XIV
SER, to be (*irregular*)

1. Present Indicative (*stem irregular*).

Singular	Plural
soy, I am	somos, we are
eres, you are	sois, you are
es, he, she, it is; you are	son, they are; you are

Preterite Indicative (*stem irregular*).

Singular	Plural
fuí, I was	fuimos, we were
fuiste, you were	fuisteis, you were
fué, he, she, it was; you were	fueron, they were; you were

2. Ser is used with a predicate noun or adjective.

es rojo, it is red
el hielo es frío, the ice is cold
es suyo, it is his
el libro es de mi padre, the book is my father's (*lit.*, of my father)

3. Nouns of trade, profession, nationality, when used predicately after **ser**, omit the indefinite article.

es sastre, he is a tailor
es soldado, he is a soldier
es inglés, he is English

In this construction, the noun is treated as an adjective; hence the omission of the definite article.

4. Certain adjectives (a) have a special meaning with **ser**, or (b) denote permanent, inherent quality.

(a) es bueno, he is good   es malo, he is bad
    él es muy cansado, he is very tiresome
(b) el vapor es caliente, the steam is hot
    es moreno, he is dark

VOCABULARY

americano, -a, American
bastante, enough
el capitán, captain
español, Spanish
francés, French
frío, -a, cold
generalmente, generally
el hielo, ice
malo, -a, bad

más, more
moreno, -a, dark, brunette
pobre, poor
el precio, price
rico, -a, rich, excellent, sumptuous
rubio, -a, blond, light
el sastre, tailor
el soldado, soldier
suficiente, sufficient, enough
todo, -a, all, every
todos los —, every

A. 1. es 2. son 3. Ud. es 4. ella es 5. somos 6. ustedes son 7. vosotras sois 8. ¿es él? 9. es suficiente 10. el hielo es frío 11. es capitán 12. sois franceses 13. es americano 14. es bueno 15. son morenos 16. fuí 17. ¿fué Vd.? 18. no fué suficiente

AA. 1. I am 2. she is 3. you (*polite*) are 4. they are 5. is he? 6. they (*feminine*) are 7. he is [a] soldier 8. she is [an] American 9. it is enough 10. the steam is hot 11. he is small 12. we are tailors 13. he is [a] tailor 14. they are Spanish 15. he is bad 16. are you French? 17. the books are red 18. the men are large 19. the lessons are easy 20. is the chalk white? 21. we were poor 22. are they good?

B. 1. ¿Son las mesas blancas o rojas? 2. No estudias más; ¿ya es suficiente la lección que tienes? 3. Los libros que los alumnos tienen son negros. 4. ¿Es frío o caliente el vapor? 5. El vapor es caliente; el hielo es frío. 6. Los hombres son diligentes, son generalmente buenos. 7. ¿Es el tío soldado o sastre? 8. La señora es una mujer feliz. 9. Hay muchos hombres felices que no son ricos ni pobres. 10. ¿Es el primo rubio o moreno? 11. El primo es rubio; la tía es morena. 12. Fué rico.

BB. 1. Is it the father's desk or the uncle's that she cleaned? 2. Is the pupil good? 3. The brothers are, the one [a] tailor, and the other [a] soldier. 4. These books are very good. 5. I am a captain. 6. The steam is hot, but the ice is cold. 7. Have you (*formal singular*) enough work? 8. The work is sufficient. 9. They are Americans. 10. The men who sold the things to the Americans are French. 11. The slates are black. 12. The windows and doors are large. 13. The cousin is blond, and the sister is a brunette.

LESSON XV
ESTAR, to be (*irregular*)

Review Lesson XIV.

1. Distinguish between the two Spanish verbs **to be**. Each verb is used only under special circumstances, and the beginner must carefully note what these are.

2. **Present Indicative** of **estar** (*stem* est-)

Singular	Plural
estoy, I am	estamos, we are
estás, you are	estáis, you are
está, he, she, it is; you are	están, they are; you are

Preterite Indicative (*stem* estuv-)

estuve, I was	estuvimos, we were
estuviste, you were	estuvisteis, you were
estuvo, he, *etc*. was; you were	estuvieron, they were; you were

3. **Estar** is used to express position of any sort.

    está aquí, he is here
    están en Francia, they are in France

4. Certain adjectives (a) have a special meaning with estar or (b) denote a temporary or transitory quality.

  (a) está bueno, he is well   está malo, he is ill
       está cansado, he is tired
  (b) esta agua está tibia (fría), this water is warm (cold)
       la pizarra está limpia, the slate is clean
       estoy listo, I am ready

VOCABULARY

(la) Alemania, Germany
cuando, when
desear, to desire, want
el ejercicio, exercise
(la) España, Spain
  este; estos, this; these (*masculine*)
  esta; estas, this; these (*feminine*)
(los) Estados Unidos, the United States
(la) Francia, France
fresco, -a, fresh, cool
(la) Inglaterra, England
limpio, -a, clean
lleno, -a, full
quedar, to remain, to stay
si, if
sucio, -a, dirty
tibio, -a, warm, luke-warm, tepid
vacío, -a, empty
el vaso, glass

ESTAR

A. 1. estuve 2. está 3. estuvimos 4. no estuvieron 5. estamos 6. están 7. Vds. están aquí 8. estuvieron 9. está lleno 10. no están vacías 11. ¿están Vds. listos? 12. sí, está aquí. 13. ¿está fresca esta agua? 14. está fría 15. no está mala 16. estamos 17. estuvieron

AA. 1. we were 2. were they? 3. we are 4. is he? 5. you (*formal singular*) are 6. were you? 7. we are good 8. they are well 9. the glass is full 10. this water is hot 11. were they ready? 12. it was 13. is he there? 14. you (*intimate plural*) were 15. were they not? 16. it was dirty 17. he is well 18. it is clean 19. yes, it is (**lo es**) 20. it was

B. 1. Las pizarras y los libros estuvieron muy sucios. 2. ¿Hay un vaso de agua fresca aquí? 3. ¿Están listos los alumnos? 4. No estuvieron malos los padres del alumno; estuvieron buenos. 5. ¿Está listo el primo del alumno? 6. Cuando ellos están aquí, hablamos de las lecciones. 7. Si no están aquí, no estudiamos. 8. No estuvieron listos los alumnos cuando nosotras estuvimos allí. 9. Los libros no son rojos, son negros. 10. El vaso está lleno de agua tibia. 11. ¿Es rubio o moreno? 12. El vaso ya está vacío, no hay más agua. 13. Nosotros estuvimos allí, pero ustedes no estuvieron. 14. ¿Está allí Juan? 15. No están en Francia, están en Inglaterra.

BB. 1. They were in America, not in England (**no en Inglaterra**). 2. Is this water warm or hot? 3. The glass is not full; it is empty. 4. Was she ill? 5. If the water is warm, they do not want to drink it (**beberla**). 6. He wanted to be in France, but we were not there, we were in Germany, and so he stayed in the United States. 7. Is he happy? 8. No, his lessons are difficult, he does not want to study, and he is not well. 10. Was the glass dirty? 11. No, it is clean, but there is no water (**no hay agua**). 12. The exercises are easy, but he does not study. 13. The children are dirty, and the mother wants to clean John's face. 14. Are you ready? 15. No, are you (and you)?

LESSON XVI
THE PASSIVE[1]

Review Lessons XIV and XV.

1. The past participle of most Spanish verbs is formed by adding -**ado** to the stem of the first conjugation, and -**ido** to the stem of the second and third conjugations.

    habl ado   hablado, spoken
    beb ido   bebido, drunk   viv ido   vivido, lived

2. The passive voice in Spanish is made up of the appropriate form of the verb **ser** plus the past participle of the transitive verb.

    es temido, he is feared

The past participle must agree with the subject in person and number.

    (vosotras) sois temidas, you are feared
    La casa fué comprada por Juan, The house was bought by John.

3. The agent (or doer) of the action with the passive is expressed in most instances by **por**.

    El verbo fué conjugado por el alumno, The verb was conjugated by the student.

With some verbs, however, in which the action is not so much material as mental, **de** is used.

    Es temido de sus enemigos, He is feared by his enemies.

4. There must be distinguished from the passive a somewhat similar form, with **estar** instead of **ser**. The distinction is this: in the real passive (the form with **ser**), an action is or was actually carried on; that is, the subject of the passive verb actually receives the effect of some

---

[1] The active voice of a transitive verb is that form of it in which the doer of an action is the subject of the verb and the receiver of the action the object of the verb. "John (doer) hits (verb, active voice) the ball" (receiver of action). The passive voice of a transitive verb is that form of it in which the receiver of the action is the subject. "The ball (receiver) was hit by (verb, in the passive) John" (doer, governed by "by").

A transitive verb is one that performs an action on a person or thing. "I see the man." An intransitive verb is one that cannot perform an action on a person or thing. "John is here." John cannot "is" anything. Intransitive verbs have no passive.

action, and an agent is expressed or implied. Cf. the English: "The ball was hit by John." In the apparent passive, however, (the form with **estar**), the past participle does not represent a real action, but is used as an adjective, without at all the force of a verb. Cf. the English: "The meat is well done." "Done" is here used as an adjective.

La casa está comprada, The house is bought.

VOCABULARY

ahora, now
amar, to love
el calcetín, sock
dar, to give
escrito, written (*irregular past participle*)
el estadista, statesman
lavar, to wash
la media, stocking
la palabra, word; speech
tocar, to touch; to play (*a musical instrument*)
la vajilla, kitchen utensils, dishes (*collective noun*)

A. 1. el verbo es conjugado por Enrique 2. los calcetines (*why not an accent?*) son buenos 3. son amados de todos 4. está escrito 5. fué escrito por Juan 6. los niños fueron lavados por la madre 7. la vajilla está vendida 8. la vajilla fué vendida por la señora 9. fué comprada por el hombre

AA. 1. *Explain why* **ser** *or* **estar** *is used in each sentence in A.* 2. *Note the agreement of the past participle with the subject of* **ser** *or* **estar** *in each sentence of A.*

AAA. 1. the socks are good 2. the verbs are being conjugated 3. it is all written 4. the child was washed by the mother 5. the letters were written by the student 6. are the socks white? 7. they were bought by the lady 8. it is sold 9. the meals were prepared by the woman 10. he is beloved of all 11. the glass is cleaned

B. 1. Estos hombres, que son muy buenos, son amados de todos los alumnos. 2. Ya está estudiada la lección, ya están escritas las cartas. 3. ¿Están vendidas las medias? 4. Los libros fueron vendidos a los alumnos por el hombre. 5. La mesa y el piano fueron comprados por el tío y dados al primo. 6. Los vasos están llenos de agua tibia. 7. La señora no es muy feliz. 8. ¿Son blancas las mesas? 9.

Vivimos en la casa que está en la calle X. 10. El hielo es frío; esta agua está tibia. 11. No están ahora en Francia; viven en Inglaterra.

BB. 1. When we are here, you do not study. 2. Were the stockings sold? 3. We lived in the house with (de) two stories. 4. Were they bought by the man? 5. The glasses are clean, but there is not [any] water. 6. Was the piano bought by the man or the woman? 7. Are the glasses washed? 8. Were they washed by you, Mary? 9. He is loved by the pupils. 10. The glass is full of cold water. 11. Is the meal prepared? 12. The books are red.

LESSON XVII
POSSESSIVE ADJECTIVES

Review Lesson V, 2 and V, 4.

1. The possessive adjectives are:

mi, my (*goes with* yo)

tu, your (*goes with* tú)

su, his, her, its; your (*goes with* él, ella; usted)

nuestro, -a, our (*goes with* nosotros, -as)

vuestro, -a, your (*goes with* vosotros, -as)

su, their; your (*goes with* ellos, -as; ustedes)

Note that the possessive adjective tu has no accent. It is thus distinguished from the pronoun subject tú; just as él, *he*, has an accent to distinguish it from el, *the*.

(yo) tengo mi casa, I have my house
(tú) tienes tu casa, you have your house
(él) tiene su casa, he has his house
Vd. tiene su casa, you have your house.

Note that su is also used for the polite **your** (**usted** takes everything in the third person).

2. Like any adjective, these possessives agree with the noun modified (**not** the antecedent).

mis casas, my houses (mis *plural to agree with* casas, *not* yo)
nuestra casa, our house (nuestra *singular and feminine to agree with* casa)

3. Only **nuestro** and **vuestro** have special feminine forms. All other possessives are used in one form for both genders.

VOCABULARY

el azúcar, sugar
la carne, meat
el café, coffee; (*plural* **cafés,**)
hallar, to find
el huevo, egg
la leche, milk
la mantequilla, butter
el pan, bread
el papá, father, "dad"; (*plural,* **papás**)
la sed, thirst
tengo sed, I am thirsty
la silla, chair
el te, tea; (*plural,* **tes**)
tengo, I have
el vino, wine

A. 1. mi 2. tu 3. su 4. sus 5. nuestras 6. sus 7. tu 8. su 9. nuestras 10. vuestros 11. mi 12. tus 13. mis 14. vuestras 15. tus

AA. 1. my 2. your 3. your (*polite*) 4. your book 5. your (*polite*) books 6. your book, Henry and John 7. our pens 8. their books 9. your exercises 10. our book 11. your (*intimate*) slate 12. my pens 13. your books, Mary 14. my pens 15. your books, Henry

B. 1. Buscamos ayer nuestras plumas. 2. ¿Hallasteis vuestras lecciones? 3. No preparamos nuestras comidas: la mujer prepara sus comidas y también las de nosotros. 4. ¿Toca usted todavía su piano, Señor X? 5. Lavamos la cara de nuestros niños. 6. ¿Fueron vendidos los libros por su hermana? 7. Sus vasos están limpios. 8. La señora no está muy feliz (lucky). 9. No hay más azúcar ni leche en mi casa. 10. Sus huevos no son buenos. 11. Tengo sed; deseo un poco de su vino. 12. ¿Tiene Vd. sed? ¿Desea Vd. te o café? 13. El vino está en la mesa, pero él busca agua. 14. No hay más sillas en la pieza.

BB. 1. His books were bought by his students. 2. Have you my pen? 3. The child is on his table—he is looking for sugar. 4. His books are always bought by his sister. 5. Do you still live in this house? 6. Her pen was not found. 7. He is hungry; but he does not want to drink coffee or (nor) tea, he wants to drink water. 8. He has no wine, he is drinking milk. 9. I want some (a little of) meat. 10. Our piano was bought by his cousin.

11. Are you thirsty, Mr. X? Do you want some water?
12. His books are clean. 13. Have you your book there, John? 14. Our pens and your pencils are all bad. 15. He is eating some (**unos**) eggs.

LESSON XVIII
INTERROGATIVE PRONOUNS AND ADJECTIVES

1. **¿Quién?** who? **¿quiénes?** (*plural*) is used as the subject of a verb or object (**whom**) of a verb or preposition.

¿Quién está aquí? Who is here?
¿A quién busca usted? Whom are you looking-for?
¿Con quién estudias? With whom are you studying?

The adjective corresponding to the above pronoun is ¿qué?

¿Qué hombre está aquí? What man is here?
¿Con qué alumno estudias? What pupil are you studying with?

Note: In Spanish, the preposition must come before the word it governs.

2. **¿Qué?** what? referring to things, subject of a verb or object of a verb or preposition, is adjective or pronoun.

¿Qué está aquí? What is here?
¿Qué cosa es? What (thing) is it?
¿Por qué estudias? Why are you studying? (What are you studying for?)

3. Other interrogative words are:

¿cómo? how?
¿cuál? ¿cuáles? which? what? (*adjective or pronoun*)
¿cúyo, -a; -os, -as? whose? (*adjective or pronoun*)
¿de quién? whose? (*literally*, of whom?)
¿cuánto, -a; -os, -as? how much? how many? (*adjective or pronoun*)

¿Cómo estás? How are you?
¿Cuál libro desea usted? Which book do you want?
¿Cuál busca usted? Which (one) are you looking-for?
¿Cúyo libro tiene? Whose book has he?
¿De quién es el libro que tiene? Whose book has he? (*lit.*, Of whom is the book that he has?)
¿Cuántas sillas hay? How many chairs are there?
¿Cuántas hay? How many are there?

INTERROGATIVE PRONOUNS AND ADJECTIVES

4. Interrogative words, whether used in an indirect or direct question, always have an accent mark written over the stressed syllable. This accent is not to indicate stress, but to distinguish the interrogative from a corresponding relative word. Cf. interrogative: "**When** did you come?" with relative: "I was there **when** he came." The two forms in Spanish are pronounced alike.

VOCABULARY

cuando, when
la cuchara, spoon
la cucharita, teaspoon
el cuchillo, knife
el plato, plate
el tenedor, fork

A. 1. ¿cuándo? 2. ¿cómo? 3. ¿cuántas plumas? 4. ¿a quién? 5. ¿quiénes? 6. ¿con qué? 7. ¿por qué? 8. ¿para qué? 9. ¿cuál? 10. ¿cúyo libro? 11. ¿cuál pluma? 12. ¿cúyas plumas?

AA. 1. why? 2. whose lessons? 3. when? 4. with what? 5. for whom? 6. whose glass? 7. how? 8. how many books? 9. which? 10. what man? 11. which man? 12. to whom? 13. whose chairs? 14. who is here? 15. when?

B. 1. ¿Qué lecciones estudiasteis? 2. ¿Con quién hablasteis? 3. ¿Cuál verbo conjugan? 4. ¿A quiénes buscaron Vds. ayer? 5. ¿Cúyo libro es el que usted tiene? —Es el que (the one which) compré ayer. 6. ¿Por qué no preparan las niñas la comida? 7. ¿No estudió el alumno? 8. ¿No está en casa? 9. ¿Quién es?—Soy yo (It is I). Somos nosotros. Él es (It is he). 10. ¿Qué platos tiene Vd.? 11. ¿Cuáles tenedores, cuchillos, y cucharas desea usted?—No deseo cucharas, deseo cucharitas. 12. ¿Por qué no comen ustedes? 13. ¿Qué hombre es el que estudia el libro rojo? 14. ¿Cuál? 15. ¿Cuántos libros hay en la mesa? 16. No hay muchos. 17. ¿Cuánto azúcar desean ustedes? 18. ¿En qué casa viven ahora?

BB. 1. Is it you (**Es usted**)? 2. It is I. It is we. It is they. 3. How many glasses are there on the table? 4. What books did you study? 5. For whom is she preparing the dinner today? 6. Why are not these diligent pupils happy? 7. Who is lazy? 8. What forks and spoons did you find? 9. Do you want the dinner now? 10. What knife is that? 11. How much water is there in the glass? 12. How are you? 13. What students are you studying with? (*Where does* **with** *come in Spanish?*) 14. What lesson is your sister studying? 15. What bread is it? 16. In whose house are you living now, Mr. X.? 17. How do you clean the slate? 18. Why don't you study more? 19. Why don't you study when they are here?

LESSON XIX

1. **Apocopation.** The adjectives below drop the **-o** of the masculine singular when coming before a noun (this is called **apocopation**).

bueno	buen	good	ninguno	ningún	none
malo	mal	bad	primero	primer	first
uno	un	a; one	tercero	tercer	third
alguno	algún	some	postrero	postrer	last

el primer ejercicio, the first exercise
un buen hombre, a good man

2. The other forms (feminine singular, and both plurals) never have apocopation: **la primera lección,** the first lesson.

As pronouns, also, these words, even in the masculine singular, do not have apocopation: **el primero y el tercero,** the first and third.

3. **Ninguno** after the verb requires **no** before it (but if **ninguno** comes before the verb, **no** is omitted):

No tengo ningún trabajo, I have no work.
Ningún trabajo tengo, I have no work. (*more emphatic*)

4. Note that **ninguno** and **alguno** require the accent when the **-o** is dropped.

ningún hombre, no man   *But* ninguno, no one (*pronoun*)

5. **Un for una** and **el for la.** Before a feminine noun in the singular beginning with a stressed **a** or **ha, una**

becomes **un** and **la** becomes **el**. This is to prevent two stressed **a** sounds from coming together. But if the feminine noun begins with an unstressed **a**, the regular form **una** or **la** is kept.

 un águila, an eagle   *But* una alumna, a pupil
 el alma, the soul   la aritmética, arithmetic

VOCABULARY

águila, eagle (*use* el *for* la)
alma, soul (*use* el *for* la)
la aritmética, arithmetic
el cuento, story, tale; account
el dinero, money
el dormitorio, bedroom
el entresuelo, ground floor
la esquina, corner (*outside corner, as of a street*)
hacha, axe (*use* el *for* la)
el jamón, ham
el pie, foot
el piso, floor (*of a house*), story
el rincón, corner (*inside corner, as of a room*)

A. 1. primera lección 2. tercer ejercicio 3. ninguna esquina 4. un vaso 5. ningún vaso 6. buen dormitorio 7. una comida 8. un vaso 9. mal trabajo 10. ningún trabajo 11. un tenedor 12. el hacha 13. la alumna 14. el tercer piso 15. un buen cuento 16. ningún dormitorio 17. algún vaso 18. el buen vaso 19. el buen vaso y el malo (*Why is the* -o *kept? Is* **malo** *adjective or pronoun?*) 20. el águila 21. un hacha.

AA. 1. some work 2. no work 3. a slate 4. the axe 5. the last glass 6. a story 7. good exercise 8. first lesson 9. third man 10. bad pen 11. an axe 12. the [*girl*] student 13. one pencil 14. the good pencil, the bad [one] 15. no exercise 16. the first exercise and the third [one]

B. 1. Un hombre cocinó la comida. 2. En la tercera esquina está una casa blanca. 3. ¿En qué dormitorio está? ¿En el tercero? 4. No está en el tercer dormitorio; está en el primero. 5. Es un buen ejercicio, el que (the one which) está en la tercera lección. 6. El hacha no es buena. 7. ¿Tienes un buen cuento? 8. Tengo un dormitorio que es muy malo. 9. ¿En qué piso está? 10. Está en el primer piso.[1] 11. No tengo trabajo. 12. No tengo

---

[1] Spanish houses of two stories have el piso bajo or los bajos, the ground floor; and el piso alto or los altos, the upper floor. Houses with several floors have:

ningún dinero. 13. ¿No tiene ningún trabajo? 14. ¿Son negros los calcetines? 15. Fueron comprados por este buen muchacho. 16. No hay buenos relojes en la casa. 17. ¿Está aquí el hombre que preparó la comida?

BB. 1. The third exercise in the book is very difficult. 2. What books did you study in your room? 3. I was studying in my bedroom, the third room on the first floor. 4. Have you any glasses? 5. I haven't a glass. 6. Have you an axe? 7. I have a very good one (one very good). 8. It is a bad exercise that you have there. 9. Is the house on the corner of the street? 10. There isn't [any] more sugar or (**ni**) milk in the house. 11. Is there a glass on the table? 12. He lives with his father and mother in the third white house. 13. The brother and sister haven't [any] work now. 14. Are their uncle and aunt here in this house? 15. No, and they live in the first white house on the corner now.

LESSON XX.
CARDINAL NUMBERS TO 99

1.

uno, -a, one	**diez y ocho,** eighteen
dos, two	**diez y nueve,** nineteen
tres, three	**veinte,** twenty
cuatro, four	**veinte y uno, -a,** twenty-one
cinco, five	**veinte y dos,** twenty-two
seis, six	**treinta,** thirty
siete, seven	**cuarenta,** forty
ocho, eight	**cincuenta,** fifty
nueve, nine	**sesenta,** sixty
diez, ten	**setenta,** seventy
once, eleven	**ochenta,** eighty
doce, twelve	**noventa,** ninety
trece, thirteen	**noventa y cinco,** ninety-five
catorce, fourteen	**noventa y seis,** ninety-six
quince, fifteen	**noventa y siete,** ninety-seven
diez y seis, sixteen	**noventa y ocho,** ninety-eight
diez y siete, seventeen	**noventa y nueve,** ninety-nine

el entresuelo, ground floor; **el piso principal,** or main floor; and the floors above are labelled consecutively: **primer piso, segundo piso, tercer piso,** etc.

Only in large cities like Madrid, Buenos Aires, Barcelona are found many houses of several stories.

CARDINAL NUMBERS

2. For **uno** becoming **un,** see Lesson XIX, 1.

3. For the numbers **veinte y uno** through **veinte y nueve,** forms like the following may be used:

veintidós, veintitrés, etc.

The forms ending in **-dós, -trés,** and **-séis** write an accent on the last syllable to indicate the irregularity of stress of the compound word.

4. For **diez y seis** through **diez y nueve,** the following forms may be used:

dieciséis, diecisiete, dieciocho, diecinueve

Here also an accent must be written on **-séis.**

5. Note the apocopation in forms like:

veintiún libros, plumas, etc.

6. **Don** and **doña.** In Spanish, two titles of address are found which have no equivalents in English. **Don** may be variously translated as **Mr., master,** or omitted entirely. Similarly, **doña** may be translated as **Mrs., mistress,** or omitted entirely.

Don and **doña** are used only with the first names of people, and give a more intimate touch than the formal **señor, señora,** or **señorita** with the surname.

don Juan, (master) John   doña Elena, (mistress) Helen

VOCABULARY

el año, year
   tiene cinco años, he is five years old
Isabel, Elizabeth

el peso, dollar (*monetary unit of most South American countries; in Spain the word* peseta *is used*).

A. 1. treinta y cuatro 2. cincuenta y siete 3. sesenta y nueve 4. veinte y dos 5. doce 6. cuarenta y tres; veintitrés 7. ochenta y nueve 8. noventa y ocho 9. noventa y nueve 10. cincuenta y cuatro 11. veinte y dos 12. nueve 13. veintitrés 14. dieciséis; diez y seis 15.

diez 16. setenta y una 17. seis 18. veinte y seis 19. veintiséis 20. dos 21. seis 22. una 23. uno 24. un hombre 25. veinte y dos hombres 26. treinta y un ejercicios 27. veintidós lecciones 28. treinta y tres plumas 29. veintiséis plumas 30. cuarenta y cuatro lápices 31. veinticinco; veintidós 32. cuarenta y ocho 33. noventa y nueve 34. veinticuatro 35. siete 36. seis 37. setenta y cuatro 38. setenta y ocho 39. sesenta y seis 40. sesenta y dos 41. treinta y cinco

AA. 1. 55 2. 49 3. 8 4. 18 5. 7 6. 14 7. eight men 8. (don) Henry 9. 22 boys (*two spellings*) 10. Miss Mary 11. 21 lessons 12. 17 books 13. twenty-one pens 14. thirty-one glasses 15. 42 slates 16. 57 17. 99 18. twenty-one 19. thirty-one glasses 20. 49 21. 71 22. 22 23. 44 24. 31 papers 25. two pianos 26. 42 pencils 27. 72 books 28. 83 slates.

B. 1. Lavamos las dos mesas. 2. El hombre toma doce libros. 3. El padre del niño es pequeño, pero los dos tíos son muy grandes. 4. ¿Limpiaste las cinco pizarras? 5. No vendieron veinte y un lápices, vendieron diez y ocho. 6. Doña Elena tiene veintitrés años. 7. Don Enrique tiene setenta y tres; noventa y tres; dieciocho; sesenta y cuatro; cincuenta y nueve; veinte y uno; cuarenta y cinco; veintidós. 8. ¿Buscas a don Juan?—No, busco a sus dos hermanos. 9. Los diez y siete alumnos de la clase son todos perezosos. 10. ¿Tiene usted trabajo para ocho hombres? 11. Todos son muy diligentes. 12. ¿Cuántos niños hay en la clase? 13. ¿Ochenta y cinco? 14. No, hay setenta y nueve. 15. Cuando vosotros estáis aquí, nosotros no estudiamos.

BB. 1. There are eighteen pupils in my room. 2. How many books have you, Helen? 3. Have you my books, too? 4. They did not sell the eighteen pencils. 5. I-am-looking-for my three cousins. 6. How many pesos have you, John? 7. Sixty-five; forty-three; eighteen; ninety-four; eighty-four; sixty-five; fifty-four. 8. They are cleaning the glasses. 9. How many glasses are there? 10. There are twelve. 11. For ten pupils there is one teacher. 12. The lady has four children. 13. In the third room there are four windows. 14. In the white house there are nine rooms. 15. The first room is my bedroom. 16. He has ten large books and twenty-three small ones.

LESSON XXI
CONJUNCTIVE PRONOUNS

1. **me,** me; myself
   te, you; yourself
   le, lo, him; you
   lo, it
   le, la, her; you
   la, it

   nos, us; ourselves
   os, you; yourselves
   los, them (*masculine*); you (*polite*)
   las, them (*feminine*); you (*polite*)

2. These forms come directly before any finite form of a verb. **Te busco,** I am looking for you. **¿Dónde lo halló?** Where did he find it? **Los buscamos,** We are looking for them. **Le busco,** I am looking for you (*see 4 below*).

3. **Lo** and **la** are masculine and feminine forms respectively. **Le** is often used for **lo** or **la,** referring to persons.

   ¿Busca usted el libro?—**Lo busco,** Are you looking for the book?—I am looking for it.
   ¿Busca usted a su hermano?—**Le (lo) busco,** Are you looking for your brother?—I am looking for him.

4. As everything referring to **usted** is in the third person, polite **you** as the object of a verb is **le (lo, la)** singular, and **los, las** plural.

   Le busco, I am looking for you (*masculine or feminine*).
   Lo busco (*masculine*); **La busco** (*feminine*), I am looking for you.

A. 1. le busco 2. la preparamos 3. ¿los limpiáis? 4. no lo lavo 5. me buscaron 6. ¿te halló? ¿le halló? 7. no nos hallaron 8. ¿os buscó? ¿los buscó? 9. no nos halló 10. me aburre 11. vendió 12. las vendió 13. la vendiste 14. no lo vendisteis 15. lo deseo 16. los lavo 17. me lavo 18. os laváis 19. nos lavamos 20. te lavas

AA. 1. he found it 2. did he look-for us? 3. she found you 4. they want it 5. did they find you (*intimate*)? 6. do you want it? 7. aren't they looking-for us? 8. he bores me 9. I am washing myself (**me**) 10. we are washing ourselves 11. did you prepare it? 12. are you drinking it? 13. they washed them 14. are you looking for me? 15. did you take it? 16. I found it 17. they cleaned it 18. we bought them 19. didn't they find you there? 20. I am-afraid-of (fear) it 21. I didn't write it 22. they bored me

B. 1. Mis padres no están aquí; los buscamos pero no los hallamos. 2. No beben el vino, ni comen el pan. 3. Es difícil hallar las cosas que buscamos. 4. ¿Dónde están las cosas que hallaron?—Las tomaron sus padres (Their parents took them). 5. Los cuchillos, los tenedores, las cucharas—los hallé todos en la mesa. 6. Estos niños perezosos me aburren—no estudian. 7. Mis primos os buscaron ayer, pero no os hallaron. 8. Limpiaron la casa de las tías; ahora la casa está limpia. 9. Cuando nos buscasteis, nos hallasteis. 10. Tomaron los libros en la mesa ayer y hoy no los hallo (I don't find them). 11. ¿Tiene usted el libro? 12. ¿Lo halló? 13. ¿Cocinan la comida ahora o no la cocinan?

BB. 1. Did you find them? 2. No, I did not find them. 3. They took the books in my room. 4. Did you find my three books? 5. No, I did not find them. 6. Did you write it? 7. No, there isn't any paper in the house. Therefore, we are not writing it. 8. Isn't there any dinner today? 9. No, I didn't prepare it. 10. Have you (*use* **usted**) ten pencils for tomorrow? 11. They haven't them—they are still looking-for them. 12. You bore me with these accounts. 13. Many find it difficult. 14. Where is the dinner?—I ate it all.

LESSON XXII

Review Lesson XX.

1. Cardinals (*concluded*).

ciento, hundred
ciento uno, a hundred and one
ciento dos, a hundred and two
ciento treinta y nueve, one hundred thirty-nine
mil, a thousand
mil tres, a thousand and three
mil ciento ochenta y cuatro, one thousand one hundred eighty-four; *or*, eleven hundred eighty-four
un millón, a million
nueve millones, nine million

Note specially the hundreds.

doscientos, two hundred
trescientos, three hundred
cuatrocientos, four hundred
quinientos, five hundred
seiscientos, six hundred
setecientos, seven hundred
ochocientos, eight hundred
novecientos, nine hundred

The ending -os is changed to -as to form the feminine.

doscientas plumas, two hundred pens

Note the forms **quinientos**, five hundred; **setecientos**, seven hundred; **novecientos**, nine hundred. The other hundreds are formed regularly by combining the regular unit with the plural (masculine or feminine) of **ciento**.

2. The conjunction y can not be used above noventa y nueve.

ochenta y ocho, eighty-eight
ochocientos ochenta y ocho, eight hundred (and) eighty-eight
mil cinco, a thousand (and) five

Note: One can not say *eleven hundred* in Spanish, only *a thousand one hundred*: **mil ciento**.

3. Hundreds as a noun is usually centenares.

centenares de lápices, hundreds of pencils

4. Thousands as a noun is miles.

miles de ovejas, thousands of sheep

5. Never use the word un before ciento or mil.

cien hombres, a hundred men
mil vasos, a thousand glasses

But **un** must be used before **millón** (in the singular), which is used only as a noun and must be followed by **de.**

un millón de dólares, a million dollars

6. Ciento coming before a noun of either gender (that is, used as an adjective) must drop **-to.**

cien soldados, a hundred soldiers

7. Contraction of Santo and Grande. Santo, saint, is contracted only before a masculine singular noun.

San Isidro, Saint Isidor
But **el santo,** the saint   **Santa Ana,** Saint Anne

Before a noun of either gender, **grande,** *great,* becomes **gran.**

un gran hombre, a great man   **una gran mujer,** a great woman

The full form, when found before a noun, is so used for emphasis.

8. Adjective as Noun. Any adjective may be used as a noun by taking the proper gender and number.

los lápices blancos y los negros, the white pencils and the black (ones).

Note that in Spanish no word is used for **ones,** as the adjective itself expresses completely the whole idea (*Cf. Lesson VII, B7*).

VOCABULARY

azul, blue   **satisfactorio, -a,** satisfactory
habitante, inhabitant

A. *Count aloud in Spanish from* one *to* eleven hundred, *omitting like combinations.*

AA. 1. ciento uno 2. doscientas plumas 3. quinientas 4. setecientas 5. noventa 6. ochocientos 7. quinientos lápices 8. trescientos 9. setecientos 10. novecientas 11. cuatrocientas 12. doscientos 13. ciento veinte y una 14. mil quinientas sesenta y cuatro 15. veinte y un mil setecientos ochenta y tres 16. gran soldado 17. ciento cincuenta y seis; mil novecientos cuarenta y uno 18. un millón (**de** *if a noun follows*) 19. ciento un lápices

20. quinientas plumas 21. San Juan 22. ciento veinte y uno 23. ciento cinco 24. mil dos 25. San Isidro 26. Santa María 27. doscientos treinta y cuatro 28. quinientos treinta y nueve 29. setecientos cincuenta y dos 30. novecientos ochenta y una 31. seiscientos sesenta y cinco. 32. trescientos cuarenta y una.

AAA. 1. 243 2. 394 3. 587 4. 725 5. 682 6. 444 7. 892 8. 154 9. 101 10. 194,382 11. a million 12. one million 13. 24,583 14. 1,999 15. Saint John 16. Saint Mary 17. 121 18. 1,005 19. Saint Isidor 20. 524 21. 983 22. 642 23. 1,001 24. 235 25. 2,534 26. 1,534 27. 27,000

B. 1. ¿Compró usted quinientos o seiscientos lápices? 2. ¿Dónde vivió San Juan? 3. Hay veinte casas en la calle. 4. En esta calle hay ciento quince casas de dos pisos y ciento una de tres pisos. 5. En todo el libro hay doscientos treinta y dos ejercicios. 6. ¿Cuántos tenedores venden ustedes todos los años? 7. No vendemos muchos tenedores, pero vendemos muchas veces hasta (as much as) quinientas o setecientas cucharas. 8. Todos los libros son azules. 9. Los ejercicios no son muy satisfactorios hoy; son muy malos. 10. ¿Cuántas alumnas hay en la escuela? —¿doscientas?—¿doscientas cincuenta?

BB. 1. There are five hundred soldiers in the street now. 2. The pupils in this school, and there are 250, are all diligent. 3. There are not many schools where all the students are industrious. 4. The two hundred exercises in the book are very satisfactory. 5. How many soldiers are there now in the street? 6. Did you buy four or six pencils? 7. In France, there are many large cities; but in the United States, there are more. 8. New York has five million inhabitants, Chicago 2,500,000, and Boston 800,000. 9. Are there twenty or twenty-one houses in the street? 10. In his house he has twenty thousand books. 11. He sells seven hundred or eight hundred books every year.

LESSON XXIII
COMPARISON

Review Lessons V and IX.

1. The comparative is formed by putting **más,** *more,* **menos,** *less,* before the positive degree of an adjective or adverb.

    grande, large   más grande, larger
                                     menos grande, less large
    despacio, slowly   más despacio, more slowly
                                     menos despacio, less slowly

The superlative of adjectives is formed by putting the definite article before a comparative degree.

    el (la, *etc.*) más grande, the largest

With adverbs, **lo** is used before the comparative.

    lo más despacio, most slowly

2. The following adjectives are irregularly compared:

bueno, good	mejor, better	el mejor, best
malo, bad	peor, worse	el peor, worst
grande, large	más grande, larger	el más grande, largest
	mayor, older	el mayor, oldest
pequeño, small	más pequeño, smaller	el más pequeño, smallest
	menor, younger	el menor, youngest

3. The following adverbs are irregularly compared:

poco, little	menos, less	lo menos, least
mucho, much	más, more	lo más, most
bien, well	mejor, better	lo mejor, best
mal, badly	peor, worse	lo peor, worst

4. Distinguish between the comparative and superlative in expressions like the following:

    el alumno más diligente, the more industrious student

(As the article is not repeated with an adjective put after the noun, the above expression could also mean):

                             the most industrious student

5. (a) **Than** is expressed by **que.**

    Él es más grande que ella, He is larger than she.

COMPARISON

(b) Before a number, **than** is **de**.

Tiene más de cinco pesos, He has more than five pesos.

But **only** or **no more than** is **no más .... que** (*note the negative*).

No tiene más que cinco pesos, He has only five pesos.

(c) If two clauses are compared, **than** is expressed by **de lo que** if adjectives or adverbs are compared; **del que** if nouns are compared, using **el, la, los,** or **las** according to the gender of the noun.

Es más grande de lo que crees, He is larger than you think.
Trabaja menos de lo que cree, He works less than he thinks.
Él tiene más trabajo del que ella tiene, He has more work than she has.
Él tiene más plumas de las que ella tiene, He has more pens than she has.

6. **In** after a superlative is expressed by **de**.

Es la casa más grande de la ciudad, It is the largest house in the city.

7. **As .... as** is expressed by **tan** (*adjective or adverb*) **como**; or **tanto** (*noun*) **como**.

No es tan grande como yo, He is not so large as I.
No tiene tantos libros como yo, He has not so many books as I.

8. **The more (less) .... the more (less)** is expressed by **cuanto más (menos) .... tanto más (menos)**. **Tanto** may be omitted.

Cuanto más trabaja, (tanto) menos tiene. The more he works, the less he has.

Mientras may be used instead of **cuanto**, in which case **tanto** must be omitted.

Mientras más trabaja, más tiene, The more he works, the more he has.

VOCABULARY

la ciudad, city
creer, to believe
la escuela, school
pocos, -as, few

A. 1. más fácil que 2. el más contento de la ciudad 3. más perezoso que 4. el más perezoso de todos 5. tan bueno como 6. mejor que 7. tan difícil como 8. el más satisfecho 9. el hombre más satisfecho 10. más pequeño, el más pequeño 11. más grande, más perezoso, mayor 12. más diligente, el más diligente 13. el más contento 14. el más perezoso de la escuela 15. mayor, el más grande, la más fría, los más ricos, más fría que, menor 16. él es más grande que usted 17. más fresco que 18. tiene más libros de los que usted tiene 19. tan caliente como 20. cuanto más tiene, menos desea 21. lo más despacio, más sucios 22. menos 23. menos satisfactorio 24. lo peor

AA. 1. as satisfied as 2. the more he has, the more he wants 3. they are smaller than we 4. happier, less satisfied, worse, youngest 5. the richest in the street 6. colder, less cold, least cold, less, less lazy 7. older, as young as, worst, colder, younger than 8. as warm as 9. she has more books than he has 10. dirtier, less diligent, laziest, oldest, as good as, richer, older, warmer than 11. he writes more than you 12. as good as 13. better than 14. they found more pens than we found, as diligent as, lazier than 15. the less he writes, the more he prepares

B. 1. No estudiamos tanto como Uds., pero preparamos mejor nuestras lecciones. 2. Es el niño más grande de la familia. 3. No está el niño tan sucio como el primo. 4. El hermano es más perezoso que la hermana. 5. Cuanto más contentos están, tanto más estudian. 6. Su trabajo es menos satisfactorio que el de su hermano. 7. ¿Es su hermano menor o mayor de lo que es usted? 8. ¿Quién tiene agua más fresca de la que está en el vaso? 9. ¿No tiene usted más libros de los que tiene él? 10. El niño que está aquí es el más perezoso de la escuela. 11. El hermano es tan bueno como lo es la hermana. 12. La hermana es mejor que el hermano. 13. La lección que nosotras estudiamos no es tan difícil como la que (the one which) ustedes estudian. 14. La que ustedes estudian es menos difícil. 15. El hermano es menor que la hermana; es el menor de todos. 16. No trabaja bien; trabaja más despacio que todos.

BB. 1. The axe is not so good. 2. Did you find as many pens as we [did]? 3. We found more pens than you found. 4. These pupils are not as diligent as the [ones] in the room Mr. X. has. 5. The less this lazy boy has, the more he wants and the less he works. 6. The dinner is much colder than it was yesterday. 7. He washes his slate more than you wash your slate. 8. Is she as young as her sister? 9. No, she is older. 10. He has more pens than his cousin has, but he does not write with them (**ellas**) much. 11. These books and lessons are not as good as the ones that you have. 12. They are lazier now than we. 13. The man is the richest [one] in the street. 14. He is as rich as my cousin. 15. And the more he has, the more he wants. 16. She is the smallest pupil in the class.

LESSON XXIV
RELATIVE PRONOUNS

Review Lesson XVIII.

1. Note that the relative pronouns differ from the corresponding interrogatives in that the interrogatives have the accent written on the stressed syllable. This accent, it must be remembered, does not necessarily indicate that the word has an irregular stress, but that the word is interrogative and so to be distinguished from a similar form which is relative.

2. Referring to persons, **que**, *who, whom, that*, is used as subject or object of a verb.

>**El hombre que está aquí es mi hermano,** The man who is here is my brother.
>**El hombre que busca no está aquí,** The man (whom) he is looking for is my brother.

Quien, *whom*, follows a preposition.

>**El hombre con quien trabajo está aquí,** The man I work with is here.

3. Referring to things, **que**, *what, which, that,* is used as subject of a verb or as object of a verb or preposition.

> **El lápiz que está en la mesa es de Juan,** The pencil which is on the table is John's.
> **El lápiz que hallé es de Juan,** The pencil that I found is John's.
> **El lápiz con que escribo es malo,** The pencil with which I am writing is bad.

4. Other relative words are:

(a) **como,** *as,* in comparisons of equality (*see Lesson XXIII, 7*)

(b) **cual, cuales,** (*adjective or pronoun*), which

> cual padre tal hijo, like father like son (*lit.,* which the father, such the son)

(c) **cuyo, cuya,** etc. (*adjective*), whose

> **El hombre cuyo libro tengo,** .. The man whose book I have, ..

De quien is equivalent to **cuyo.**

> **El hombre de quien tengo el libro,** .. The man whose book I have, ..

(d) **cuanto, cuanta,** etc. (*adjective or pronoun*) how much, as much as; as many as (*See Lesson XXIII, 8*)

> **De cuantos hay, nadie habla con Juan,** Of as many as there are, no one is speaking with John.

(e) **cuando,** when; **donde,** where

> **Cuando usted está en Nueva York, donde está mi hermano,** ... When you are in New York, where my brother is, ...

5. Neither relative pronoun nor antecedent may be omitted in Spanish.

> **el libro que lee,** the book (which) he is reading
> **Me dijo lo que hallaron,** He told me (that which =) what they found.

6. The antecedent and pronoun should be as close together in Spanish as possible; and a preposition can come only directly before the word it governs.

> **No hallé al hombre de quien usted me habló,** I didn't find the man of whom you spoke to me. (I didn't find the man you spoke to me of.)

RELATIVE PRONOUNS

VOCABULARY

bajo, under
dice, (he, she, it) says; you say
dicen, (they) say; you say
dijo, (he, she, it) said; you said
enseñar, to point out, to show; to teach
existir, to exist
mismo, -a, same, very; (*after noun or pronoun*) -self
la mosca, fly
la pimienta, pepper
preguntar, to ask (a question)
la tinta, ink

A. 1. de quien 2. con quien 3. que es 4. con quien hablamos 5. que es 6. a quien buscamos 7. que hallé 8. con quien 9. que buscaba 10. como hallo 11. cuantos libros perdieron 12. el libro de que hablaron 13. los lápices que usted halló (*can you omit* que?) 14. los veinte pesos que usted halló 15. cuantos vasos limpiaron 16. con quienes hablamos 17. que hallé .18. que deseamos 19. cuales libros desearon 20. con quien habla

AA. 1. who 2. when he found 3. when you found 4. when did you find? 5. with which 6. whom he spoke with 7. with whom he spoke 8. which he looked-for 9. how much he wants 10. how he works 11. which books she found 12. whose pen I am writing with 13. the less he finds, the more he loses 14. the man I spoke with 15. I found the man who . . . . 16. how many pens you (*polite singular*) found 17. as many pens (as) he has, he has not enough 18. like father like son

B. 1. Conjugan los veinte primeros verbos del libro. 2. Los alumnos que no estudian son perezosos. 3. Los hombres a quienes buscamos no están aquí. 4. Los alumnos cuya pizarra lavamos ya no están aquí. 5. Me dijo cuántos pesos hallaron cuando buscaron la pluma bajo la mesa. (*Why is there an accent on* **cuántos**? *Note that an indirect statement or question is always a noun clause, whereas a relative clause is adjectival or adverbial.*) 6. Enseña a su hermano cómo cocina las comidas. 7. Vendieron la casa en que vivieron, y ahora tienen que buscar otra. 8. Los lápices que hallaron son de nuestras tías. 9. Las lecciones que estudiamos no son tan fáciles ni tan buenas como las que estudiamos ayer. 10. Me dijo cómo halló los libros que nosotras perdimos. 11. No me dijo quién está ahora en el piso alto. 12. Me dijo cuántos libros hay en el dormitorio de su hermano donde los dos estudian. 13. Enseño cuántos libros hay en el dormitorio. 14. No dijo a quién buscaron ayer en la calle donde viven sus primos. 15. El lápiz que está en mi mesa es de mi hermano. 16. No dijo cúya casa compró ni de quién es la otra casa que vendió.

BB. 1. The fifteen men whom we spoke to are not all soldiers. 2. The boys who live on the upper floor are not my cousins. 3. The books I looked-for (*see paragraphs 5 and 6 above*) are my brother's. 4. He did not say how many exercises he wrote. 6. He did not show how he worked. 7. Did he tell whose house his father bought? if it is the red [one] or the white [one]? 8. The man we looked-for is no longer here; he is in Paris (**París**). 9. Where is the man you gave (**dió**) the five hundred dollars to? 10. The more he has, the more he wants; and the more he wants, the less he has. 11. He told me (**me**), when he cooked the meal, that he wants to drink water when he eats, that he does not want milk. 12. Is the man who is over there (over there = **por allí**) your father? 13. No; the man I spoke of is my cousin. 14. He showed which books he is reading. 15. And which [ones] are they? 16. He told me what they said when they were here.

LESSON XXV

RELATIVE PRONOUNS (*Concluded*)

Review Lesson XXIV.

1. The relative pronoun has an inflected form, composed of the definite article plus either **que** or **cual**.

el que	la que	los que	las que, who, which, what
el cual	la cual	los cuales	las cuales

Note that **cual** has a plural **cuales**.

2. Where the antecedent of a relative pronoun may be confused with some other word, the inflected form is used to avoid confusion.

> El tío de la niña, la cual (la que) es muy pequeña, pregunta ...
> The girl's uncle, who (*the girl*) is very small, asks ...

3. **Which**, referring to a general idea, as that contained in an entire phrase or clause, is **lo cual, lo que** (*for the form* **lo**, *see also Lesson XII, 3*).

> Ella habla siempre, lo cual me aburre mucho, She is always talking, which bores me greatly.

4. **Quien** is sometimes used as a combination of antecedent plus relative, meaning **he (she, they) who; whoever.**

> Quien siempre habla, no dice siempre la verdad, He who (Whoever) is always talking, does not always tell the truth.

VOCABULARY

antiguo, -a, old, ancient
el empleado, clerk, employee
después de, after (*preposition of time*)
madrileño, -a, (native) of Madrid
moderno, -a, modern
la montaña, mountain
ni por mucho, not by a good deal
pasar, to pass, to go
el sendero, path
sevillano, -a, (native) of Seville
tanto, so much (*adverb*)
tantos, -as, so many

A. 1. Él no vive en la calle en que vivimos nosotros. 2. El padre de la alumna, el que no trabaja, es muy rico. 3. La tía de mi padre, la que está ahora en la casa, preguntó la misma cosa. 4. Los primos de mi amigo, el que es muy perezoso, estudian mucho y son alumnos muy buenos. 5. ¿Quién es el hombre que dijo que quien no trabaja es muy feliz? 6. La madre del niño, la cual vive en la casa blanca, prepara la comida para toda la familia. 7. Todo lo que el hombre dice, lo cual no es la verdad, nos aburre mucho. 8. Quien estudia mucho no es perezoso. 9. ¿Prepararon ellos mismos la comida que comieron? 10. Un madrileño es un hombre que vive en Madrid; y un sevillano es un hombre que vive en Sevilla. 11. Madrid es una ciudad muy antigua, y está en España. 12. Los hombres pasaron por un sendero que hallaron después de mucho trabajo. 13. ¿Tiene V. un empleado muy bueno?

14. Yo tengo uno que es muy bueno. 15. Los libros modernos, que usted lee tanto, no son todos, ni por mucho, buenos. 16. ¿Hay muchas moscas aquí? 17. Cree que la tinta que compró es buena. 18. No halla muy satisfactoria la tinta que su hermana compró.

AA. 1. There are many flies in this room. 2. Sevillians are men who live in Seville, not in Madrid. 3. The man's daughter, who (*the daughter*) is talking now, is a pupil in this school. 4. The girl, who (**la que**) is the largest pupil in the school, is lazy; she does not study much. 5. The girl who is writing there is my sister. 6. The [one] who is studying is my cousin. 7. The man who is his cousin is [a] tailor. 8. He went through a path which we found. 9. The glasses which are full of cold water are my mother's. 10. The books you are looking-for are on the table. 11. My brother's daughter, who is in Mrs. X's school (in the school of the Mrs. X.), is very diligent. 12. We found the red books of that man in the house. 13. What verbs are you conjugating?—We are conjugating the [ones] we prepared yesterday. 14. I don't want the ink which is black; I want red ink. 15. That path which he is pointing out to John is very old. 16. What are **madrileños**? 17. My house, which is on the corner of the street, is very large. 18. He who prepares a meal is not always the [one] who eats it.

LESSON XXVI

IMPERFECT (PAST DESCRIPTIVE) TENSE

Review Lessons IV, VIII, and X.

1. **hablar,** to speak (*stem* **habl-**)

hablaba, I was speaking, used to speak
hablabas, you were speaking, used to speak
hablaba, he, she, it was speaking, used to speak
hablábamos, we were speaking, used to speak
hablabais, you were speaking, used to speak
hablaban, they were speaking, used to speak

IMPERFECT (PAST DESCRIPTIVE) TENSE

beber, to drink (*stem* **beb-**)

bebía, I was drinking, *etc.*
bebías, you were drinking, *etc.*
bebía, he, she, it was drinking, *etc.*

bebíamos, we were drinking, *etc.*
bebíais, you were drinking, *etc.*
bebían, they were drinking, *etc.*

escribir, to write (*stem* **escrib-**)

escribía, I was writing, *etc.*
escribías, you were writing, *etc.*
escribía, he, she, it was writing, *etc.*

escribíamos, we were writing, *etc.*
escribíais, you were writing, *etc.*
escribían, they were writing, *etc.*

2. The second and third conjugations have the same endings. Note that the accent on all forms is written on the -í-.

The first conjugation has -ab- instead of -í-, and the accent is written only on the first plural.

3. The imperfect is used to denote (a) continued or (b) habitual action.

(a) **Trabajaba en Nueva York**, He was working in New York.
    Estudiaba cuando yo le hallé, He was studying when I found him.
(b) **Escribía un ejercicio todas las tardes**, He used to write (He would write) an exercise every afternoon.

VOCABULARY

ganar, to gain, to earn
la tarde, afternoon
todo, -a; -os, -as, all, whole

toda la ciudad, all the city, the whole city
todas las tardes, every afternoon

A. 1. quedaba 2. limpiábamos 3. cocinaban 4. lavaba 5. tomabais 6. no toca 7. ¿escribías? 8. usted deseaba 9. ¿no preguntabais? 10. hablaban 11. conjugaban 12. cocinábamos 13. tocábamos 14. aburríamos 15. bebían 16. tomaban 17. escribíamos 18. estabais

AA. 1. they were washing 2. you were writing 3. I used to write 4. it was boring 5. she would drink 6. would they eat? 7. he used to speak 8. were they taking? 9. he wasn't playing 10. he used to conjugate 11. you were buying 12. were you (*use* **estar**)? 13. he was 14. they used to take 15. you would write 16. we used to write 17. we were living 18. we would speak

B. 1. Escribían cuando nosotros cocinábamos la comida.
2. Vivíamos en la calle X. cuando vendió la casa a su tío.
3. Ningún hombre trabaja allí. 4. Comía en la casa de mi primo. 5. Cuando nosotros estábamos aquí, usted no estudiaba. 6. ¿Es usted?—Sí, yo soy (soy yo). 7. El hombre que vivía en la casa blanca ya no está aquí. 8. Vivía en la esquina de la calle X. 9. Siempre preguntaba las mismas cosas. 10. Comían siempre en la casa de mis tíos, que ahora están en Francia. 11. No deseaba una cuchara, deseaba un cuchillo. 12. ¿Buscaba V. a Juan o a Elena? 13. Buscaba a Elena, pero hallé a Juan. 14. No escribía más que cinco ejercicios. 15. Él estaba en París cuando nosotros lo buscábamos en Madrid.

BB. 1. The two men from Madrid whom we looked-for in Paris were tailors who were on X. Street (the street X.). 2. We were looking-for our cousins, but we did not find them. 3. He was showing the work every afternoon. 4. We used to live in the mountains, but now we are living in the city. 5. We used to live on the third floor. 6. They used to write some very satisfactory exercises. 7. She was looking for her brother's things. 8. The more he used to work, the less he used to earn. 9. The hundred men who used to work for my uncle did not earn very much. 10. He used to eat and drink at my parents' (in house of my parents). 11. He used to cook at my uncle's, but now he is working at the captain's (*see BB, 10*). 12. He would study with my cousins, but now they are in Paris, and he is very lazy—he does not study now. 13. What books were you studying? Are they as interesting as the [ones] which we were studying? 17. He is showing the books he was studying yesterday. 18. He has only eight now.

[Before taking lesson XXVII, study Appendix B, p. 208. Beginning with Lesson XXVII, the student should pay special attention to idiomatic expressions.]

LESSON XXVII
TENER, to have

1. Present Indicative (*stem irregular*).

tengo, I have, *etc.*
tienes, you have, *etc.*
tiene, he, she, it has; you have, *etc.*

tenemos, we have, *etc.*
tenéis, you have, *etc.*
tienen, they have; you have, *etc.*

2. Imperfect Indicative (*stem* **ten-**)

tenía, I had, *etc.*
tenías, you had, *etc.*
tenía, he, she, it had; you had, *etc.*

teníamos, we had, *etc.*
teníais, you had, *etc.*
tenían, they had; you had, *etc.*

Preterite Indicative (*stem* **tuv-**)

tuve, I had
tuviste, you had
tuvo, he, she, it had; you had

tuvimos, we had
tuvisteis, you had
tuvieron, they had; you had

2. (a) The present tense is somewhat irregular. Note the **-g-** in the first person singular, and the change of **-e-** to **-ie-** in the second and third singular and in the third person plural. The other endings are regular.

(b) The imperfect is wholly regular.

(c) The preterite changes the stem from **ten-** of the infinitive to **tuv-**. The endings of the first and third persons singular are the same as those of the first conjugation, but are unaccented; the other endings are the regular second conjugation endings.

3. The verb **tener** means **to have** in the sense of *possess*, and has that meaning only (do not use **tener** as the auxiliary, as in **I have seen**, where there is no idea of possession).

Tengo un libro, I have a book.
Teníamos nuestras comidas en casa de nuestra tía, We used to have our meals at our aunt's.
Tuvo un lápiz, He had a pencil.

4. **Tener**, when it takes a direct personal object, does not

have the preposition **a** (this is an exception to Lesson XII, 2).

Tengo un hermano, I have a brother.

5. Note the idioms:

(a) ¿**Qué tiene usted?** What is the matter with you? (*lit.*, What have you?)
No tengo nada, Nothing is the matter with me. (*lit.*, I have nothing.)
(b) ¿**Tiene usted frío?** Are you cold? (*lit.*, Have you cold?)

Frío is a noun, hence must be modified by an adjective. The Spanish does not say: "I am very cold," but "I have much cold."

Tengo mucho frío, I am very cold. (*lit.*, I have much cold.)

This construction is used only of persons. Cf. XIV, 2 and XV, 4.

(c) ¿**Cuántos años tiene usted?** How old are you? (*lit.*, How many years have you?)
Tengo diez y siete años, I am seventeen years old. (*lit.*, I have seventeen years.)

VOCABULARY

el aire, air
el año, year
¡ca! not at all! no, indeed!
el calor, heat
 tiene mucho calor, he is very warm
Dios, God
¡Por Dios! For heaven's sake!
(la) hambre, hunger
tiene hambre, he is hungry
llorar, to weep, to cry
el miedo, fear; tenemos miedo, we are afraid
nada, nothing (*pronoun*)
nada, not at all (*adverb*)
el sueño, sleep
tiene sueño, he is sleepy

A. 1. tenía 2. tuvieron 3. ¿tenía ella? 4. ¿no tenía él? 5. usted tiene 6. ¿no tienen? 7. tuvimos 8. ¿tuve yo? 9. no tuviste 10. ¿no tenía yo? 11. ¿cuántos años tenía? 12. ¿tienes calor? 13. tengo frío 14. tienen mucho frío 15. tengo 16. tenemos 17. teníamos 18. tuvimos 19. tenía 20. tiene 21. tuvo 22. tuvisteis 23. tenéis 24. tienes 25. tiene 26. teníais 27. tengo un libro 28. tengo dos tías 29. ¿qué tienes? 30. no tengo nada 31. V. no tiene 32. ¿tenía Vd.?

AA. 1. they are twenty and twenty-five years old 2. I had 3. they have 4. had they? 5. were you having?

6. I am holding. (**tengo**) 7. were they cold? 8. how old are you? 9. is he very old? 10. she was eighteen years old 11. what is the matter with you? 12. nothing is the matter with her 13. are you cold? 14. we are very warm 15. we had 16. did he have? 17. they were having 18. did you use to have? 19. you would have (you used to have)

B. 1. El aire en esta pieza está muy caliente; ¿no tiene usted mucho calor? 2. No tenía el libro. 3. No tuve miedo; pero yo soy muy pequeño y él es muy grande. 4. ¿Qué tenía?—No tenía nada. 5. Halló al niño, y el niño lloraba. 6. ¿Quién tuvo mi libro? ¿Juan o Enrique?—Fué Elena. 7. ¿Cuánto dinero tuviste ayer? 8. Mi madre no tenía ni cuchara ni tenedor; Juan los tenía. 9. Escribía una carta cuando yo entré en el dormitorio. 10. Don Enrique tiene mucho frío; ya tiene setenta años. 11. ¿Dónde tenías la tinta, Elena?—En la mesa de mi dormitorio. 12. Los amigos de mi primo, los que tenían la casa blanca de la esquina, son muy perezosos. 13. La vajilla que está en la pieza está muy sucia. 14. La ciudad donde tiene sus casas no es muy grande. 15. Vivieron allí mucho tiempo.

BB. 1. What have you in your bedroom? 2. I have some books there today, but I did not have them there yesterday. 3. Were you very cold yesterday? 4. No, indeed, I was warm; but the room was cold. 5. Are you afraid? 6. How old are your sister's children now? 7. She is eight years old, and her father is forty-five. 8. Did they conjugate again the verbs the student pointed out? 9. No, they were conjugating them when I entered the room. 10. Did you find the man?—No, he wasn't in the house. 11. I like to have books, but I have not many. 12. Did you want the book I was reading? 13. No, I wanted the book John had. 14. They had the third exercise, but they did not write. 15. Didn't they study the lesson?—No, indeed.

LESSON XXVIII
HABER, to have

Review Lesson XXVII.

1. Present Indicative (*stem irregular*)

he, I have, *etc.*
has, you have, *etc.*
ha, he, she, it has; you have, *etc.*

hemos, we have, *etc.*
habéis, you have, *etc.*
han, they have; you have, *etc.*

Imperfect Indicative (*stem* hab-)

había, I had, *etc.*
habías, you had, *etc.*
había, he, she, it had; you had, *etc.*

habíamos, we had, *etc.*
habíais, you had, *etc.*
habían, they had; you had, *etc.*

Preterite Indicative (*stem* hub-)

hube, I had
hubiste, you had
hubo, he, she, it had; you had

hubimos, we had
hubisteis, you had
hubieron, they had; you had

2. (a) The present tense is irregular. Note the first person singular ending and the -as, -a of the second and third persons. In the plural, the first and third persons are also irregular. The second person plural, **habéis**, is the only regular form. In the other five forms, the stem is shortened to **h-**.

(b) The imperfect tense is wholly regular.

(c) The preterite changes the stem from **hab-** of the infinitive to **hub-**. The endings of the first and third persons singular are unaccented, but have the same vowels as the first conjugation preterite (*cf.* **tener** *in Lesson XXVII, 2c*).

3. **Hay**, made by adding **y** to the third person singular of the present, is an impersonal verb form meaning **there is** or **there are**.

Hay un lápiz en la mesa, There is a pencil on the table.
Hay dos plumas en mi pieza, There are two pens in my room.

In the other tenses, the third person singular is similarly used, but without adding **y**.

Había un lápiz en la mesa, There was a pencil on the table.

Note expressions like **debe haber**, there must be (**debe**, it ought).

4. **Hay** is used in certain idioms.

hay viento, it is windy (*lit.*, there is wind)
hay sol, it is sunny (*lit.*, there is sun)
hay neblina, it is foggy (*lit.*, there is fog)

5. **Haber** is used most commonly as the auxiliary to form the perfect tenses.

Perfect Indicative, **hablar**

he hablado, I have spoken	**hemos hablado,** we have spoken
has hablado, you have spoken	**habéis hablado,** you have spoken
ha hablado, he, she, it has spoken; you have spoken	**han hablado,** they have spoken; you have spoken

Pluperfect Indicative, **hablar**

había hablado, I had spoken	**habíamos hablado,** we had spoken
habías hablado, you had spoken	**habíais hablado,** you had spoken
había hablado, he, she, it had spoken; you had spoken	**habían hablado,** they had spoken; you had spoken

Perfect Indicative, **beber**   Perfect Indicative, **vivir**

he bebido, I have drunk	**he vivido,** I have lived
has bebido, you have drunk, *etc.*	**has vivido,** you have lived, *etc.*

Pluperfect Indicative, **beber**   Pluperfect Indicative, **vivir**

había bebido, I had drunk	**había vivido,** I have lived
habías bebido, you had drunk, *etc.*	**habías vivido,** you had lived, *etc.*

He hablado con su padre, I have spoken with your father.
Lo había escrito, He had written it.

In questions, the subject, if expressed, follows the whole compound.

¿**Lo había escrito Juan?** Did John write it?

VOCABULARY

después, afterwards (*adverb*)   **después que,** after (*conj.*)

A. 1. hay viento 2. hay 3. ¿había? 4. había neblina

5. había 6. habíamos aburrido 7. no habíamos conjugado
8. había neblina 9. hubo 10. ¿había? 11. no hay 12. no hubo 13. tú has vivido 14. ¿ha habido sol? 15. ha habido viento 16. no hay 17. hay viento 18. ¿no había viento? 19. vosotras habéis lavado

AA. 1. was it foggy? 2. there is 3. there are 4. there wasn't 5. it was sunny 6. there were 7. were there? 8. it is windy 9. was it windy? 10. there are 11. it is not windy 12. he has drunk 13. he had written 14. you have hastened 15. she had gone out 16. we had had 17. had we had? 18. she has prepared

B. 1. ¿Ha hablado a su padre del libro que compró ayer? 2. Hay mucho viento y yo tengo mucho frío. 3. ¿Ha hablado usted con algún hombre ayer de las cosas de su padre? 4. ¿Hay mucho sol hoy? 5. ¿Hay muchos alumnos en esta escuela? 6. Sí, hay muchos. 7. Ayer había mucho viento, pero hoy no hay viento. 8. No tiene lección para hoy; ayer había estudiado toda la lección y después escribió el ejercicio. 9. El hombre que preparó la comida no la comió. 10. No hemos hallado los lápices que buscábamos. 11. Ayer había sol, pero hoy no hay sol. 12. Mis primos han vivido en Madrid, pero ahora viven en Barcelona. 13. Yo he tenido mi dormitorio en el piso alto; pero ahora lo tengo en el piso bajo. 14. El alumno ha preparado sus lecciones para hoy.

BB. 1. Have they written their exercises yet? 2. It is very sunny and windy today. 3. Had they studied their lessons when you came into their room? 4. No, and they have not studied them yet. 5. They are very lazy; the man who teaches in their school must (**debe**) be good. 6. Have you bought the pencils they want? 7. Who wants them?—The man whose son is studying in our room. 8. The man who lived in the house had bored me a great deal. 9. It was very foggy when we entered Paris. 10. We have not studied as much as you have studied, but we have studied more lessons than you have studied and we have prepared them better. 11. The lessons we have prepared are the most difficult in (*how expressed?*) the book. 12. After we ate the dinner, we washed the dishes. 13. Had she finished washing the glasses when you were there? 14. As much money as he has, he wants more.

LESSON XXIX
IDIOMS WITH TENER AND HABER

Review Lessons XXVII and XXVIII.

1. The following very common expressions are formed with **tener** and **haber**:

(a) **tener que**, have to, must

> Tengo que escribir el ejercicio, I have to (must) write the exercise.

The **que** may be separated from the verb, and then the expression is to be translated:

> Tengo un ejercicio que escribir, I have an exercise to write.

(b) **Haber de** plus the infinitive means **am to, are to**, etc.

> He de escribir dos ejercicios para mañana, I am to write two exercises for tomorrow.

(c) **Hay que** (**había que**, *etc.*) is an impersonal expression, the meanings of which are best learned from examples.

> Hay tres lecciones que estudiar para mañana, There are three lessons to be studied for tomorrow.
> No hay nada que hacer, There is nothing to be done. (*lit.*, nothing to do.)
> Hay que hacerlo, It must be done, It ought to be done. (*lit.*, There is to do it.)

Note pronoun object following and joined to infinitive.

2. Note the following idioms. Similar expressions can readily be formed.

> ¡Pobre de usted! You poor fellow!
> ¡Infeliz de Juan! Unhappy fellow that John is!
> ¡Ay de usted! Woe to you! You poor fellow!
> No ve lo buenos que son, He doesn't see how good they are.

3. Present Indicative of Ver, to see (stem v-)

veo, I see
ves, you see
ve, he, she, it sees; you see

vemos, we see
veis, you see
ven, they see; you see

VOCABULARY

la camisa, shirt
el cuello, collar
la chaqueta, jacket, coat
hacer, to do, to make

infeliz, unhappy, unlucky
pobre, poor
el zapato, shoe

A. 1. ¡infeliz de nosotros! 2. han de ... 3. tenía que ... 4. tenemos un libro que estudiar 5. ha tenido que lavar 6. teníamos que ... 7. tenemos lecciones que estudiar 8. hay que hacer 9. hay mucho que hacer 10. hay que ver 11. había de verlas 12. tenemos que entrar 13. ha tenido que estudiar 14. hay que leerlo 15. había que leer 16. hemos tenido que escribir 17. ¡pobre de Juan! 18. ¡ay de María

AA. 1. we have a lesson to write 2. poor fellows! 3. poor John! 4. did we have to come in? 5. is he to speak? 6. was he to play the piano? 7. we have had to study 8. there is much to be done 9. has he had to clean? 10. there is nothing to be cleaned 11. you should have seen the mist! (¡había que ver la neblina!) 12. was he to play the piano? 13. they have had to live in that (aquella) house 13. you should have read the book! 14. you ought to see the house! 15. poor fellow!

B. 1. ¿Tenían que comprar zapatos sin medias? 2. ¡Hay que ver el sombrero que tiene! 3. Había de tocar el piano cuando usted entró en la pieza. 4. Compraron cuatro camisas y doce cuellos y después no los hallaron en la casa cuando los desearon. 5. Cuanto más tenían que estudiar, tanto menos estudiaron. 6. ¿Ha tenido usted frío en su dormitorio? 7. Tenemos que preparar la comida para hoy. 8. ¡Hay que ver cuánto comen! 9. ¡Pobre de Juan! no trabaja ni tiene dinero. 10. Hemos tenido que trabajar mucho para preparar la lección. 11. Ha habido mucho viento, pero ahora hay sol. 12. ¡Infelices de ustedes! ¿Por qué no prepararon mejor su lección? 13. Había de tocar el piano ella, no él. 14. ¿Quién ha lavado la vajilla? ¡Hay que ver lo sucia que está! 15. ¡Había que ver lo bien que escribía!

BB. 1. Did they have to study the lessons yesterday or are they studying today? 2. You ought to see the exercises he wrote! 3. You poor fellow! 4. I am to eat dinner with my uncle today. 5. He was to come in the room with us, but he didn't finish studying. 6. There were so many things to do that I didn't do (**no hice**) anything (**nada**). 7. Did you have many verbs to conjugate? 8. No, we had few. 9. As many lessons as he had to study, none did he study well. 10. He didn't have as much money as I. 11. But he was much happier. 12. Whose books did you have? 13. I had John's. 14. The water is warm; we didn't have cold water. 15. They have had to live in the white house because they didn't buy the other. 16. Poor children! It was so windy that they didn't see the city. 17. Are you cold?—Is the air in the room cold?

LESSON XXX

DEMONSTRATIVE ADJECTIVES AND PRONOUNS

1. Masculine   Feminine

Masculine		Feminine	
este, this	**estos**, these	**esta**, this	**estas**, these
ese, that	**esos**, those	**esa**, that	**esas**, those
aquel, that	**aquellos**, those	**aquella**, that	**aquellas**, those

(a) **Este** is readily understood from the English equivalent.

(b) **Ese** is used of objects relatively near, and **aquel** of objects relatively distant.

Yo tengo este libro, I have this book.
Tú tienes (Vd. tiene) ese libro, You have that book.
Él tiene aquel libro, He has that book.

(c) **Ahí** means **there** (rather near) and **allí** also means **there** (but distant from the speaker).

¿Qué tienes ahí? What have you there?
¿Qué tiene Juan allí? What has John there?

(d) Note the endings of the masculine singular.

2. The demonstrative adjectives are also used as pronouns; but in writing, an accent mark is placed over the stressed syllable to distinguish pronoun from adjective.

éste, this (one)   **éstos,** these   **ésta,** this (one)   **éstas,** these
ése, that (one)   **ésos,** those   **ésa,** that (one)   **ésas,** those
aquél, that (one) **aquéllos,** those   **aquélla,** that (one) **aquéllas,** those

3. In such phrases as: "I think not," "I think so," "I believe so," the **not, so,** etc. take the place of a clause (e. g. "I think that it is so"). In Spanish, therefore, they must be preceded by the conjunction **que,** since a conjunction cannot be omitted before the subordinate clause.

Creo que sí, I think so. (*lit.*, I think that yes.)
Me parece que no, I think not. (*lit.*, It seems to me that not.)

VOCABULARY

aquí, here
cerca de, near
eléctrico, -a, electric
el estudiante, (college) student
la luz, light
parece, it appears, it seems
me parece, it seems to me, I think
el petróleo, kerosene

A. 1. éstas 2. ésos 3. aquélla 4. ésas 5. estos niños 6. estas plumas 7. esta agua 8. este reloj 9. aquellos dormitorios 10. estas virtudes 11. estas pizarras 12. esta tiza 13. ésos 14. aquéllos 15. esta mesa 16. estos zapatos 17. aquellas camisas 18. esos cuellos 19. esta comida 20. aquellas niñas

AA. 1. these 2. that meal 3. this house 4. that 5. these 6. this truth 7. that chalk 8. those women 9. this cousin 10. that slate 11. these students 12. those verbs 13. these meals 14. that 15. those 16. these 17. this ice 18. that water 19. this sugar 20. these chairs 21. those eggs 22. those houses 23. that coffee

B. 1. ¿Has hallado los libros rojos y los blancos?

2. ¿Son estos libros de su señor tío?[1] 3. ¿Cuáles libros son los que usted ha hallado en mi dormitorio? 4. ¿Han hallado tantos libros en éste como en aquél? 5. Estos lápices son mejores que los de Juan. 6. ¿En qué calle de Madrid viven ustedes? 7. ¿Qué tienes ahí? ¿Es un libro? 8. Estos vasos están vacíos, pero aquéllos están llenos de agua. 9. ¿Cúyo piano es éste?—¿Lo toca Juan? 10. En aquella esquina hay una casa blanca, en donde (where) vive mi primo, don Enrique. 11. Mis padres ya no viven en esta ciudad; viven ahora en Madrid. 12. Aquí hay luz eléctrica, pero ahí tienes que tener la luz de una lámpara de petróleo. 13. ¿Es buen alumno su primo? —Me parece que sí. 14. Yo creo que no. Me parece que no es muy bueno como estudiante. 15. ¿Está aquí su señora madre?

BB. 1. Was it windy yesterday? This man doesn't think so. 2. There are now seven hundred soldiers in this city. 3. How many soldiers are there in your (= that) city? 4. This child is younger than that one, but he is larger. 5. Who is that man who says that he who does not work is very happy? 6. Everything this man says bores me greatly. 7. What did they have there? 8. Are these books as difficult as John's? 9. The more these children study, the less, it seems to me, they learn (**aprenden**). 10. These forks and spoons are my aunt's; I found them today. 11. Are these children here your cousin's? 12. This thin child is my cousin, but that one is not (it), he is my cousin's friend. 13. These chairs and tables are no good. 14. What is that thing there near you, John? —Is it a book? 15. I think not. 16. Is your father in Madrid now?

---

[1] **señor, (señora, señorita)**, may be put before a noun, in speaking to a person, to make the expression more polite.

¿Cómo está su señor padre? How is your father?
¿Está aquí su señora madre? Is your mother here?

LESSON XXXI
DEMONSTRATIVES (*Concluded*)

Review Lesson XXX.

1. Éste (*adjective or pronoun*) may mean **the latter;** and **aquél, the former.**

> Juan y María están aquí; ésta es mi prima y aquél mi amigo, John and Mary are here; the latter is my cousin and the former my friend.

2. Expressions like **my brother's** are rendered in Spanish by **that of my brother.**

> mi dinero y el de mi primo, my money and my cousin's

The demonstrative is sometimes used to give more emphasis.

> este niño y aquel que encontramos ayer, this child and the one that we met yesterday

Note that the demonstrative does not have the accent here.

3. Each of the demonstrative pronouns has a neuter form: **esto, eso,** and **aquello.** As there are no neuter demonstrative adjectives (for there are no neuter nouns), no accent has to be written over the forms. These pronouns refer to a clause, phrase, or general or vague idea.

There is no plural for these forms. Note that it is the neuter forms, and not the masculine, that end in **-o.**

> ¿Qué es eso? What is that?
> Todo eso que usted dice es la verdad, All that you say is the truth.
> Él las ha hallado.—Eso no es la verdad, He found them.—That is not the truth.

4. En ésta has the special meaning of **in this town; en ésa, in that town** (the town of one's correspondent, to whom one is writing).

> En ésta no hay novedad, There is nothing new in this town (here).

VOCABULARY

bajar, to go down, to descend
el brazo, arm
un cabello, [a] hair
los cabellos, hair (*collective*)
el carro, street car, trolley
 (*South-American word*)
 castaño, -a, chestnut-colored
el dedo, finger
 derecho, -a, right; straight
duele, (it) hurts
el pie me duele, my foot hurts
encontrar, to meet, find, come across
enfermo, -a, sick, ill, sore
flojo, -a, lazy
izquierdo, -a, left
tomar, to take
el tranvía, street car, trolley
 (*word used in Spain*)

A. 1. aquél 2. éste 3. mi libro y el de mi hermano 4. eso 5. aquello 6. ésta 8. éste 9. aquél 10. aquélla 11. mi tiza y la del niño 12. su ejercicio y el de su primo 13. Juan y María; ésta y aquél .... 14. este libro y aquél 15. ¿Qué es eso? 16. Eso es (That's so)

AA. 1. What's that? 2. this 3. that 4. this book 5. this [one] 6. that [one] 7. my slate and my cousin's 8. those 9. that's so 10. that's right (that is so) 11. the former and the latter 12. the latter and the former 13. that is so 14. the former 15. the former and the latter 16. the former 17. it seems to me that is the truth 18. the former and the latter 19. in this town 20. in your town 21. there (in your town)

B. 1. Éste no está muy sucio; pero hay que lavarlo. 2. ¿Qué dice el niño de (with) los cabellos castaños? 3. ¿Qué niño? ¿Aquél? Sus cabellos son rubios, no castaños. 4. Tomamos el tranvía en esta calle, que es la calle X., y bajamos por la calle Z. 5. El dedo me duele. 6. ¿En qué calle vive? 7. En ésta hay muchas casas blancas; en ésa, son todas rojas. 8. En aquella escuela hay muy pocos alumnos; en ésta, hay muchos; pero éstos son muy flojos, aquéllos, muy diligentes. 9. Este pie me duele; lo tengo muy enfermo (it is very sore). 10. Me parece que este niño está muy contento.—Sí, lo es. 11. Aquéllos ya no están en Francia; están en Inglaterra. 12. ¿Le duele mucho la cara?—Ya me parece que no. 13. En ésta hay mucha neblina. 14. Sus niños y los de su tío son muy diligentes; estudian mucho en esta escuela.

15. No tomamos el carro en esta calle; lo tomamos en aquélla.

BB. 1. Those are my cousins; they live in this street. 2. This arm hurts; it is very sore (I have it very sore). 3. These men went by a path they found after much trouble (work). 4. That child with the blond hair is my sister; the one with the dark hair is my cousin (*see B, 2*). 5. The boy's fingers hurt; they are very sore. 6. Is X. Street near this one?—I think so. 7. These pupils are very diligent; they have prepared their work well. 8. Did you take the car?—No, no one showed us where to take it. 9. Is it sunny in your city?—No, it is windy here. 10. My right foot hurts me very much; it is very sore. 11. Those children are very lazy; they do not study the easy lessons, much less (so-much [the] less) the hard [ones]. 12. He is conjugating the first verb in this book. 13. He has finished conjugating those in my book and in my brother's also. 14. She was buying the books when we found her. 15. That man is the father of this pupil, who goes to our school.

LESSON XXXII

1. Future Indicative of hablar, to speak (*stem* hablar-)

hablaré, I shall speak
hablarás, you will speak
hablará, he she, it will speak; you will speak

hablaremos, we shall speak
hablaréis, you will speak
hablarán, they will speak; you will speak

beber, to drink (*stem* beber-)

beberé, I shall drink
beberás, you will drink
beberá, he, she, it will drink; you will drink

beberemos, we shall drink
beberéis, you will drink
beberán, they will drink; you will drink

escribir, to write (*stem* escribir-)

escribiré, I shall write
escribirás, you will write
escribirá, he, she, it will write; you will write

escribiremos, we shall write
escribiréis, you will write
escribirán, they will write; you will write

Note:

(a) The future endings are alike in all three conjugations.

(b) They are added to the whole infinitive, not to the stem. (Certain irregular verbs, however, have a modified infinitive stem. Cf. A, 20 and 21, below.)

(c) Note that the first plural is the only form without a written accent.

2. Conditional.

hablar, to speak (*stem* **hablar-**)

hablaría, I should speak	hablaríamos, we should speak
hablarías, you would speak	hablaríais, you would speak
hablaría, he, she, it would speak; you would speak	hablarían, they would speak; you would speak

beber, to drink (*stem* **beber-**)

bebería, I should drink	beberíamos, we should drink
beberías, you would drink	beberíais, you would drink
bebería, he, she, it would drink; you would drink	beberían, they would drink; you would drink

escribir, to write (*stem* **escribir-**)

escribiría, I should write	escribiríamos, we should write
escribirías, you would write	escribiríais, you would write
escribiría, he, she, it would write; you would write	escribirían, they would write; you would write

Note:

(a) The conditional endings are alike in all three conjugations.

(b) They are added to the whole infinitive. (Certain irregular verbs, however, have a modified infinitive stem.)

(c) The accent is written on all six forms.

3. The future and conditional are generally used as in English.

Mañana estaré en Madrid, Tomorrow I shall be in Madrid.
Mañana estaría en Madrid si . . . Tomorrow I should be in Madrid if . . .

4. The future has also a special meaning in Spanish: it expresses probability in the present. For "He is probably here," or "He must be here," the Spanish often says:

Estará aquí, He is probably here, He must be here, *etc.*
No estará aquí, He can't be here, He isn't here likely, *etc.*
But
Está probablemente aquí may be used.

5. The same idea of probability, likelihood in past time, is expressed by the conditional.

Estaría aquí ayer, He was probably here yesterday.
But
Estaba probablemente aquí ayer could also be used.

VOCABULARY

antes, before (*adv. of time*)
considerar, to consider
cumplir (con), to fulfill; to complete
cumplió hoy diez años, he is ten years old today; he reached his tenth birthday today
el deber, duty
detrás de, behind
juzgar, to judge
listo, -a, ready
llegar, to arrive

A. 1. viviré 2. ¿bebería él? 3. usted hablará 4. ella escribiría 5. tú quedarías 6. lavaré 7. cocinaréis 8. conjugaré 9. hallarás 10. ¿estudiarían? 11. comprarás 12. lavarán 13. prepararían 14. acudirán 15. tú escribirías 16. ¿no aburriría? 17. tocará el piano 18. sería 19. no estaré 20. tendremos (*note that* **tener** *has the stem* **tendr-** *in the future and conditional*) 21. **habrá** (*note that* **haber** *has the stem* **habr-** *in the future and conditional*) 22. **habré** tenido

AA. 1. would they wash? 2. I shall not clean 3. he will hasten 4. you would cook 5. I shall find 6. will you play the piano? 7. he would clean 8. will they have? 9. I shall be 10. would he have? 11. you would bring 12. would they study? 13. you will buy 14. they will clean 15. would they prepare? 16. they will hasten 17. you would write 18. wouldn't he bore? 19. he will play the piano 20. would he be? 21. I shall not be

22. will he not have? 23. they will not have had 24. I shall have the books

B. 1. Sin un buen libro no estudiaré bien los verbos españoles. 2. Desearía hablar un poco con usted. 3. ¿Estará aquí su hermano? 4. Comeré la comida que ella preparó. 5. No, es para Juan. 6. ¿Vivirá usted en esa casa blanca si la compramos? 7. ¿Venderá usted sus libros si yo los compro? 8. ¿Tocarán ellos el piano antes o después? 9. Detrás de la mesa está la silla y sobre la silla hay un reloj muy grande. 10. ¿Cómo estará su primo hoy? ¿Estará todavía enfermo? 11. ¿Cuántos años tendrá (*future of* **tener**) su hermano ahora? 12. No tendrá más que quince años. 13. Hablaron con sus amigos después de la comida. 14. ¿Qué tendrán allí? 15. Probablemente está aquí.

BB. 1. Can your brother be here now? 2. Where is my brother? He is probably studying. 3. If he works, we study; but when we are working, he plays the piano. 4. As he will not be here tomorrow, they are not writing the exercise. 5. The more we [shall] work, the less we shall have. 6. We shall not have the house in which we lived; our father has already sold it. 7. We shall have written (**Habremos escrito**) the exercises when you (will) arrive. 8. What does your brother judge of a man who does not fulfil (**cumple con**) his duty? 9. Can your mother have bought (**Habrá comprado su señora madre**) your books already? 10. Don't you consider that he is a very industrious student? 11. He isn't here now, but he will probably arrive today. 12. He can't have much work today, but yesterday he had a-lot (much). 13. Do you think your brother is ready? (Will your brother be ready?) 14. I shall not have all my lessons for tomorrow; I have not studied much today. 15. He is fifteen years old today.

LESSON XXXIII
NOUNS AND ADJECTIVES

1. **Gender.** Nouns and adjectives of nationality ending in a consonant add -a to form the feminine.

alemán, German (*masculine*)   **alemana,** German (*feminine*)
escocés, Scotch   **escocesa,** Scotch
español, Spanish   **española,** Spanish

2. Adjectives ending in **-ón, -or,** or **-án** add **-a** to form the feminine.

socarrón, sly (*masculine*)   **socarrona,** sly (*feminine*)
burlón, humorous, joking   **burlona,** humorous, joking
hablador, talkative   **habladora,** talkative
traidor, treacherous   **traidora,** treacherous
haragán, lazy   **haragana,** lazy

Exceptions are comparatives in **-or**: **mejor, peor, menor,** and **mayor** (*See Lesson XXIII, 2*).

3. Review Lessons V and VI.

El día, day, is masculine; **la mano,** hand, is feminine, in spite of the ending.

Nouns ending in **-ma, -ta** are usually masculine.

el cometa, comet   **el planeta,** planet   **el programa,** program
el telegrama, telegram   **el dentista,** dentist

Note:

el *or* **la espía,** spy   **el** *or* **la guía,** guide   **el mapa,** map
el presidente, la presidenta, president   **la centinela,** sentinel

4. **Position.**

Review Lesson VII, 2.

Adjectives of number (**first, second,** etc.; **one, two,** etc.); all the articles (**a, the, this, his, which, such,** etc.); usually, a few very common adjectives (**pretty, good, some,** and a few others) precede the noun. All other adjectives—such as adjectives of color, shape, size, nationality—follow the noun. Briefly, limiting adjectives precede; descriptive adjectives follow.

NOUNS AND ADJECTIVES

el hombre, the man
este niño, this boy
su pizarra, his slate
tres libros, three books
primer ejercicio, first exercise
pequeños libros, small books
bonitas casas, pretty houses
ciertas niñas, certain children
algunas sillas, some chairs

pluma negra, black pen
mesa redonda, round table
hombre enorme, huge man
ejercicio español, Spanish exercise
sombrero de paja, straw hat
carta escrita, written letter
niño flojo, lazy child
alumno diligente, industrious student
muchacha haragana, lazy girl

5. If two or more adjectives are used, each follows the normal rule for position.

> las dos pizarras negras y cuadradas, the two square black slates
> tres libros de mucho valor, three books of great value

6. Some adjectives that usually follow may precede when used in a poetic or figurative sense.

> un soldado grande, a large soldier
> un gran soldado, a great soldier
>
> mi hermana pequeña, my little (small) sister
> mi pequeña hermana, my little (young) sister
>
> cosa cierta, sure (reliable) thing
> cierta cosa, a certain thing (some thing)
>
> niño pobre, poor (poverty-stricken) child
> pobre niño, poor (unhappy) child
>
> el blanco pan, white-bread (*as a sort of compound word*)
> la pura verdad, the whole truth

VOCABULARY

cuadrado, -a, square (*adjective*)
chico, -a, small
desagradable, disagreeable
entonces, then
largo, -a, long
la nieve, snow
la paja, straw
el poema, poem
ronco, -a, hoarse
turco, -a, Turkish
el trueno, thunder
el valor, worth, value
la voz, voice

A. 1. el poema 2. traidora 3. burlona 4. española 5. escocesa 6. peor (*what is the feminine of this word?*) 7. peores 8. el ronco trueno 9. la nieve blanca 10. voz ronca 11. gran hombre 12. un telegrama 13. centinela 14. el cometa 15. la mano 16. la mano derecha 17. niña burlona 18. el día 19. hombres turcos 20. alumnas

haraganas 21. verdad cierta 22. ciertas verdades
23. hombre grande 24. bonito niño 25. niño muy bonito
(**bonito** *follows the noun because it is itself modified;* **bonito** *usually precedes*)

AA. 1. the day 2. a certain lesson 3. a telegram
4. a sure guide 5. treacherous spy 6. the sentinel
7. funny (humorous) child 8. a hand 9. the comet
10. humorous 11. hoarse voice 12. my program 13. sly
fellow 14. great soldier 15. talkative woman 16. Scotch
women 17. some books 18. large girl 19. pretty red
house 20. very pretty child 21. straw hat 22. a sure
thing 23. a telegram

B. 1. No tengo bonitos vasos para la comida. 2. Los
espías pasaron por el camino. 3. No hallé un programa
y por consiguiente no deseaba quedar allí. 4. Este niño
grande, que está en nuestra escuela, vive con sus padres
en aquella gran casa blanca (**gran** *is here put before the noun to balance* **blanca**). 5. Volvió a hablar de aquella
muchacha habladora. 6. Cuando entré en la pieza, hallé
un telegrama muy largo de mi hermano. 7. Escribió el
primer ejercicio en su pizarra, el segundo en papel, y el
tercero en su libro. 8. Aquel niño traidor, ¡no le tendría
en mi casa! 9. Aquel día no hallé mi dinero; pero hoy
lo hallé en su dormitorio. 10. Me ha hablado de ciertas
cosas que no deseo creer. 11. ¿Cuándo estará aquí el
cometa? 12. Un gran hombre no es siempre un hombre
rico; y un hombre rico no es siempre un hombre haragán.
13. No había tantos ingleses como escoceses en Madrid.
14. Tienen algunos pequeños libros rojos, en que escribían
sus ejercicios de español. 15. Tienen también pizarras,
en que escriben con tiza. 16. Un gran hombre no es
siempre un hombre grande. 17. ¿Son sus tíos?—Sí, los
son (Yes, they are).

BB. 1. They found the telegram they had from their
cousins. 2. The books will be here today. 3. Are they
Scotch or English (the) [ones] who live in the house now?
4. There used to be several Englishmen who lived in that

red house on S. Street in Santiago, but now Germans live there. 5. This lazy fellow has a hard disagreeable task (work), a thing which seems very tiresome to him. 6. These boys are writing a long exercise in Spanish for tomorrow. 7. That sly fellow will not show me how he works. 8. Did you show (to) John how to do it? 9. Did you find my program? 10. John took it from the table. 11. She is very talkative, she talks very much, and bores me always. 12. Certain friends showed John a white house, which he bought. 13. It is a sure truth that a large man is not always a great man, but many great men are large. 14. They wrote the first exercise and then the second, and then remained (in order) to talk of the third. 15. A certain man showed me the house in which they live. 16. They had just bought it. 17. They have found their Spanish books, but they did not have to write [any] exercises.

LESSON XXXIV
PLURAL

Review Lessons IX and XII.

1. Nouns ending in an accented vowel or diphthong form the plural by adding -es (as do words ending in a consonant).

el rubí, ruby   **la ley**, law
los rubíes, rubies   **las leyes**, laws

2. Words in unstressed -es and -is have the same form in the singular and plural. This is important chiefly for the names of the days of the week.

lunes, Monday   **viernes**, Friday
martes, Tuesday   **(sábado)**, Saturday
miércoles, Wednesday   **(domingo)**, Sunday
jueves, Thursday   (*all masculine; note small letter*)
la tesis, thesis   **las tesis**, theses

3. A number of words may be considered as **irregular**, being too rare for classification.

el papá, father, "dad"   los papás, fathers, "dads"
　　　　　　　　　　　　　　　　(*familiar form*)
la mamá, mother　　　　 las mamás, mothers (*familiar form*)
el pie, foot　　　　　　　 los pies, feet
el canapé, couch　　　　 los canapés, couches (*also*, canapées)
el cortaplumas, penknife　los cortaplumas, penknives
el te, tea　　　　　　　　 los tes, teas
el café, coffee　　　　　　los cafés, coffees

4. Surnames are usually unmodified in the plural, but are preceded by the definite article in the plural.

los García, the Garcías　　los hermanos Gálvez, the Gálvez brothers

5. As an adjective in the masculine plural may modify at the same time feminine and masculine nouns, so a masculine noun may refer to objects of both genders. (*Cf. Lesson IX, 3*).

　　mis tíos, my uncle and aunt, my uncles, my uncles and aunts
　　mis padres, my parents

VOCABULARY

el bambú, bamboo　　　　　el rey, king
　barato, -a, cheap, inexpensive　la semana, week
　caro, -a, dear, expensive　　　todavía, still, yet
　cursi, cheap, vulgar　　　　　usar, to use; to wear
la hipótesis, hypothesis　　　　el maravedí, farthing
la mies, (*pl.*) mieses, corns, grains

A. 1. bambúes 2. mis hermanos 3. rubíes 4. reyes 5. canapés 6. los lunes 7. reyes 8. cafés 9. las tesis 10. los miércoles 11. los hermanos Hernández 12. cursis 13. mis tíos 14. los tes 15. los cortaplumas 16. papás 17. mamás 18. los jueves 19. pies 20. maravedíes 21. mis primos, Juan, Enrique, y María 22. rubíes 23. cafés 24. canapés

AA. 1. kings 2. laws 3. couches 4. penknives 5. my uncle and aunt 6. my uncles and aunts 7. my uncles 8. Wednesdays 9. feet 10. my cousins, Mary and John 11. my parents 12. Friday 13. (the) Fridays 14. rubies 15. cheap penknives 16. theses 17. fathers (*use familiar word*) 18. teas 19. farthings 20. thesis 21. the Gutiérrezes 22. the Gutiérrez sisters 23. mammas

B. 1. Mis tíos beben su te ahora; toman [el] te con sus amigos todos los miércoles. 2. ¿Han comido ya los García? ¿Están con ellos sus padres? 3. Hoy día (Today) no hay muchos reyes. 4. Tengo los pies muy enfermos. 5. Compraron un canapé, pero todavía no ha llegado a la casa. 6. No acabó de beber su café cuando sus primos, Juan y María, entraron en la pieza. 7. ¿Cuántos rubíes compró su primo para su hermana? 8. Hemos hallado dos lápices (*singular* **lápiz**) en esta pieza; ¿son de usted o de su padre?—Son de mis primos, Juan y Enrique. 9. ¿Qué es cortaplumas en inglés? 10. Los lunes y los miércoles son días de la semana. 11. Los rubíes que enseñó son muy caros. 12. Tenemos que comprar dos canapés. 13. Las leyes tienen que ser buenas, pero no lo son siempre. 14. Su papá está ahora en Madrid, y mañana estará en Barcelona. 15. Escribió una tesis, pero no es muy buena. 16. Los García son muy cursis.

BB. 1. How many days are there in a week?—There are seven: the first days are Monday, Tuesday, and Wednesday. 2. Every Thursday he has to write three exercises in his Spanish class. 3. In Spanish, the word dentist is **dentista**. 4. The two theses he wrote are on my table; I found them in my room the Friday that you were here. 5. They will eat here today. 6. Are there any couches in the house? 7. We are very sleepy and want to stay. 8. His feet are very sore. 9. The Gálvez brothers are here; they want to study. 10. They had a telegram, but we did not find it on the table. 11. There aren't many rubies here. 12. Every Friday he prepares his lessons for all the week. 13. Not all (the) laws are good. 14. As he did not study when he was in (the) school, he does not speak Spanish well. 15. He bought tables, chairs, and couches for his house.

LESSON XXXV

RADICAL-CHANGING VERBS: CLASSES I AND II

Review Lessons IV, X and XI.

1. In Spanish, certain verbs change an -e- or -o- of the stem to -ie- or -ue- when the stress falls on that vowel. This happens in all three persons singular of the present indicative and in the third person plural.

The verbs below, classes I and II, are exactly alike.

Class I, first and second conjugations.

mostrar, to show (*Radical-changing I*)

muestro, I show	mostramos, we show
muestras, you show	mostráis, you show
muestra, he, she, it shows; you show	muestran, they show; you show

pensar, to think, to intend (*R-ch. I*)

pienso, I think	pensamos, we think
piensas, you think	pensáis, you think
piensa, he, she, it thinks; you think	piensan, they think; you think

volver, to return (*R-ch. I*)

vuelvo, I return	volvemos, we return
vuelves, you return	volvéis, you return
vuelve, he, she, it returns; you return	vuelven, they return; you return

encender, to kindle, to light (*R-ch. I*)

enciendo, I kindle	encendemos, we kindle
enciendes, you kindle	encendéis, you kindle
enciende, he, she, it kindles; you kindle	encienden, they kindle; you kindle

Class II, third conjugation.

dormir, to sleep (*R-ch. II*)

duermo, I sleep	dormimos, we sleep
duermes, you sleep	dormís, you sleep
duerme, he, she, it sleeps; you sleep	duermen, they sleep; you sleep

RADICAL-CHANGING VERBS

sentir, to feel; to be sorry (*R-ch. II*)

siento, I feel
sientes, you feel
siente, he, she, it feels; you feel

sentimos, we feel
sentís, you feel
sienten, they feel; you feel

2. These verbs are conjugated exactly like any other regular verb as regards the **endings**, the only difference being that where the stress falls on the **stem**, the **-e-** changes to **-ie-** and the **-o-** to **-ue-**.

3. Not all verbs with a stem **-e-** or **-o-** change that vowel. **Deber**, for instance, does not change the stem **-e-**; debo, debes, etc.; so **tocar**: toco, tocas, etc.

VOCABULARY

acostar (ue), to put to bed
almorzar (ue), to lunch, to breakfast
así, thus, so, and so
cerrar (ie), to close, to shut
confesar (ie), to confess; to admit
contar (ue), to count, to relate
deber, ought, must; owe
dormir (ue), to sleep
encerrar (ie), to shut in, to lock up
entender (ie), to understand
joven, young; el joven, youth; la joven, girl
jugar (ue, *as though the stem had an -o-*), to play (games)
llover (ue), to rain
mentir (ie), to lie (*tell a falsehood*)

morir (ue), to die
nevar (ie), to snow
¿no?
¿no es verdad?
¿verdad?
¿no es así?
 — isn't that so? isn't it true? won't he? didn' they; aren' you? etc.
perder (ie), to lose
para (*plus infinitive*), in order to
poder (ue), to be able, can
querer (ie), to wish; (*plus a noun*) to love, to like
sentar (ie), to seat
la silla, chair
tarde, late
temblar (ie), to tremble
tiembla de frío, he is trembling with cold
el tiempo, time; weather
tronar (ue), to thunder
volver (ue), to return

A. 1. *Conjugate on the above models the radical-changing verbs:* almorzar temblar cerrar perder morir confesar tronar (*in the third person singular only*); nevar (*in the third person singular only*); encender volver sentir

AA. *Locate the form and give the infinite of:*
1. confieso 2. confesó 3. sentimos 4. ¿contáis? 5. siento
6. llueve 7. siento 8. mentís 9. nieva 10. mienten
11. quiero 12. juega 13. entendemos 14. vuelves 15.

duermo 16. encierro 17. cierro 18. volvemos 19. cuento 20. tiemblan 21. almuerzo

AAA. 1. they eat 2. I return 3. it is snowing 4. he isn't counting 5. are you shutting it [up]? 6. I am breakfasting (lunching) 7. are you having-breakfast? 8. you are returning 9. it is raining 10. they are dying 11. I am sorry 12. they are not feeling 13. do you want? 14. he understands it 15. he is not lying 16. he doesn't confess it 17. does she understand? 18. they are trembling

B. 1. Si ella cuenta las lecciones, hallará treinta y ocho en el libro. 2. Quiero sentar al niño en la silla porque está cansado y tiene sueño. 3. ¡Pobre de la niña! ¡Su padre se (*do not translate*) muere y ella es tan joven! 4. No confiesa que ha perdido su dinero; pero lo perdió. 5. ¿Truena hoy?—No hay sol, y lloverá después. 6. La hermana juega tanto como el hermano, pero estudia más. 7. No puede estudiar tan bien como ellas, porque no tiene tanto tiempo. 8. Tiene que trabajar todos los días. 9. La madre acuesta a los niños porque ya es muy tarde. 10. Enciende la luz en el dormitorio porque quiere leer. 11. No juega ahora porque tiene que tocar el piano. 12. ¿Ha cerrado usted la puerta? 13. ¿Tienes frío, mi hijo? 14. Me cuenta que su padre ha comprado aquella casa grande que está en la calle X.

BB. 1. Does he understand that we can't study the lessons today? 2. It is thundering, isn't it? 3. The children are playing, and we can't put them to bed yet. 4. He isn't counting his money; he has no money to count. 5. They are very sorry not to have studied their lesson for tomorrow. 6. And now they have no time (in-order)-to play the piano, either. 7. I want to seat the child on the chair near the table, where he can eat. 8. What are you telling me! He is dying (*put* se *before the verb*)! 9. If he is lying, we cannot speak with him [él] again. 10. If they are tired, they can sleep in my bedroom; I shall sleep on the couch. 11. It is raining now; the children cannot play in the street. 12. Are you cold? You are trembling. 13. They put the children to bed, but the latter are now playing in their bedroom. 14. They are eating again because they are very hungry. 15. She does not want to close the window, because she feels warm. 16. He is sorry to have played the piano because he did not understand that the child was sleeping.

LESSON XXXVI
RADICAL-CHANGING VERBS (*Continued*)

Review Lesson XXXV

1. Class III of Radical-changing verbs has only one vowel change, and that is -e- to -i- under the accent (includes third conjugation only).

repetir, to repeat (*Radical-changing III*)

repito, I repeat	repetimos, we repeat
repites, you repeat	repetís, you repeat
repite, he, she, it repeats; you repeat	repiten, they repeat; you repeat

This change is parallel with that in Classes I and II, and the same remarks apply, the only difference being that here only the -e- changes, and that to an -i-.

2. Class II also changes -o- to -u- and -e- to -i-; and Class III changes -e- to -i-, when the ending begins with a diphthong. This occurs, in the indicative, in the preterite third singular and plural (two forms).

sentir, to feel (*R-ch. II*)

sentí, I felt	sentimos, we felt
sentiste, you felt	sentisteis, you felt
sintió, he felt; you felt	**sintieron**, they felt; you felt

dormir, to sleep (*R-ch II*)

dormí, I slept	dormimos, we slept
dormiste, you slept	dormisteis, you slept
durmió, he, she, it slept; you slept	**durmieron**, they slept; you slept

repetir, to repeat (*R-ch. III*)

repetí, I repeated	repetimos, we repeated
repetiste, you repeated	repetisteis, you repeated
repitió, he, she, it repeated; you repeated	repitieron, they repeated; you repeated

VOCABULARY

competir (i), to compete
contestar, to answer
despedir (i), to dismiss
derretir (i), to melt
dieron, (they) gave; you gave
dió, (he, she, it) gave; you gave
gracias, thanks
impedir (i), to hinder, to prevent
no hay de qué, not at all
nunca, never
pedir (i), to ask (a favor); to ask-for (*dative of person*)
repetir (i), to repeat
servir (i), to serve
vestir (i), to dress

A. 1. *Like* **repetir**, *conjugate in the present and preterite:* pedir vestir competir impedir despedir derretir

2. *Conjugate in the preterite:* morir mentir sentir

AA. *Locate the form and give the infinite of:*
1. pidió 2. pido 3. pedimos 4. viste 5. compite 6. compitieron 7. sirven 8. repetís 9. repetisteis 10. derritió 11. despedisteis 12. vistieron 13. competí 14. pedisteis 15. derritieron 16. vistieron 17. despidió 18. compites 19. despedís 20. repite 21. derrite 22. pido 23. impides

AAA. 1. they are asking 2. I prevent 3. they dressed 4. is she repeating? 5. they competed 6. are you serving? 7. you didn't repeat 8. they are melting 9. you are dressing 10. is she competing? 11. they prevented 12. they dismissed 13. will you prevent? 14. I asked 15. they prevented 16. did you prevent? 17. you are competing 18. they are serving 19. they melt

B. 1. Piden a Juan (They ask John for) el dinero que él halló. 2. No podemos competir con sus primos porque estamos enfermos. 3. Repitió que ellos dieron quinientos dólares a este hombre y que él los dió a Enrique. 4. La madre vistió muy bien a los niños, pero ellos están muy sucios ahora. 5. Me pide (He asks me for) un poco de dinero, pero yo no tengo dinero. 6. Contestó que no podía hacerlo. 7. ¿Por qué no repite lo que ha preguntado? 8. Porque no quiere contestar. 9. No pide ninguna cosa (**anything**) a su padre; nada quiere. 10. Compite con alumnos de catorce años; siempre compite con niños. 11. No contestó cuando su padre le habló (spoke to him). 12. Tú no le quieres, ¿no es verdad? 13. Sí, es verdad. 14. No quieren estudiar.

B. 1. They are melting the ice in a glass of water. 2. Aren't you repeating the work you had yesterday? 3. They are studying it again, aren't they? 4. They have just studied it; there is no reason for (**no hay para qué**) studying (*use infinitive with pronoun object joined to it*) it again. 5. They asked their uncle for the money, but he had none for them (**ellos**). 6. The woman dressed her child, and then it went out (**salió**) and played in the street. 7. Then the mother put the child to bed. 8. They served me a glass of hot milk, but I wanted cold water. 9. The first glass had warm water; the second, cold. 10. When I asked (*use correct form of* **preguntar**) if she had cold water, she did not answer. 11. He repeated what he said. 12. He said that it was raining. 13. Is it raining now? 14. No, it is snowing. 15. Yesterday, it was sunny; today, it is windy and it is snowing.

LESSON XXXVII

1. Formation of Present Participle. The present participle is formed by adding **-ando** to the stem of the first conjugation, and **-iendo** to the stem of the second and third conjugations.

habl	**ando**	hablando, speaking
beb	**iendo**	bebiendo, drinking
escrib	**iendo**	escribiendo, writing

Note **siendo** (ser) **estando** (estar)
　　　teniendo (tener) **habiendo** (haber)

2. Review Lesson XXXVI, 2. Radical-changing verbs

of Classes II and III undergo the second change (-o- to -u- and -e- to -i-).

> durmiendo (dormir)   sintiendo (sentir)   vistiendo (vestir)
> *But* mostrando (mostrar)   pensando (pensar)   volviendo (volver)

3. The verb **estar** with the present participle of a verb may form a progressive tense. Thus **hablo**, while it may mean "I am speaking," is not as vividly progressive as **estoy hablando**.

> está hablando, he is speaking (*in the act of speaking*)
> estaba comiendo, he was eating

4. **Preguntar** and **Pedir**. **Preguntar** means to ask (a question) whereas **pedir** means to ask (for something, to ask a favor).

> Me pregunta si mi hermana está aquí, She asks me if my sister is here.
> Me pide un libro, He is asking me for a book.

Note that after **pedir**, a thing is the direct object and a person the dative object.

> Pide un poco de dinero a su hermano, He is asking his brother for a little money.

5. **Prepositional Adjectives.** Prepositional adjectives may be formed like the models below. Note that the noun governed by the preposition is not inflected even when the sense of the compound is plural.

pluma de oro, gold pen (*pen of gold*)
vaso de leche, glass of milk
taza de te, cup of tea
taza para te, teacup (*cup for tea*)
sombrero de paja, straw hat
lección de español, Spanish lesson (*lesson about Spanish*)
leccion en español, Spanish lesson (*lesson conducted in Spanish*)
anteojos de plata, silver spectacles
billete de banco, banknote

plumas de oro, gold pens
vasos de leche, glasses of milk
tazas de te, cups of tea
tazas para te, teacups
sombreros de paja, straw hats

6. **Mismo.** **Mismo** before a noun means **same**; after a noun it means **-self, very**.

> el mismo hombre, the same man
> el hombre mismo, the man himself
> la casa misma, the very house

FORMATION OF PRESENT PARTICIPLE

VOCABULARY

Learn the expressions above.

el hierro, iron   el acero, steel

A. 1. está comiendo 2. estaban bebiendo 3. el mismo niño 4. están sirviendo 5. ¿estás durmiendo? 6. no estaba durmiendo 7. ¿qué está preguntando? 8. ¿qué pide? 9. pide dinero al tío 10. pregunta si ellas están estudiando 11. sombrero de paja. 12. taza para café 13. el niño mismo 14. lección de inglés 15. taza de te 16. billetes de banco 17. lápiz de plata 18. estamos escribiendo 19. estábamos conjugando

AA. 1. will they be serving? 2. gold pen 3. coffee cup 4. we are writing 5. they were sleeping 6. straw hat 7. are you counting? 8. they are lighting 9. the same house 10. were they drinking? 11. she is studying 12. banknotes 13. are you speaking? 14. they are counting 15. silver eyeglasses 16. English lessons (*conducted in English*) 17. gold pen 18. the money itself

B. 1. Me pide un poco de dinero, porque nada tiene él. 2. ¿Qué está preguntando su hermano?—Pregunta si hemos estudiado nuestra lección. 3. ¿Tenían ustedes tenedores y cucharitas de plata y tazas para te muy pequeños? 4. No, teníamos tazas para café, pero las vendimos. 5. ¿Puedes beber tantos vasos de leche como yo? 6. Cuando le pregunté si vivían en la primera casa blanca de la esquina, dijo: No. 1. Cuantos billetes de banco tiene, y tiene más de cincuenta, todos son de cien pesos. 8. Le pedí el dinero porque él es el hombre más rico de la ciudad. 9. No podemos tocar el piano ahora porque mi padre está durmiendo. 10. El hombre mismo que dice que quien no trabaja es muy feliz, él mismo no trabaja, y sin embargo (nevertheless) no me parece muy feliz. 11. Hoy tenemos una lección en inglés y mañana tenemos una en español. 12. ¿Qué estás contando? 13. No tengo dinero; he perdido el billete de a diez pesos (ten peso bill) que usted ha hallado. 14. ¿No es Vd. el mismo hombre que estuvo aquí ayer? 15. ¿Qué pidió usted a su hermana?—Pedí su libro, pero no lo tenía. 16. ¿Están ustedes estudiando la lección para mañana? 17. No, estamos estudiando la de hoy. 18. No quiero preguntar si han estudiado sus lecciones, porque nunca estudian.

BB. 1. Were they speaking of their work when you entered the room? 2. Did you ask your father if he liked the house? 3. We drank the tea in small cups. 4. Are you writing with a gold pen, Henry? Can you write better with a gold one? 5. No, sir; I am studying my lessons, I am not writing. 6. Are you the boy who found a peso? 7. I haven't any money today; I lost it all. 8. The boy has just finished writing his exercise, but he has not studied the lesson well. 9. Have you a straw hat?—No, I have no hat; I lost the one I had. 10. You ought to see the house I bought! 11. He is asking me for (**Me pide**) his book, but I have lost it. 12. What are they studying now? 13. They are not studying; they are playing. 14. I haven't a gold pen; I have a steel pen. 15. He is asking me (**me**) if my arm is sore. 16. Did you buy a straw hat?—No, because I did not like the straw hats they showed me (**me**).

LESSON XXXVIII

CONJUNCTIVE PRONOUNS

Review Lesson XXI (direct object).

1. Indirect Object.

me, to me, me	**nos,** to us, us
te, to you, you	**os,** to you, you
le, to him, him; to her, her; to you, you; to it, it	**les,** to them, them; to you, you

2. In the first and second persons singular and plural, the indirect forms are the same as the direct.

Me da el libro, He gives the book to me. (*Cf.*, **Me ve,** He sees me.)

3. In the third person, singular and plural, the same indirect form, **le**, serves for both genders and polite **you**.

Le da el libro, He gives **her** the book. (He gives **him** the book.)
Le hablo, I am speaking to **you**.

4. The indirect pronoun object always precedes the direct.

Me lo da, He gives it to me. (He gives me it.)

5. **Se as Indirect Object.** When both pronoun objects are of the third person, the indirect is always **se**, no matter what the original gender, person, or number.

se lo da, he gives it to him
                to her
                to them
                to you (*formal singular or plural*)

6. **Position of Pronoun with Infinitive or Present Participle.** A pronoun used as object of an infinitive or present participle follows and is joined to it.

Quiere venderme el libro, He wants to sell me the book.
Quiere vendérmelo, He wants to sell me it.
Está bebiéndolo, She is drinking it.

Note that the accent may be required in some cases.

7. **Object Pronoun** with **ser**. (Review Lesson XII, 3.) The pronouns **lo, la, los, las** are used predicately after **ser** when referring to a noun already mentioned.

¿**Es la hermana? — Sí, la es,** Is it the sister? — Yes it is (she).

VOCABULARY

el caballo, horse
la carrera, trip, circuit; race
el coche, coach, carriage
  da, (he, she, it) gives; you give
  dan, (they) give; you give
la dificultad, difficulty
  en casa de, at the house of
  hace, (he, she, it) makes, does; you make, do

interesante, interesting
ligero, -a, swift, light, rapid
nadie, no one, nobody
pintoresco, -a, picturesque
rápidamente, rapidly
rápido, -a, rapid
sin embargo, nevertheless

A. 1. lo conjugó 2. ella me los dió 3. me hablaron 4. ¿te lo dió? 5. no me lo dió 6. os lo enseñaron 7. lo hallaron 8. le escribió una carta 9. le escribió 10. se la escribió 11. prepararon la comida 12. la preparó 13. me da un lápiz 14. se lo dió 15. se la da 16. se las da 17. se las dan 18. se los dió 19. le da la tiza 20. se la da 21. me dice 22. me lo dice 23. os dice 24. os lo dice 25. te enseñaron la lección 26. te la enseñaron 27. os la enseñaban 28. me da la mano 29. se la da 30 enseñándomelos 31. desea verlas 32. ¿es la hermana? 33. la es

AA. 1. he gave me the shoes 2. he gave them to me 3. he is showing me the exercise 4. he shows them to me 5. he passed me the cup and knife 6. he passed them to me 7. he is passing them to you 8. he wants to pass them to us 9. he is passing them to them 10. passing them to her 11. they want to pass them to you (*polite singular*) 12. he is writing me a letter 13. he is writing me it 14. he wrote it to me 15. this book pleases my uncle 16. it pleases me 17. I like it (it pleases me) 18. it pleases you 19. she likes it 20. he gave 21. he gave the pens to me 22. he gives me them 23. I give you them 24. he gives them to them 25. he gave them to them 26. he gives them to you (*polite plural*)

B. 1. ¿Por qué no me enseñaste la lección que acabas de estudiar?—Porque no había estudiado el ejercicio. 2. No dió el libro a Juan; lo dió a su hermano. 3. ¿Quiere Vd. tomar mi libro?—No, gracias; tengo uno. 4. Hace una carrera por la ciudad en coche. La ciudad es muy pintoresca y la ve por primera vez. 5. Me dió un coche y sin embargo no acabé de ver toda la ciudad. 6. El caballo que compró es muy ligero; ¿quiere usted vendérmelo? 7. Es amado de todos los alumnos porque les enseña muy bien. 8. ¿Con quién y para quién prepara ella las comidas? 9. Las prepara para su hermano; se las prepara todos los días. 10. No me gusta estudiar todo el tiempo; quiero jugar un poco. 11. ¿Por qué les enseñó V. la cuchara que halló?—Ellos son los que la perdieron. 12. Se lo dijo. 13. ¿Tienes el libro?—No, él quiere dármelo, pero yo no

CONJUNCTIVE PRONOUNS

lo quiero. 14. No acabó de estudiar cuando su hermano entró en la pieza. 15. ¿Enseñó usted el ejercicio a Juan?—Se lo enseñé porque él no había estudiado todavía la lección. 16. ¿Dió usted los libros a su hermano?—No quiero dárselos.

BB. 1. Have you the book?—Yes, thanks; John gave it to me. 2. Does he see us? 3. No, he doesn't see us; he isn't here now. He gave me a very light (**ligero**) carriage, and so we have been able to see all that picturesque city. 4. Did John give you the bill he found yesterday? 5. He did not give it to me, and now he has no money. 6. What is the matter with you? 7. What have you? Spanish books? Who gave them to you? 8. No one gave them to us; we found them in the house. 9. Do you want to give them to us? 10. We can not give them to you because they are John's. 11. Are you taking a trip today in [a] coach to see this interesting city? 12. We don't want to see it because we haven't the time. 13. He gave me these things because they are my father's. 14. He didn't give it to my father because my father wasn't at home (in house). 15. He does not want to give them to him because he isn't at home.

BBB. 1. He gave me the paper because it is my brother's. 2. He gave it to me because it was not his paper. 3. Doesn't he want to give it to you, Mr. X.? 4. Don't they want to give them to you, John? 5. We want to take a ride in a fast coach to see this picturesque city. 6. We want to take a ride in order to see it. 7. Did they prepare the dinner or didn't they prepare it? 8. I don't like this city; it isn't interesting. 9. Is that your cousin's piano? Do you play it? 10. Where is your exercise? 11. Didn't you have to write it? 12. Don't you understand that I can't study it today? 13. Where are the children?—The mother put them to bed. 14. These pupils are very diligent; they prepared their work well yesterday and they are preparing it well today. 15. Did

you find the man of whom I was speaking? 16. Do you
see them? 17. Are their uncle and aunt here? 18. Do
you see her? 19. Who is the man whom I was speaking of?

LESSON XXXIX
RADICAL-CHANGING VERBS (*Continued*)

Review lessons XXXV and XXXVI

1. Summary of Radical-changing verbs treated thus far:
(a) R-ch. verbs of Class I

(1) are recruited from conjunctions 1 and 2;

(2) change -e- to -ie- and -o- to -ue- under the accent.

These changes occur in all the present singular forms
and third plural.

(b) R-ch. verbs of Class II

(1) are recruited from conjugation 3.

(2) change -e- to -ie- and -o- to -ue- under the accent.

These changes are in all the present singular forms and
third plural.

(3) change -e- to -i- and -o- to -u- when the ending
begins with diphthong.

These changes occur in the third singular and plural of
the preterite indicative; and in the present participle.

(c) R-ch. verbs of Class 3

(1) are recruited from conjugation 3 (hence, distinguish such verbs from those in **b**)

(2) change -e- to -i- (there are no verbs with the
stem in -o-) either under the accent or when the ending
begins with a diphthong.

These changes occur in all the present singular forms
and third plural; in the third singular and plural of the
preterite indicative; and in the present participle.

2. The radical-changing verbs **errar** and **oler** change -ie- and -ue- to -ye- and -hue- respectively. This is due to a Spanish rule of spelling that a word cannot begin with a written diphthong **ie** or **ue** (the pronunciation, however, is the same).[1]

errar, to err (*R-ch. I*)

yerro, I err	**erramos,** we err
yerras, you err	**erráis,** you err
yerra, he, she, it errs; you err	**yerran,** they err; you err

oler, to smell (*R-ch. I*)

huelo, I smell	**olemos,** we smell
hueles, you smell	**oléis,** you smell
huele, he, she, it smells; you smell	**huelen,** they smell; you smell

VOCABULARY

la apuntación, note (*as, to take notes*)
brillante, brilliant
completo, -a, complete
costar (ue), to cost
el cuaderno, notebook
el examen, examination
el éxito, (favorable) outcome, result
el hielo, ice
el helado, ice cream
la hoja, leaf; page
el hueso, bone
morder (ue), to bite
la nota, mark (*in class*)
el profesor, teacher; professor
la profesora, teacher; professor
recibir, to receive; to pass (*a student in a subject*)
sobresaliente, excellent (*mark in class*)
suelto, -a, loose

A. 1. huele 2. yerro 3. olemos 4. oliendo 5. errado 6. yerra 7. erramos 8. hueles 9. oléis 10. erráis 11. yerran 12. sienten 13. pide 14. repetimos 15. tiemblas 16. tembláis 17. compito 18. almuerzan 19. vuelve 20. juegas 21. huelen 22. jugando 23. vistes 24. llueve 25. yerro 26. huele 27. jugamos 28. jugarán 29. juego 30. huelen

AA. 1. he is playing 2. they dress 3. it smells 4. I am mistaken 5. they smell it 6. do they smell? 7. they are asking 8. I am putting them to bed 9. is he playing? 10. they err 11. you are mistaken 12. do we make a mistake (do we err)? 13. does it smell? 14. she is mistaken

---

[1] Cf. hielo, hueso, huevo. The hie- of hielo and the ye- of yerro are pronounced alike; both avoid the initial ie-.

15. they don't smell 16. doesn't it smell? 17. they don't smell 18. aren't they mistaken 19. is he playing? 20. they will play 21. playing 22. I err 23. did it rain?

B. 1. El perro ve el hueso. 2. ¿No yerran cuando dicen que este niño es el menor? 3. No juegan, trabajan; hacen apuntaciones en sus cuadernos. 4. ¿Qué notas tuvisteis?— Malas; no me recibieron. 5. No hay examen para mañana; el profesor está enfermo. 6. El hielo es frío, pero se derrite rápidamente. 7. Me cuentan que los niños no escriben sus ejercicios ahora en cuadernos. 8. El agua huele a café (smells of coffee); ¿no está limpio el vaso? 10. Los alumnos escribieron sus exámenes con éxito completo; ahora están jugando. 11. Llueve, pero tenemos que trabajar. 12. Las alumnas compiten la una con la otra, y así son muy diligentes. 13. Veo el caballo, pero me parece que no es muy ligero. 14. El perro halló un hueso y lo mordió. 15. El niño juega con el perro. 16. Si usted dice eso, yerra mucho; eso no es la verdad.

BB. 1. This boy is mistaken when he says that; the truth is that he does not study. 2. If the water smells of tea, I don't want it; I want fresh water. 3. We ate the dinner, and then the dog had a bone. 4. They are asking me for the money, but I haven't got it (I haven't it). 5. Does the dinner smell of onions (**cebollas**)? 6. He is probably here; but he is mistaken if he thinks we'll show him those things. 7. We do not have to study, for we have studied already. 8. The dinner will be ready soon. 9. He is asking his brother for his book, but his brother hasn't studied it enough yet. 10. He is making good notes in his notebook, for he is a brilliant student and always receives excellent marks. 11. In the examinations, he had (a) complete success. 12. The dog is biting the bone. 13. Is he asking-for more fresh water?

LESSON XL
POSSESSIVE PRONOUNS
Review Lesson XVII

1.

Singular	Plural
el mío, la mía, mine	los míos, las mías, mine
el tuyo, la tuya, yours	los tuyos, las tuyas, yours
el suyo, la suya, his, hers; yours	los suyos, las suyas, his, hers; yours
el nuestro, la nuestra, ours	los nuestros, las nuestras, ours
el vuestro, la vuestra, yours	los vuestros, las vuestras, yours
el suyo, la suya, theirs; yours	los suyos, las suyas, theirs; yours

2. These pronouns may be used in any of the ordinary pronoun relations—subject or object of a verb, object of a preposition.

¿Dónde está el libro? Where is the book?
El mío no está aquí, Mine isn't here.
Juan tiene el mío, John has mine.
Juan estudia con el mío, John is studying with mine.

3. The pronouns (like the adjectives) agree with the thing possessed in gender and number.

Yo tengo la pluma de Juan y él tiene la mía, I have John's pen, and he has mine.
¿En qué calle tiene él las casas?—Las suyas están en la calle X. On what street has he the houses?—His are on X Street.

Las suyas agrees with **casas**, the thing possessed, feminine plural; and not with **él**, the possessor.

4. When the possessive pronouns are in the predicate after the verb **ser**, the article is ordinarily dropped.

Esta casa es mía, This house is mine.
Esos lápices son nuestros, Those pencils are ours.

5. The forms without the article are also used as adjectives after the noun if:

(a) the noun is preceded by a number or an indefinite adjective.

dos primos míos, two cousins of mine (*But*, mis dos primos, my two cousins)
el tercer ejercicio mío, the third exercise of mine (*But*, mi tercer ejercicio)

(b) in direct address, especially at the heading of a letter.

Muy amigo mío: My dear Friend: (*salutation in letters*)

6. The definite article often replaces the possessive adjective (either the forms in 5 above, or those in Lesson XVII).

No tiene el sombrero aquí, He hasn't his hat here.
Metió el dinero en el bolsillo, He put the money in his pocket.

VOCABULARY

el bolsillo, pocket
la carta, letter
(la) China, China
decir, to say, to tell
dentro de, within (*prep.*)
el hombro, shoulder
mandar, to send
el momento, moment
los muebles, furniture (*plural in Spanish*)
las noticias, news
el renglón, line (*of writing*)

A. 1. el mío 2. las nuestras 3. las suyas 4. el vuestro 5. el suyo 6. los suyos 7. la mía 8. el nuestro 9. el de Juan 10. las de mi amigo 11. ciertos libros nuestros 12. dos niños suyos 13. un amigo mío 14. cierta amiga suya 15. sus noticias 16. un caballo vuestro 17. los suyos 18. la nuestra 19. el mío 20. los tuyos 21. mi amigo 22. amigo mío 23. padre nuestro 24. padre mío

AA. 1. theirs 2. mine 3. ours 4. yours 5. a dog of mine 6. some book of theirs 7. theirs 8. yours 9. yours (*formal*) 10. yours (*intimate, plural antecedent*) 11. yours (*intimate, singular antecedent*) 12. mine 13. his (*modifying feminine plural noun*) 14. his (*modifying masculine singular noun*) 15. yours 16. hers 17. good news 18. three boys of hers 19. her three boys 20. some cousins of theirs 21. certain cousins 22. My dear Friends:

B. 1. ¿Dónde están las plumas? Buscábamos las nuestras ayer, pero no las hallamos. 2. Ciertos amigos nuestros que están aquí tienen notas muy buenas; pero las nuestras

POSSESSIVE PRONOUNS

son siempre malas. 3. ¿Toca usted todavía su piano?—No toco el mío ahora, porque lo vendí; toco el de mi hermano. 4. Las nuestras son noticias muy ciertas; ustedes pueden creerlas. 5. Metió en el bolsillo el dinero que había hallado. 6. Ya había perdido todo el suyo, y tenía mucha hambre. 7. ¿No tienes ni te ni café? En la casa de mi tía los hay (there is some). 8. Amigo mío, ¿quiere usted enseñarme la lección para mañana? 9. ¿Dónde estarán esos amigos suyos (of yours) que habían de llegar hoy? 10. Cuando el padre halló al niño, el niño lloraba. 11. Muy amigo mío: escribiré una cosa que no va a (that you will not) creer. 12. Cierto amigo mío me dijo que usted estaría aquí dentro de pocos días. 13. Sus dos hijos tienen diez años el uno y quince años el otro. 14. Aquí tengo mis libros; ¿dónde tiene usted los suyos?

BB. 1. His books were bought by his students, but his brother bought his furniture. 2. Their father has not so many houses as mine has; but he has better ones (he has them better). 3. Some friend of mine is studying with him. 4. Have you any of their tea now?—No, I am drinking mine, but they are sending me some (a little) from China. 5. Our piano was bought for us by our parents, and theirs was bought for them by theirs. 6. My dear Friends: I can write you a long letter because I have much time today. 7. He tells me the sure news that three friends of his are coming today. 8. I have your hat; where did you put mine? 9. The more we work, the better are our exercises and yours. 10. Our pens and yours are all bad.' 11. Father, will you give me your pen a moment? 12. Have you much to write? 13. He put the money in his pocket and entered the room. 14. Some cousins of theirs are to arrive this afternoon. 15. The mother had the little daughter by the hand as they came (entered) into the room. 16. Your children and mine are playing in the house.

LESSON XLI

NEGATION

Review Lesson VIII, 4 and 5

1. **No** before the verb makes it negative, with the mere idea of **not** or **no**.

> **No lo escribí,** I did not write it.

2. Other negative words are used:

(a) alone before the verb or (b) after the verb but with **no** before the verb.

(a) **Nada veo,** I see nothing. (b) **No veo nada,** I see nothing.
    A nadie veo, I see nobody.   **No veo a nadie,** I see nobody.

3. **Alguno** following a noun is negative in meaning.

> **No me ha enseñado cosa alguna,** He hasn't showed me a thing.

Before the noun it means **some**.

> **Tiene algunas cosas que son muy raras,** He has some things which are very rare.

4. **Pero, mas,** and **sino**. The ordinary Spanish conjunction for **but** is **pero** (**mas**, occasionally found, should not be used by the student, as it is used only in literary style).

> **Yo leo, pero Juan escribe,** I am reading, but John is writing.

Sino is used in a *phrase* which contradicts a previous *clause*.

> **No escribo en francés sino en español,** I am not writing in French, but in Spanish.

Sino que is used if there is a verb in the second part of the sentence.

> **No escribo en francés sino que escribo en español,** I am not writing in French, but I am writing in Spanish.

VOCABULARY

jamás, never
nada, nothing; not at all
nadie, no one, nobody
ni siquiera, not even
ni . . . ni, neither . . . nor
no . . . más, no more, no longer
nunca, never

amarillo, -a, yellow
ancho, -a, wide
angosto, -a, narrow
aplicado, -a, diligent
el bacalao, cod
la clase, kind, sort; class

de ninguna manera, in no way, not at all
detenidamente, carefully
el entusiasmo, enthusiasm
examinar, to examine, to look at carefully
la especie, kind, sort, class
indiferente, indifferent
la lata, can
en lata, canned. tinned
el paño, cloth, goods
el pescado, fish (*caught*)
el pez, fish (*not caught, in water*)
raro, -a, rare, unusual
la sardina, sardine
la seda, silk

A. 1. ningún entusiasmo 2. algún pescado 3. pescado alguno 4. algún pescado 5. ¡ca! 6. no duermen, estudian 7. no comieron carne sino pan 8. no estudiaba nunca 9. casa alguna 10. ninguna cosa 11. ninguna 12. no buscamos a nadie 13. a nadie buscamos 14. no juego con ninguno de sus amigos 15. ni el libro ni el cuaderno son míos 16. no escribió ni en el libro ni en el cuaderno 17. ni la pluma ni el cuaderno son suyos 18. no juega con ninguno de sus amigos 19. a nadie se lo ha dado 20. no se lo ha dado.

AA. 1. not at all! 2. I never write 3. no man 4. I do not see 5. no man 6. neither his uncle nor his aunt is here 7. his uncle is here, but his aunt is not here 8. not his (el) uncle but his aunt is here 9. they never write 10. they never showed them to me 11. they didn't show 12. they showed it to you 13. they will show them to no one 14. no! 15. not at all 16. he never works

B. 1. No son perezosos, sino indiferentes. 2. En la clase estudiamos detenidamente toda clase de paño—seda, et cétera. 3. Hay que limpiar todo—ninguna cosa está limpia, todo está sucio. 4. Pasamos por aquella calle angosta, donde no había ni siquiera luz de petróleo.

4

5. Como teníamos hambre, compramos una lata de sardinas, con un poco de pan. 6. No me gustan sardinas de ninguna manera. 7. No todos los alumnos son tan diligentes como estos dos. 8. ¿Quiere usted comprar este paño?—¡Ca! No me gusta de ninguna manera. 9. No podemos examinar su paño porque no tenemos mucho tiempo. 10. No estoy escribiendo a Juan sino a Enrique. 11. No preparó la comida sino que la comió. 12. ¿Quiere usted trabajar aquí?—¡Jamás! 13. No tiene nada. 14. No vendió la casa sino el piano.

BB. 1. We didn't find the French books, but the notebooks. 2. I don't see anyone in the street. 3. Did you ever prepare the dinners? 4. No, but I have eaten them. 5. I have never prepared any meal. 6. Don't you have to write the exercises for tomorrow? 7. Not at all! We aren't preparing any work for tomorrow. 8. Don't you have to play the piano tomorrow? 9. These children are not hard-working, but lazy. 10. If you are hungry, you can eat some canned sardinas. 11. We don't like this can of sardines. 12. What kind of sardines are they? 13. Don't you like them? 14. He didn't buy the silk cloth; he only examined it, and then he said that he would certainly not (in no way) buy it. 15. But he did buy a silk shirt. 16. These glasses are not dirty—they are yellow. 17. The street is not narrow, but wide. 18. He didn't study the lesson, but he wrote it in his notebook.

LESSON XLII

DISJUNCTIVE (PREPOSITIONAL) PRONOUNS

Review Lessons XIII and XXXVIII.

1.
mí, me	nosotros, -as, us
ti, you	vosotros, -as, you
él, him, it; ella, her, it	ellos, -as, them
usted, you	ustedes, you

DISJUNCTIVE (PREPOSITIONAL) PRONOUNS

2. These pronouns are used exclusively as the objects of prepositions.

Ese libro es para mí, That book is for me.
Lo presenté yo a usted, I introduced him to you.

With the exception of the first and second persons singular, the prepositional pronouns are the same in form as the subject pronouns.

The first person singular **mí**, *me*, has an accent to distinguish it from the possessive adjective **mi**, *my*.

3. With the preposition **con, mí** and **ti** combine to form **conmigo** and **contigo**.

Juan hablaba conmigo, John was speaking with me.

4. The prepositional forms are used for the indirect pronoun when the direct form is a person.

Yo quiero presentarlo a ella, I want to introduce him to her.

5. The prepositional form is also used to distinguish between persons or to emphasize a pronoun (*review XXXVIII, 3 and 5*). In this use, it often repeats a conjunctive pronoun already used.

Los veo a él y a ella, I see him and her (I see them, him and her)
Se lo doy a él,   I am giving it to him
    a ella,   to her
    a usted,   to you
    a ellos,   to them
    a ellas,   to them
    a ustedes,   to you
A mí me lo da (Me lo da a mí), He is giving it to me.

VOCABULARY

acompañar, to accompany, to go with
al lado de, beside; **a su lado,** at his side, beside him
correr, to run
diré, I shall say; **dirás,** you will say; *etc.*
hacia, towards
haré, I shall do; **harás,** you will do, *etc.*
el lado, side
presentar, to introduce, to present
según, according to
solo, -a, only, alone (*adjective*)
sólo, only (*adverb*)
visitar, to visit

A. 1. con él   2. sin nosotras   3. con ustedes   4. contigo

5. con ella 6. cerca de nosotros 7. según vosotros
8. conmigo 9. para ella 10. se lo doy a él 11. a mí me
hablaron 12. conmigo 13. por él 14. sin nosotros 15. sin
usted 16. hacia ellos 17. no estudiarán 18. se lo enseñaremos 19. hacia nosotras 20. a ustedes, no a ellos
21. se lo enseñaron a ustedes, no a ellos 22. al lado de
Juan 23. a su lado 24. al lado de él 25. a su lado de él
26. a su lado de ella 27. harán 28. diremos 29. haré

AA. 1. with me 2. without them 3. towards us
4. I'll show it 5. I'll show it to them 6. to me 7. they'll
show them to her 8. beside them 9. near us 10. beside
him 11. not to her 12. with you (*intimate singular*)
13. with me 14. with her 15. with them 16. with you
(*intimate singular*) 17. with you (*intimate plural*)
18. with you (*polite singular*) 19. with me 20. without
me 21. with me 22. toward you (*formal plural*) 23. according to her 24. according to them (*feminine*)

B. 1. Mi padre está aquí, pero no le busco a él sino a
mi madre. 2. A mis primos los buscaron ayer, pero no los
hallaron. 3. ¿Me buscas a mí? 4. No te busco a ti. 5. Se
lo daré a él, no a ella. 6. ¿Quién estudia contigo? 7. No
quieren estudiar contigo; quieren estudiar solos. 8. A
Juan no lo veo a él sino a su hermano. 9. Mis primos os
buscaron ayer, pero ni él ni ella os encontraron. 10. No
se lo dió el libro a Juan sino al hermano. 11. Se los pasa
los cuadernos a Juan, pero Juan no los quiere tener (*for*
no quiere tenerlos). 12. A mí me dió un coche muy ligero,
y sin embargo no acabé en cuatro horas de ver toda la
ciudad. 13. Pasan por el sendero hacia nosotras, pero no
esperaremos. 14. A mí me dió mi libro. 15. Mi tío desea
leer aquel libro; no le gusta leer éste. 16. ¿Por qué no
estudias conmigo? 17. A mí no me dará una buena nota
porque no estudio bastante. 18. Corre y juega con sus
hermanos, pero es mucho más joven que ellos. 19. ¿No
son sus hermanos?—Sí, los son.

BB. 1. What will they give to **you**? 2. They won't

give **me** a very good mark because I did not study. 3. Neither he nor she are good students; they don't study enough. 4. They were running towards us and so we passed to one side. 5. He gave it to me, not to them, because it is mine. 6. Will he give it to me because it is **mine (el mío,** *full form for emphasis*)? 7. The man of whom I was speaking—did you find him? 8. Did he give the books to you or to him? 9. Didn't you give them to him? 10. Shan't you wait for them? 11. No! 12. What will they do with this book? 13. What will they do with it? 14. What did he say to you? 15. I'll tell it to you but not to them. 16. They are working with me. 17. Aren't they with you (*intimate singular*)? 18. They introduced me to her. 19. Did they introduce you to them? 20. Never! 21. He passed along the path, and his sister was beside him. 22. He visited me yesterday, and their brother was with him. 23. Isn't she your cousin?—She is **(La es),** yes. 24. Who was with you?

[Study Appendix C as introductory to Lesson XLIII and the following lessons on the subjunctive.]

LESSON XLIII.
PRESENT SUBJUNCTIVE.

1. **hablar,** to speak (*stem* **habl-**)

hable, (that) I speak, *etc.*	**hablemos,** (that) we speak, *etc.*
hables, (that) you speak, *etc.*	**habléis,** (that) you speak, *etc.*
hable, (that) he, she, it speaks; *etc.*	**hablen,** (that) they speak; you speak, *etc.*

beber, to drink (*stem* **beb-**)   **escribir,** to write (*stem* **escrib-**)

beba	bebamos	escriba	escribamos
bebas	bebáis	escribas	escribáis
beba	beban	escriba	escriban

2. The characteristic vowel of the present subjunctive of the first conjugation is **e** in all six forms; of the second and third conjugations, **a**.

3. The following verbs have certain irregularities in the stem or ending.

ser, to be (*stem* **se-**)

sea	seamos
seas	seáis
sea	sean

estar, to be (*stem* **est-**)

esté	estemos
estés	estéis
esté	estén

tener, to have (*stem* **teng-**)

tenga	tengamos
tengas	tengáis
tenga	tengan.

haber, to have (*stem* **hay-**)

haya	hayamos
hayas	hayáis
haya	hayan

decir, to say (*stem* **dig-**)

diga	digamos
digas	digáis
diga	digan

ver, to see (*stem* **ve-**)

vea	veamos
veas	veáis
vea	vean

4. When the main verb is present or future, the subordinate subjunctive tense is present.

Es preciso que estén aquí, It is necessary that they be here.
Será preciso que estén aquí, It will be necessary that they be here.

VOCABULARY

el automóvil, automobile
  conducir, to lead; to drive
el dependiente, clerk
  dudar, to doubt (*takes subjunctive*)
durante, during
en seguida, then, next, at once
imposible, impossible
es imposible, it is impossible
  (*takes subjunctive*)
necesario, necessary
es necesario, it is necessary
  (*takes subjunctive*)
la playa, beach, shore
posible, possible
es posible, it is possible
  (*takes subjunctive*)
es preciso, it is necessary
  (*takes subjunctive*)
estar bueno de salud, to be in good health
es tiempo de que, it is time (to)
  (*takes subjunctive*)
las vacaciones, vacation
viajar, to travel
Viña del Mar, Viña del Mar (*a beach in Chile*)

A. *Give the infinitive and locate the form of:*

1. que estemos 2. que sea 3. que seamos 4. que seáis vosotras 5. que acudan 6. que escribamos 7. escribimos 8. que cocine 9. que limpien 10. que tema 11. que tengáis 12. que usted tenga 13. que vendamos 14. vendemos 15. que tengan 16. tienen 17. que me aburran

PRESENT SUBJUNCTIVE

18. que usted viva 19. que comamos 20. que halléis 21. que ustedes escriban 22. que lloremos 23. que él estudie 24. que tengamos 25. que estudien 26. que sean 27. que digan 28. que digáis 29. que reciban 30. que lo presentemos a ellas

AA. *Use subjunctive with phrases introduced by* that.

1. that we sell 2. that you have 3. that they are 4. that we are 5. that she is well 6. that they cook 7. that his brother is 8. that he is tiring 9. that we introduce them to her 10. that you find 11. you find 12. that we clean 13. we clean 14. that they are studying 15. that we believe 16. we believe 17. that they are 18. that they have 19. that I have 20. that I may have 21. I have 22. that she believes 23. that you have 24. that we have to write 25. that she has 26. that they have 27. that they see 28. they see 29. I see 30. that I am seeing 31. that I have found

B. 1. Es preciso que los niños de mi tía estudien. 2. Es tiempo de que estudien. 3. No es necesario que limpiemos los vasos ahora. 4. Dudo que estén aquí. 5. Dudan que él esté aquí. 6. Duda que sea necesario que estudiemos ahora. 7. ¿Es imposible que lo vendan? 8. Será posible que nos vea. 9. El dependiente duda que pase las vacaciones en la playa de Viña del Mar. 10. Es posible que el alumno viaje en automóvil durante las vacaciones. 11. Dudamos que Vds. escriban las cartas hoy. 12. Dudo que Vd. se lo escriba hoy. 13. El hombre no quiere conducir el automóvil porque no es suyo. 14. Dudo que lo pueda conducir, porque está tan enfermo. 15. Será tiempo de que vuelva a la casa. 16. Es imposible que viajemos durante estas vacaciones. 17. Será preciso que laven los cuchillos y las cucharas en seguida. 18. Dudo que tengan el tiempo para eso. 19. Dudo que vuelvan a hacerlo.

BB. 1. They doubt that she is here. 2. Is it possible they doubt it? 3. It is time that she washes the glasses.

4. It is time for her to wash the glasses (It is time that she washes the . . .). 5. It is time for them to wash them (It is time that they wash . . .). 6. It will be necessary that he study more. 7. It is necessary for him to study today. 8. It must be time for them to read the lesson. 9. I doubt that they will be (that they are) here today. 10. It isn't necessary for them to study the whole day (*See BB, 6*). 11. It is time they receive good marks. 12. I doubt that he will travel in an auto this vacation. 13. It isn't possible that he passes all his vacation at Viña del Mar. 14. It is time they were (are) here. 15. It will be impossible for him to study here. 16. It is impossible for him to study here. 17. It will be impossible for him to study all these lessons for tomorrow. 18. It isn't possible—he will not study them. 19. You doubt that they are studying now. 20. It is time they wash their face and hands, and study. 21. During the vacation it will be impossible for us to study. 22. I doubt that they are telling the truth. 23. Don't you doubt it, too?

LESSON XLIV
PAST SUBJUNCTIVE

Review Appendix C.

1. **hablar**, to speak (*stem* **habl-**)

hablase, (that) I spoke, *etc.*	hablásemos, (that) we spoke, *etc.*
hablases, (that) you spoke, *etc.*	hablaseis, (that) you spoke, *etc.*
hablase, (that) he, she, it spoke; you spoke, *etc.*	hablasen, (that) they spoke; you spoke, *etc.*

beber, to drink (*stem* **beb-**)   **escribir**, to write (*stem* **escrib-**)

bebiese	bebiésemos	escribiese	escribiésemos
bebieses	bebieseis	escribieses	escribieseis
bebiese	bebiesen	escribiese	escribiesen

Note in the past subjunctives that the endings of all three conjugations are alike except that the first has -a- where the second and third have -ie-.

PAST SUBJUNCTIVE

The stress is on the same syllable throughout, the first plural having a written accent.

estar, to be (*stem* **estuv-**)

estuviese	estuviésemos
estuvieses	estuvieseis
estuviese	estuviesen

ser, to be (*stem* **fu-**)

fuese	fuésemos
fueses	fueseis
fuese	fuesen

haber, to have (*stem* **hub-**)

hubiese	hubiésemos
hubieses	hubieseis
hubiese	hubiesen

tener, to have (*stem* **tuv-**)

tuviese	tuviésemos
tuvieses	tuvieseis
tuviese	tuviesen

decir, to say (*stem* **dij-**)

dijese	dijésemos
dijeses	dijeseis
dijese	dijesen

ver, to see (*stem* **v-**)

viese	viésemos
vieses	vieseis
viese	viesen

Note that **dijese,** *etc.* and **fuese,** *etc.* lack the **-i-** of the diphthong **-ie-**.

2. There is another form of the past subjunctive which differs from that above in having **-ra**[1] for the final **-se**.

hablar, to speak (*stem* **habl-**)

hablara, (that) I spoke, *etc.*	habláramos, (that) we spoke, *etc.*
hablaras, (that) you spoke, *etc.*	hablarais, (that) you spoke, *etc.*
hablara, (that) he, she, it spoke; you spoke, *etc.*	hablaran, (that) they spoke; you spoke, *etc.*

beber, to drink (*stem* **beb-**)

bebiera	bebiéramos
etc.	*etc.*

escribir, to write (*stem* **escrib-**)

escribiera	escribiéramos
etc.	*etc.*

estar, to be (*stem* **estuv-**)

estuviera	estuviéramos
etc.	*etc.*

ser, to be (*stem* **fu-**)

fuera	fuéramos
etc.	*etc.*

haber, to have (*stem* **hub-**)

hubiera	hubiéramos
etc.	*etc.*

tener, to have (*stem* **tuv-**)

tuviera	tuviéramos
etc.	*etc.*

decir, to say (*stem* **dij-**)

dijera	dijéramos
etc.	*etc.*

ver, to see (*stem* **v-**)

viera	viéramos
etc.	*etc.*

3. The past subjunctive is used in the subordinate clause

---

[1] In general, the -ra subjunctive is common in South America, the -se in Spain.

after a conditional, imperfect, or preterite in the main clause.

> **Dudaría que estuviesen aquí,** I should doubt that they were here.
> **¿Era posible que estuviesen aquí?** Was it possible that they were here?

4. The perfect takes a present or past subjunctive according to the sense.

Compound forms of the subjunctive are regularly formed with **haber.**

> **Ha mandado que yo estudiara,** He ordered that I study (*then*).
> **Ha mandado que yo estudie,** He ordered that I study (*now*).
> **Dudó que lo hubieran escrito,** He doubted that they had written it.

VOCABULARY

mandar, to order, to command
quisiera, I should wish, I should like, I wish
a veces, at times, sometimes

A. 1. que estuviéramos 2. que estuviésemos 3. que fueran 4. que hubiéramos bebido 5. que escribieran 3. que fueran 4. que hubiéramos bebido 5. que escribieran 6. que escribiesen 7. que dijese 8. que dijera 9. que tuviéramos 10. que lavara 11. que aburriera 12. que comiese 13. que fuera 14. que escribieran 15. que vendiera 16. que hubiera 17. que lavasen 18. que hablásemos 19. que habláramos 20. que viera 21. que dijeran 22. que viesen 23. que dijeses 24. que hayan comido 25. que tuvieran 26. que hubieras 27. que comiéramos 28. que bebiera 29. que lavara 30. que viviéramos

AA. *Use subjunctive with phrases introduced by* that.

1. that they had 2. that they have spoken. 3. that they said 4. that we washed 5. that you had 6. that he saw 7. that they had eaten 8. that they have bored 9. that we drank 10. that she spoke 11. that they wrote 12. that we ate 13. that you had travelled 14. that we doubted 15. that he said 16. that he had had 17. that I had had 18. that she saw 19. that we had 20. that you wrote 21. that they ate 22. that they had eaten 23. that I wrote 24. that we had written 25. that we had 26. that we had spoken 27. that she had cleaned

PAST SUBJUNCTIVE

B. 1. Quisiera que ellos se lo hubieran enseñado.
2. Dudaba que fuera necesario que estudiásemos. 3. Mandé que Juan tocase el piano hoy, pero no lo tocó. 4. Dudamos (*what tense is this?*) que escribiera todas las cartas ayer. 5. Fué preciso que lavase los cuchillos ayer. 6. Fué preciso que lavara los cuchillos y las cucharas. 7. El dependiente ha dudado que pasara las vacaciones en Viña del Mar. 8. Sentimos mucho que ella lo hubiera dudado. 8. ¿Fué posible que el alumno pasara las vacaciones en la playa? 9. ¿No quería el hombre conducir el automóvil? 10. No fué preciso que los viese ayer. 11. Sentí mucho que ella no la escribiese. 12. Dudé que el hombre enfermo pudiese conducir el automóvil. 13. Fué imposible que lo vendieran. 14. Fué necesario que mis primos estudiaran todo el día. 15. Quisiera que Vd. preparase (*or* **prepare**, *according to the sense*) muy bien esta lección. 16. Fué tiempo de que dijeran la verdad. 17. ¿No fué tiempo de que nosotros escribiésemos los dos ejercicios? 18. Sintió que ellos no se lo hubieran enseñado.

BB. 1. They doubted that she was there. 2. It wasn't necessary for them to play the piano the whole day. 3. I wish we had written the exercise yesterday. 4. It has been impossible at times for her to study. 5. It wasn't impossible to learn the whole lesson for today. 6. It was time for them to wash the glasses. 7. We were sorry (*takes subjunctive*) that we had not studied the two lessons. 8. During the vacations it was impossible for us to study much. 9. I doubted that they would be here today. 10. We have had to work, or we should be sorry that we did not work. 11. You doubted that they had studied. 12. He ordered us to finish writing the exercise. 13. It was time that they cleaned their slates. 14. It was impossible that he had to have them for yesterday. 15. They have ordered us to write the exercises. 16. I doubted that they were telling the truth. 17. I ordered them to tell the whole truth. 18. I wish we had played the piano yesterday.

LESSON XLV
CONDITIONAL SENTENCES

Review Appendix C.

1. There are two kinds of conditions to distinguish: (a) fact conditions, and (b) contrary-to-fact conditions.

(a) Fact conditions are conditions in which the condition stated actually has occurred or, so far as we know, will occur. Here the **if** may be equivalent to **when** or **whenever**. These conditions have identically the same construction in Spanish and in English, and in Spanish are always in the indicative.

> Si está aquí temprano, estudiamos juntos, If (whenever) he is here early, we study together.
> Si está aquí temprano, estudiaremos juntos, If he is here early, we shall study together.

(b) Contrary-to-fact conditions are conditions in which the **if**-clause states the opposite of what happens or happened. In Spanish, contrary-to-fact conditions have one clause, sometimes both clauses, in the subjunctive.

2. In conditions contrary to fact, the **if**-clause may have the **-se** or **-ra** past subjunctive, and the result clause the conditional (as in English). Or the **if**-clause may have the **-se** past subjunctive, and the result clause the **-ra** subjunctive.

> Si él { estuviese / estuviera } aquí, estudiaríamos juntos ⎱ If he were here,
> Si él   estuviese   aquí, estudiáramos juntos   ⎰ we should study together.
>
> Si él { hubiese / hubiera } estado aquí, estudiaríamos juntos
> Si él   hubiese   estado aquí, hubiéramos estudiado juntos
> If he had been here, we should have studied together.

3. **Si = Whether.** Note that after **si**, in the sense of **whether**, only the indicative may be used.

> Quiero saber si están aquí, I want to know whether they are here.

VOCABULARY

en vez de, instead of
la guerra, war
juntos, -as, together
el liceo, high school, academy

prestar, to lend, to pay (*attention*)
el sofá, sofa
temprano, -a, early

A. 1. Si tuviera ocho mil dólares, compraría la casa. 2. ¿Cuántos soldados habría en esta ciudad ahora si hubiese guerra? 3. No tuviéramos que estudiar tanto si preparásemos nuestras lecciones tan bien como ustedes. 4. Me habría enseñado dónde están los libros en su casa si hubiera tenido mucho tiempo. 5. Trabajando aquel hombre (If that man worked), estaría mucho más contento. 6. Si ella no preparase bien una comida, él no la comiera. 7. ¿Dónde habríamos vivido si hubiésemos vendido la casa? 8. Si dijese esto, no hablaría con verdad. 9. Si tuviese veinte años, no estaría en el liceo. 10. Si la vajilla estuviese sucia, ella la lavara. 11. Si yo tuviera calor, no cerraría la ventana. 12. Si ayer Vd. hubiera hablado a su padre de estos libros, él los habría comprado. 13. Si usted estuviese en Madrid, ¿en qué calle viviría? 14. Si los alumnos preparasen sus lecciones mejor, ¿tendrían mejores notas? 15. Si hubiese un sofá en la casa, él dormiría allí. 16. Si encendiera la luz en el dormitorio, leería. 17. Si yo tuviera dinero, compraría el paño hoy mismo. 18. Si aquel hombre dijera que quien no trabaja es feliz, no diría la verdad. 19. Si me hubiese enseñado la lección, yo habría acabado de estudiar ahora.

AA. 1. If you had your book there, would you lend it to me? 2. How many soldiers would there be here now if there were still war? 3. The young pupils would not be so diligent if they did not have to study. 4. If they had sold their house, where would they be living now? 5. If they had sold it, where would they live now? 6. If the girl had not washed the dishes, she would have finished studying already. 7. If he had spoken to his father yesterday about the book, then he would have it today. 8. If I had my verbs to conjugate now, I should not be playing the piano. 9. If this child were younger, he would not be so large. 10. If he found his book, he would have to study. 11. If we had nine thousand dollars, we should buy the house. 12. I should not have all my lessons ready if I had not studied all day yesterday. 13. If you had found the program, wouldn't you have given it to them? 14. If they had had a telegram, they would not be here now. 15. If they had put the children to bed, they would not have to read to them. 16. If there were coffee instead of tea, I should drink it. 17. If he had good notes in his notebook, he would have better marks. 18. If we found his hat, we should not have to buy him another.

LESSON XLVI
SUBJUNCTIVE (*Continued*)

1. **Subjunctive with Impersonal Expressions.** The subjunctive is used with many impersonal verbs expressing possibility, necessity, emotion, opinion, and the like.

>**Es tiempo de que estudien,** It is time that they studied.
>**Es posible que lo tenga,** It is possible that he has it.

Other expressions are:

es imposible, it is impossible	**importa,** it is important
es importante, it is important	**es preciso,** it is necessary
es lástima, it is a pity	

2. Many impersonal expressions substitute an infinitive for the **que** clause with subjunctive. Here a dative of the personal pronoun is used with the finite verb.

>**Es imposible que esté aquí,** It is impossible that he is here.
>**Le es posible estar aquí,** It is possible for him to be here.

But avoid the infinitive where the impersonal expression has a noun.

>**Es tiempo de que esté aquí,** It is time that he were here.

3. Present Tense, **saber**, to know (*stem* **sab-**)

sé, I know	**sabemos,** we know
sabes, you know	**sabéis,** you know
sabe, he, she, it knows; you know	**saben,** they know; you know

VOCABULARY

demasiado, too much
esta noche, tonight
por lo común, generally

saber, to know; to know how; to taste of
a tiempo, on time

A. 1. Es tiempo de que ella la vea. 2. Es tiempo de que lavemos. 3. Es posible que nos aburran si estamos allí mucho tiempo. 4. Es preciso escribir los ejercicios difíciles tan bien como los fáciles. 5. Es necesario que nos escriban todos los días. 6. No sé si están aquí o no; pero sí[1] sé que estarán. 7. Es imposible que tenga un mal ejercicio porque siempre está estudiando. 8. No me dijo si estaría aquí, pero creo que sí estará.[1] 9. Si ellos le dicen eso, yo quisiera saberlo. 10. No sabe si son madrileños o sevillanos; pero sí sabe que son españoles. 11. ¿Es posible que hayan pasado tanto tiempo en la playa? 12. No le fué posible viajar en automóvil porque costaba demasiado. 13. Era posible hacerlo. 14. Era preciso que cocináramos todos los días una comida para veinte y un hombres. 15. Me fué preciso preparar la comida para toda la familia.

AA. 1. I had to write (*use construction with* **era preciso** *or* **necesario**) two exercises because I had not written one the day before. 2. I don't know whether they are studying now; but generally they do not prepare their work on time. 3. Do you know whether they were here with their parents? 4. It was impossible for them to say it. 5. Do they know yet whether they had good marks? 6. Wasn't it possible for them to get better marks? 7. Couldn't they study more every day? 8. It was impossible for them to buy the ink because they didn't have much time; and now we can't write our exercises. 9. It is time for us to have good marks. 10. It was time that they did (**hiciese**) their work; they are the laziest children in the class. 11. Did they know whether the González[es] would be here tonight? 12. It wasn't necessary for them to work, because their parents were rich. 13. But it was a pity that they didn't work.

---

[1] Sí is inserted in statements to make them more emphatic. Cf. A, 8.

LESSON XLVII

1. Dative of Taking Away. Verbs meaning *to take away, buy, ask*, etc., take the dative of the person, the accusative of the thing.

> Nadie se lo robó, No one robbed him of it.
> La compraron al señor X, They bought it from Mr. X.
> No lo preguntó a María, sino a Juan, He didn't ask Mary that, but John.

2. Past Anterior (Secondary Pluperfect).

hablar, to speak

hube hablado, I had spoken
hubiste hablado, you had spoken
hubo hablado, he, she, it had spoken; you had spoken

hubimos hablado, we had spoken
hubisteis hablado, you had spoken
hubieron hablado, they had spoken; you had spoken

beber, to drink

hube bebido,
hubiste bebido
etc.

escribir, to write

hube escrito
hubiste escrito
etc.

The past anterior has exactly the same meaning as the pluperfect, but is found only after conjunctions of time, such as **cuando,** *when;* **después (de) que,** *after;* **luego que,** *as soon as.* Even here, however, the ordinary pluperfect or even the preterite may be used.

> Después de que hubo (había) hablado, partió, After he had spoken, he left.

VOCABULARY

adelante, on, ahead
el abogado, lawyer
así que, and so
bajo, under, beneath
cantar, to sing
el derecho, law
la medicina, medicine
el médico, doctor
el negociante, business man, merchant
los negocios, business
olvidar, to forget
partir, to leave, to depart
pedir (i), to ask for
pedir prestado, to borrow
quitar, to take away
robar, to rob, to steal

A. 1. el mismo alumno 2. se lo pido a usted 3. después de que hubo trabajado 4. os lo robaron a vosotros 5. te las robó a ti   6. cuando hubimos estudiado   7. me lo preguntaba   8. se lo pidió prestado a él   9. la niña misma   10. cuando hube lavado   11. Juan mismo   12. el hombre mismo   13. los mismos papeles   14. me las tomaron   15. te las robaron   16. os lo pidió   17. se lo preguntamos   18. nos los quitaron   19. ¿se lo quitó a usted?

AA. 1. he asked me for it   2. they robbed him of it   3. after they had come-in   4. after coming-in (after they had come-in)   5. they will take it from you   6. he is asking you for them   7. did they take it from him?   8. after they had eaten   9. when they had asked him for them   10. John himself   11. after I had left   12. the same man   13. the man himself   14. Mary herself   15. the same man   16. the very books   17. they had robbed him of them   18. when they had departed   19. the same children   20. the children themselves

B. 1. Después de que hubo hablado, tomó su sombrero y partió.   2. El mismo Juan (That very John) con quien acabamos de hablar estudia medicina—pero nunca será médico.   3. Cuando hubimos comprado el paño, visitamos a mi hermana.   4. Robaron mucho hierro a aquel negociante, así que ahora no puede seguir adelante en su negocio.   5. Se lo pedimos a nuestro padre, pero él no tenía nada de eso.   6. El mismo hombre que nos dijo eso antes, ahora no dice lo mismo.   7. Quiero lo mío (*note the neuter use of* **lo** *to denote indefinite meaning*)—no lo tuyo.   8. Compró el piano al señor X.   9. Conjugas los mismos veinte verbos que conjugaste ayer; pero antes de mañana los olvidarás otra vez.   10. A mí también me preguntaron si había estudiado la lección, y contesté que no.   11. Estos lápices son mejores que los de María.   12. Estos mismos lápices son mejores de los que tiene María.   13. Se los quité a Juan.   14. Después de que hubo tocado el piano, cantó.   15. ¿Le duele el mismo diente?   16. ¿Qué juzga usted de un hombre que roba dinero a un niño?   17. Quiero sentar al niño en la misma silla donde estaba antes.   18. La señora tomó los lápices de la niña (*how translated?*) y se los dió al hermano de Juan. 19. La señora quitó los lápices a la niña (*cf. with 18*).

BB. 1. No one robbed the merchant of anything; he lost his money. 2. Did you conjugate the same verbs as those your brother was conjugating yesterday? 3. These very pens are the ones your brother lost. 4. He wants to seat the child at the table. 5. Him too they asked whether he liked the cloth; but he said, No. 6. After we had studied the lessons hard (**mucho**), we wrote all the exercises. 7. Mary herself studied all the lesson, but the brother never works. 8. After she had worked a long time, she took her hat and left. 9. If they ask their father for the money, he will not give it to them. 10. Did they buy the table and chairs from Mr. S.? 11. They did not buy them for Mr. S. 12. After they bought the piano, they found it was not a good one. 14. Did they ask **him** too for the money? 15. The lady took the books from her children, and then they wrote the exercises.

LESSON XLVIII

REFLEXIVES AND RECIPROCALS

Review Lessons XXI and XXXVIII.

1. **Conjunctive forms** (direct and indirect).

me, myself
te, yourself
se, himself, herself, itself; yourself

nos, ourselves
os, yourselves
se, themselves; yourselves

Disjunctive forms.

mí, myself
ti, yourself
sí, himself, yourself, itself; yourself

nosotros, -as, ourselves
vosotros, -as, yourselves
sí, themselves; yourselves

Note the forms **conmigo, contigo, consigo** (*Cf. Lesson XLII, 3*).

2. Do not mistake the intensive pronoun for the reflexive. Cf. the English:

I myself (*intensive*) see myself (*reflexive*). **Yo mismo me veo.**

3. The conjunctive pronouns are used reflexively or reciprocally; the disjunctive only reflexively.

(a) Reflexively, a pronoun denotes that the subject acts on itself.

Me veo en el espejo, I see myself in the glass.

(b) Reciprocally, the individuals of a plural subject (**nosotros,** *etc.*) act on one another. If there are two individuals, we say in English: "We write each other." If there are more than two individuals, we say: "We write one another."

Se escriben a menudo, They write to each other (one another) frequently.

4. To prevent a reciprocal verb from being mistaken for a reflexive, or vice-versa (cf. the translations of (a) and (b) above), the Spanish often adds **el uno** (**la una,** *etc.*) **al otro** (**a la otra**). The article may be omitted.

Nos escribimos la una a la otra, We write to each other.

Distinguish also:

Se escriben el uno al otro, They write to each other.
Se escriben unos a otros, They write to one another.

Note that some verbs require the preposition **de.**

Nos acordamos la una de la otra, We remember each other.
Se ríen uno de otro, They laugh at one another.

5. Reflexive verbs are given in vocabularies with **-se** added to the infinitive. In inflection, however, the student must use the proper form of the reflexive.

peinarse, to comb oneself
me peino, I comb myself

VOCABULARY

aburrirse, to bore oneself; to be bored
acordarse (ue) de, to remind oneself of, to remember
afeitarse, to shave oneself
a menudo, frequently, often
bañarse, to bathe oneself, to take a bath
convencerse, to convince oneself, to be convinced
decidirse, to decide oneself, to make up one's mind
dirigirse, to make one's way (to), to go
escaparse, to escape, to run away
el espejo, mirror, looking glass
felicitarse, to congratulate oneself, each other
holgarse (ue), to be idle, to have a good time
lejos, far
mutuamente, mutually, each other, one another
ocupado, -a, busy
ocuparse de, to occupy oneself with
preocuparse de, to be preoccupied with
pues, for; well
salvarse, to save oneself; to run off
sentarse (ie), to seat oneself, to sit down

A. 1. Nos acordamos una de otra muy bien; pues, siendo niñas, habíamos estudiado en la misma escuela. 2. No nos habíamos escrito porque no habíamos tenido mucho tiempo para eso. 3. No tiene nada consigo. 4. Me veo en el espejo. 5. No se ríen unos de otros porque son todos muy diligentes. 6. ¿No te ves en este espejo? 7. Se felicitan mutuamente en sus cartas porque se quieren mucho. 8. Ustedes pueden felicitarse porque tienen hijos tan buenos. 9. ¿Se escriben muy a menudo? 10. No; no se escriben una a otra casi nunca; y viven en dos ciudades que son muy lejos una de otra. 11. Yo me veo a mí mismo en el agua, pero no te veo a ti. 12. No tenían nada consigo. 13. No hablan nunca de sí; siempre hablan de otros. 14. ¿No se acuerdan ustedes uno de otro? 15. Siendo niños, ustedes vivían en la misma calle donde vivía yo también. 16. Pero como no se han escrito uno a otro, ya no se acuerdan el uno del otro.

AA. 1. Do you see yourself in the glass? 2. Don't they write each other frequently? 3. They don't write each other as frequently as they used to (write to each other). 4. Can't you see yourself in the glass? 5. We remember each other very well, for as (= being) children we lived in the same street. 6. We don't laugh (**reímos**) at each other (*cf. A, 5*), for he is too diligent and I am as diligent as I can be (it). 7. After they had not written each other, they had no more news of each other. 8. What has he with him? 9. I see **you** in the glass, but I can't see **myself** in it. 10. They don't live in the same city now, and so they write each other frequently. 11. Those good friends congratulate each other, for they like each other very much. 12. They aren't talking to each other now, for they are too busy. 13. We don't write to ourselves, we write to each other.

LESSON XLIX

REFLEXIVES AND RECIPROCALS (Concluded)

Review Lesson XLVIII.

1. (a) The reflexive as used in Spanish sometimes corresponds to the English.

Me veo en el espejo, I see myself in the glass.
Se preocupa de sus negocios, He busies himself with his affairs.

(b) In some cases, the reflexive is used explicitly in Spanish where it is only implied in English.

Me visto, I dress (myself).
Se lava, he is washing (himself).

(c) In some cases, the reflexive meaning is not obvious and must be looked for in the original meaning of the verb.

se acuerda de, he remembers (recalls to himself)
Se sienta, He sits down (seats himself).
Se desayuna, He has breakfast (breaks to himself the fast).

(d) In some cases, there is no plausible accounting for the reflexive.

ir, to go	**irse,** to go off
reír, to laugh	**reírse de,** to laugh at
salvarse, to run off	**escaparse,** to run away

Se lo llevó, He carried it off with him.

2. In Spanish, the reflexive usually takes the place of the English passive.

Se aburre, He is bored. (He bores himself.)
Aquí se habla español, Spanish is spoken here.

Cf. also:

Aquí se trabaja mucho, Much work is done here. (*Lit.*, Here it works itself much.)
Se le dijo que . . , He was told that . . .

3. Note the double expressions below:

me imagino, se me imagina, I imagine
me figuro, se me figura, I fancy, imagine
me olvido de, se me olvida, olvido, I forget

Note that **se** precedes any other form of the conjunctive pronoun.

4. Where a reflexive is used, the Spanish often has a definite article for the English possessive.

Se pone el sombrero, He puts on his hat. (To himself he puts on the hat.)

VOCABULARY

antojarse (*impersonal*), to fancy, to have a whim
calzar (se), to put on (shoes)
comerse, to eat up
el cuarto, room
desayunarse,[1] to have breakfast
desnudar (se), to undress
despertar (ie), to wake up (*transitive*); -se, to awaken (*intransitive*)
etcétera, et cetera, and so forth
fabricar, to manufacture
figurarse, to imagine
el gusto, taste
imaginar, to imagine
levantar, to raise, to lift; -se, to rise, to get up
llevarse, to carry off
olvidar (-se de), to forget
seguro, -a, sure, certain
siguiente, following
el traje, suit (of clothes)
tranquilo, -a, tranquil, quiet, calm

A. 1. se dice 2. se pone los calcetines 3. nos vestimos 4. ¿te despertaste? 5. se escaparon 6. se fueron 7. me olvidé de eso 8. me acuerdo 9. no se estudia (it is not studied) 10. se me figura 11. me imagino 12. se ven a menudo 13. se hace mucho trabajo 14. se habla inglés 15. se les antoja 16. se toca mucho el piano en esta escuela

---

[1] Distinguish between **desayunarse**, to have breakfast (first meal of the day— coffee or chocolate and a roll) and **almorzar**, to have lunch (second meal, about ten to one o'clock, depending upon the person or social environment). The English often call this Spanish meal their breakfast because it is the first hearty meal of the day.

17. se juega mucho 18. se afeita 19. nos lavábamos 20. me desayuné 21. me acostaré 22. os despertaréis 23. nos sentamos 24. que me lave 25. me decidí (por) 26. que Vd. se vista 27. se huelga 28. se limpiaban los dientes 29. se pasa el tiempo 30. se lavó

AA. 1. we shall go to bed 2. French is spoken 3. I was told (it told itself to me) 4. they dressed 5. they are putting on their shoes 6. you imagine 7. we breakfasted 8. I breakfast 9. they are sitting down 10. that we woke up 11. there is much piano playing (plays itself much the piano) 12. you fancy 13. the piano is played much 14. we woke up 15. we forgot it 16. they went away 17. little work is done here 18. he went off 19. they play much in (the) school 20. there is a good time here 21. he will have breakfast 22. (the) time is spent 23. she will forget it 24. he imagines 25. we have a good time 26. he went to bed

B. 1. Cuanto más la niña lava los vasos, (tanto) más sucias están. 2. Ahora tiene que lavarse. 3. ¿No te lavaste ya? 4. No se afeitarán porque no tienen tiempo. 5. ¿No se acuerda usted de cuando, siendo jóvenes, estudiábamos juntos en mi cuarto? 6. Aquí puede usted estar tranquilo porque aquí se habla español. 7. Me imagino que no estudiarán las lecciones para mañana porque son siempre tan flojos. 8. No os reís de ellos, estoy seguro. 9. La madre le pone el sombrero y los zapatos al niño, y él se escapa. 10. Cuando me despierto temprano, me afeito, me lavo, y me desayuno. 11. Tú no te afeitas porque nunca tienes tiempo para eso en la mañana. 12. Nos acostamos temprano porque tuvimos que levantarnos al día siguiente a las seis (at six o'clock). 13. Aquí se aburre uno mucho porque no hay nada que hacer. 14. ¿Qué se fabrica aquí? ¿Calzados? 15. No se habla de nada sino de sombreros, de calzados, de trajes, etcétera. 16. Se le dijo a mi hermano que no había clases hoy. 17. A él se le antoja que pueda hacer todo a su gusto. 18. En esta escuela se estudia mucho. 19. Nos lo llevamos.

BB. 1. Why doesn't the mother put the child's shoes and stockings on him? 2. One is bored very much here, because there is nothing to do. 3. Nothing will be spoken of except (**sino**) hats, shoes, dresses, and so forth. 4. She fancies she can do anything to her liking (taste). 5. On the next day they went to bed early because they were very tired. 6. The more this child washes, the dirtier he is. 7. Spanish is spoken here—but we can't (**sabemos**) speak it. 8. The children must wash—they are very dirty. 9. If you don't shave, you can't go with me. 10. They imagine that their son can study eight hours a (**por**) day. 11. Will you wash the dishes today? 12. What is manufactured here? 13. They are putting on their hats already—they are going off at once. 14. What was spoken of yesterday? 15. Nothing is said of that and so it is done many times. 16. Have you forgotten what they said to you? 17. They ran away, and we didn't find them again. 18. You aren't laughing at them, I'm sure. 19. A good breakfast can be had (it breakfasts itself well). 20. They carried it off with them.

LESSON L

1. **Conjunctions with the Indicative.** Common conjunctions used with the indicative are:

después (de) que, after
antes (de) que, before
cuando, when
de manera que, so that
  (*result clause*)
luego que, as soon as
o . . . o, either . . . or
no solamente . . . sino que, not only . . . but also
porque, because
pues, for
tanto (*noun*) **como,** as much . . . as
tan (*adj. or adv.*) **como,** as . . . as

  No lo compró, pues no tenía dinero, He didn't buy it, for he had no money.

2. **Conjunctions with the Infinitive.** If the subject of the main verb and that of the subordinate clause are the same, **de** may usually be substituted in compound conjunctions ending in **que** and the infinitive used in the subordinate clause.

Después de estudiar la lección, escribió el ejercicio, After studying the lesson, she wrote the exercise.

(a) Some prepositions do not require **de.**

No lo compró por no tener dinero, He did not buy it because he did not have any money.

(b) **Para** before the infinitive denotes purpose.

Pidió el dinero para comprar un piano, He asked for the money in order to buy a piano.

But verbs of motion take **a**, except that **para** may be used to denote very strong purpose.

Vino a verme, He came to see me.
Vino para verme a mí, He came in order to see me.

3. Infinitive as Noun. An infinitive may be used as the subject of a verb.

(El) no estudiar es malo, Not studying (Not to study) is bad.

On with a present participle form in English is rendered in Spanish by **al** (**a** plus **el**) with the infinitive.

Al verme se fué, On seeing me, he went off.

VOCABULARY

la cobardía, cowardice, act of cowardice
dejar (de), to stop (doing)
el desayuno, breakfast
mirar, to look at
vino, (he, she, it) came; you came

A. 1. al escribirlo 2. después de 3. cuando 4. después de 5. cuando hubo hablado 6. al comprarlos 7. no solamente los hombres, sino también los niños 8. tan grande como 9. después de estudiar 10. antes de hacer 11. después de que hubimos 12. antes de que estaba 13. antes de llegar ellos 14. no solamente estudió sino que escribió 15. para pedirlo prestado 16. después de sentarse 17. al despertarse 18. para comprar 19. de manera que fué

AA. 1. after writing it 2. before awakening 3. in order to have 4. on doing it 5. not only did he look-at but he bought it 6. on washing them 7. on writing it 8. as lazy as 9. the lazier he is, the less he works 10. in order to be 11. on saying 12. before doing 13. after he spoke 14. as soon as he had written 15. they didn't study because they did not have 16. so that she took 17. in order to look for

B. 1. No escribió los ejercicios después de estudiar la lección porque estaba demasiado cansado. 2. Cuanto más miraba el piano, tanto más lo deseaba. 3. No lo compró pues no le gustaba. 4. Para comprar una casa, hay que tener mucho dinero. 5. No se compra una casa con poco dinero, no solamente en ésa sino también en ésta. 6. Al decir esto, se puso (put on) el sombrero y salió del cuarto. 7. Después de hacer una carrera en coche por la ciudad, nos dijo que quedaría cuatro días más. 8. Cuanto más compraba, tanto más deseaba comprar. 9. Pide el libro a su hermano por tener el suyo en casa. 10. Jugar demasiado es peor que estudiar poco. 11. No podemos examinar el paño ahora pues no tenemos mucho tiempo. 12. Después de escribir los ejercicios, se los pasa los cuadernos a Juan (*are* **se los** *necessary?*). 13. Después de estudiar usted mejor, tendrá mejores notas. 14. El no decir esto sería una cobardía, si lo que usted dice es la verdad. 15. Sintieron que sus primos no se lo enseñasen después de que lo hubieron hallado. 17. El mismo hombre que nos lo dijo antes al preguntárselo nosotros, ahora no dice la misma cosa. 18. Los lápices no son tan grandes como nos dijo su hermano. 19. Contesta las cartas.

BB. 1. After seeing us, they took their books and studied again. 2. On looking through the window, we saw them on the path. 3. These books are not as large as those you showed us yesterday, but they are better. 4. After they had bought the piano, they did not like it. 5. In order to buy the piano, he had to ask his uncle for more money. 6. Without saying anything (nothing), he studied three hours in his room, and then he went to bed. 7. To study too little is as bad as studying too much. 8. When they had eaten, they washed the dishes and then went to bed. 9. He didn't buy the house because he did not like it. 10. The same children who told us that, now say that it isn't the truth. 11. They were sorry we didn't give it to them before returning home (**a casa**). 12. After he said that, he put on (*see B, 6*) his hat and left the house without saying anything more. 13. To play the piano so much is better than doing nothing. 14. If you don't say that, it would be an act of cowardice. 15. The more pencils he bought, the more he lost. 16. In order to play the piano, one must work hard. 17. Before taking a ride around the city, we must look for a carriage. 18. Did you find the child yesterday before you reached home? 19. They not only studied the grammar, but they also wrote the exercise. 20. It was necessary for them to do it in order to arrive there.

LESSON LI
ORTHOGRAPHIC CHANGES

Review Lessons I and XII, 1 (See Appendix E)

1. The consonant **sound** with which a verb stem ends (most verb stems end in a consonant) must be maintained throughout the verb. Now, as the endings of verbs start with the vowels **-a, -e, -i,** or **-o,** it is necessary sometimes to make certain changes in **spelling** (called **orthographic changes**) in order to preserve the original consonant sound. For instance, as **c** before **a** is pronounced like **k**, *sacar*, in order to indicate the **k** sound before the subjunctive endings of the present (which begin with **-e**), must change the **c** to **qu**.

Some of the common changes work according to the scheme below.

(a) **-car** verbs change **c-** to **qu-** before **-e**.
    sacar, to pull out (*stem* **sac-**, *sound* **k**)

        preterite indicative: **saqué**
        present subjunctive:
            saque, saques, saque; saquemos, saquéis, saquen

(b) **-quir** verbs change **qu-** to **c-** before **-o** or **-a**.
   delinquir, to be delinquent (*stem* **delinqu-**, *sound* **k**)
   present indicative: **delinco**
   present subjunctive:
   delinca, delincas, delinca; delincamos, delincáis, delincan

(c) **-gar** verbs change **g-** to **gu-** before **-e**.
   llegar, to arrive (*stem* **lleg-**, *sound* **g** *as in* **good**)
   preterite indicative: **llegué**
   present subjunctive:
   llegue, llegues, llegue; lleguemos, lleguéis, lleguen

(d) **-ger** and **-gir** verbs change **g-** to **j-** before **-o** or **-a**.
   coger, to catch (*stem* **cog-**, **j** *sound in back of throat*)
   present indicative: **cojo**
   present subjunctive:
   coja, cojas, coja; cojamos, cojáis, cojan

   elegir, to choose, to elect (*stem R-ch. III*, **j** *sound in back of throat*)
   present indicative: **elijo**
   present subjunctive:
   elija, elijas, elija; elijamos, elijáis, elijan

(e) **-guar** verbs put a diaeresis on the **ü-** before **-e**.
   averiguar, to ascertain (*stem* **averigu-**, *write* **-ü-** *before* **-e**)
   preterite indicative: **averigüé**
   present subjunctive:
   averigüe, averigües, averigüe; averigüemos, averigüéis, averigüen

(f) **-guir** verbs change **-gu** to **-g**.
   distinguir, to distinguish (*stem* **distingu**, *drop* **-u-** *before* **-o** *or* **-a**)
   present indicative: **distingo**
   present subjunctive:
   distinga, distingas, distinga; distingamos, distingáis, distingan

(g) **-jar** verbs keep **j-** always (*the change to* **g-** *is not made*).
   dejar, to leave (*stem* **dej-** *always*)
   preterite indicative: **dejé**, *etc.*

Note that (a), (c), and (e) change in the same seven forms; and that (b), (d), and (f) change in the same seven forms.

Verbs in -jer and -jir, e. g., **tejer**, *to weave,* and **crujir**, *to creak,* also keep the **j-** unchanged.

2. Verbs of the second or third conjugation with the stem ending in -ll or -ñ drop the -i- of the third person singular and plural preterite indicative, and all the past subjunctives. The fact that ll and ñ are pronounced as though the -i- were present anyway accounts for the dropping of the written -i-.

bullir, to boil (*stem* **bull-**)

preterite indicative:
bullí, bulliste, bulló; bullimos, bullisteis, bulleron
past subjunctive:
bullese, bulleses, bullese; bullésemos, bulleseis, bullesen
bullera, bulleras, bullera; bulléramos, bullerais, bulleran

teñir, to stain, to dye (*stem R-ch. III*)

preterite indicative:
teñí, teñiste, tiñó; teñimos, teñisteis, tiñeron
past subjunctive:
tiñese, tiñeses, tiñese; tiñésemos, tiñeseis, tiñesen
tiñera, tiñeras, tiñera; tiñéramos, tiñerais, tiñeran

The same change also occurs in the present participle.

bullendo   tiñendo

VOCABULARY

alojar, to lodge, to dwell
el animal, animal
(la) arma, arm, weapon
brincar, to jump, to skip
bruñir, to burnish, to polish
entregar, to hand over, to give over
gruñir, to grunt

es menester, it is necessary
pagar, to pay
rajar, to split, to cleave
rezar, to pray
rogar (ue), to beg, to ask, to request
sacar, to pull out, to draw out
venir, to come

A. 1. toqué 2. tejer 3. que dejen 4. que lleguemos 5. que crujan 6. que bullese 7. pagué 8. dirijo 9. que cruja 10. alojé 11. gruñeron 12. que dirijamos 13. que averigüéis 14. bulló 15. que mengüen 16. que bruñésemos 17. rajé 18. que recemos 19. averigüé 20. que

paguen 21. que mengüen 22. distingo 23. gruñeron
24. que delinca 25. pagué 26. que rueguen 27. que ruegue
28. que juguemos 29. alojé

AA. 1. it boiled 2. they offended 3. that it creaks
4. I take 5. that they distinguish 6. they burnished 7. I
lodged 8. that he ascertain 9. I prayed 10. that we direct
11. I am directing 12. that they offend 13. I played
14. that it is lacking 15. I offend 16. that it creaks 17. I
paid 18. I have paid 19. that we pay 20. that you (*intimate singular*) pay 21. that he pay 22. I arrived 23. I shall arrive 24. they boiled 25. that we distinguish 26. that we arrive 27. I asked (*use form of* **rogar**)

B. 1. Gruñeron los animales y el niño se fué corriendo. 2. Lo cogí por el brazo y entonces me dijo la verdad. 3. Saqué un poco de dinero de mi bolsillo y se lo entregué. 4. Crujió la puerta cuando entramos en el cuarto. 5. Pagué diez pesos por el paño, pero después no me gustó. 6. Averigüé que lo que él dijo era la verdad. 7. Es preciso que recen todos los días. 8. Dejé la escuela antes de escribir los ejercicios. 9. Es preciso que toques el piano todos los días antes de venir de la escuela. 10. Distingo entre los alumnos diligentes y los flojos; éstos tienen notas muy malas, aquéllos las tienen muy buenas. 11. Es preciso que alojemos aquí porque no hay otra casa en el camino. 12. Es tiempo que usted me entregue la carta que tiene para mí. 13. Bruñeron sus armas. 14. A los quince años no tocaba todavía el piano.

BB. 1. ¿Es preciso que la puerta cruja cuando entras en el cuarto? 2. No distingo entre los alumnos grandes y los pequeños, sino entre los flojos y los diligentes. 3. No es preciso que paguemos por la comida ahora. 4. Lo cogí por el brazo y le tenía (held him) hasta no tener más fuerzas. 5. El soldado bruñía sus armas. 6. ¿Fué menester que las bruñese? 7. Es necesario que los niños recen todos los días. 8. Nos dejó allá, y entró en su cuarto, donde volvió a estudiar. 9. Toqué el piano. 10. Alojé en una casa de la calle X., la más grande de la ciudad. 11. Es preciso

SUBJUNCTIVE OF RADICAL-CHANGING VERBS 127

que averigüemos la verdad de lo que él dijo. 12. Es tiempo que dejemos todo eso. 13. Es tiempo de que lleguemos si hemos de comer con ellos hoy. 14. Es menester que averigüéis la verdad.

BBB. 1. Was it necessary for the door to creak when they went out? 2. Did he have to leave the school when he was only sixteen (years)? 3. It was time that you left them there. 4. We must distinguish between the large and the little children. 5. Why did the soldiers have to burnish their arms? 6. That day I played the piano, because my brother was ill and could not play it himself. 7. I took the money from my pocket and paid him. 8. I ascertained the truth. 9. It was necessary for them to lodge there, for they could not go to your town the same day. 10. He left the child with his brother, and went off. 11. It is necessary for you to play the piano today, for John's brother will not be here.

LESSON LII

SUBJUNCTIVE OF RADICAL-CHANGING VERBS

Review Lessons XXXV and XXXVI.

1. In Class I, Radical-changing verbs change in the subjunctive all the singular and the third plural of the present (just as in the indicative).

volver, to return (*stem R-ch. I*)		**encender**, to kindle (*stem R-ch. I*)	
vuelva	volvamos	encienda	encendamos
vuelvas	volváis	enciendas	encendáis
vuelva	vuelvan	encienda	enciendan

2. In Class II, Radical-changing verbs change (a) in the present subjunctive the same forms as in the indicative (-o- to -ue- and -e- to -ie-); and

(b) in the first and second persons plural present

subjunctive, the present participle, and all the past subjunctives (-o- to -u- and -e- to -i-).

sentir, to feel, to be sorry (*stem R-ch. II*)

present	past		present participle
sienta	sintiese	sintiera	
sientas	sintieses	sintieras	
sienta	sintiese	sintiera	sintiendo
sintamos	sintiésemos	sintiéramos	
sintáis	sintieseis	sintierais	
sientan	sintiesen	sintieran	

morir, to die (*stem R-ch. II*)

muera	muriese	muriera	muriendo
mueras	murieses	murieras	
muera	muriese	muriera	
muramos	muriésemos	muriéramos	
muráis	murieseis	murierais	
mueran	muriesen	murieran	

3. Class III has only the change e to i. This change is found in every case where either change occurs in Class II above.

repetir, to repeat (*stem R-ch. III*)

repita	repitiese	repitiera	repitiendo
etc.	etc.	etc.	

4. **hacer**, past subjunctive

hiciese	hiciera
hicieses	hicieras
hiciese	hiciera
hiciésemos	hiciéramos
hicieseis	hicierais
hiciesen	hicieran

VOCABULARY

despedirse (i) de, to take leave of
durante, during
equivocarse, to be mistaken
la pregunta, question
pronto, soon, quickly
propio, -a, own
romper, to break

A. *Conjugate the present and past subjunctives and give the present participle of:* cerrar pedir despedirse contar volver sentir sentarse dormir morir vestirse encender

SUBJUNCTIVE OF RADICAL-CHANGING VERBS 129

AA. 1. que pidiera 2. que cerremos 3. que nos pidan 4. que pidiésemos 5. que se acostasen 6. que nos depidamos 7. nos despedimos 8. que me siente (*what is the infinitive?*) 9. que sienta (*what is the infinitive?*) 10. que sintamos 11. que nos sentemos 12. que me vista 13. que volvamos 14. que volviéramos 15. que volviésemos 16. que perdamos 17. que repitamos 18. que repitan 19. que mienta 20. que mintamos 21. que llueva 22. que cerrásemos 23. que cerraran 24. que impidiera 25. que impida 26. que confiese 27. que tiemblen

AAA. 1. that he should shut 2. that we dressed 3. that they were sorry 4. that I return 5. that they returned 6. that they return 7. that it was raining 8. that we asked-for 9. they took leave 10. that it is raining 11. that he is dressing 12. that we are counting 13. that we slept 14. that he is sleeping 15. that we are sleeping 16. that he lies 17. that he had lied 18. that you lied 19. that you are lying 20. that they have repeated 21. that I am repeating 22. that she seated the child near the table 23. that it is not snowing 24. that it did not snow 25. that he confessed 26. that we prevented

B. 1. Es lástima que tiemblen de frío. 2. Es tiempo de que nos despidamos si hemos de llegar a tiempo. 3. Es preciso que la hermana llegue temprano. 4. Sienten mucho que nosotros no hayamos tocado el piano. 5. Fué preciso que la madre vistiese muy bien a los niños, pero ellos ya estaban muy sucios. 7. ¿Fué necesario que los niños contestasen al hombre? 8. Si lloviese, estudiaríamos en casa todo el día. 9. Si tú me lo hubiese pedido, te lo hubiera entregado. 10. No es necesario que vuelvas a comer; ya has comido demasiado. 11. Dudo que volviesen a decirlo al profesor. 12. Si no durmiera durante el día, no trabajaría en la tarde. 13. Es posible que los niños no la quieran; sin embargo, es su propia tía. 14. ¿No fué posible que repitieran mal el mismo trabajo? 15. Dudamos mucho que hubiera por qué volver a estudiarlo. 16. Es posible que pueda derretir el hielo en un vaso, pero ahora no está derritiéndolo.

BB. 1. It is possible that he did not ask for it, but I do not remember that. 2. You doubt that we asked for it. 3. If he had asked me, I should have answered him. 4. We doubt that they will do it again. 5. It was a pity that they dressed so early. 6. We are sorry that you are trembling so much with cold, but it is very cold in this room—it is necessary to shut the windows. 7. If he wanted to melt the ice in the glass, he would break it first. 8. We doubt that the pupils compete with each other, because they are brothers. 9. If we did not sleep during the day, we should not sleep during the night either. 10. It is necessary for us to eat again because we are hungry. 11. It is a pity that they did not ask for it because he would have given (*use* **entregar** *in correct form*) it to them. 12. It is time that you took leave. 13. It was time that they took leave. 14. I am very sorry that we did not have breakfast before leaving. 15. Is it possible that the children don't like their own uncle?

LESSON LIII

SUBJUNCTIVE IN ADVERBIAL CLAUSES

Review Appendix C.

1. The subjunctive is used in adverbial clauses (clauses introduced by **when, where, so that, although,** etc.) when they are indefinite in sense. (Cf. the English: "He wanted to finish it before they arrived." The time of arriving is still uncertain. "I finished it just before they arrived." The time they arrived is a known fact; hence the indicative is used here.)

2. Some of the commonest conjunctions that may introduce the subjunctive in adverbial clauses are:

SUBJUNCTIVE IN ADVERBIAL CLAUSES

a fin (de) que, in order that
a menos que, unless
antes que, before
a pesar de que, in spite of the fact that
aunque, although
cuando, when
dado que, considering
de manera que, so that (*purpose*)
de modo que, so that (*purpose*)

después (de) que, after
en caso (de) que, in case
hasta que, until
luego que, as soon as
no sea que, unless
para que, in order that
por (*adjective*) que, however ...
siempre que, whenever; provided
sin que, without

3. If the subject of the main verb and the subject of the subordinate clause are identical, substitute **de** for **que** (this can be done with most compound conjunctions; but note that **hasta**, **para**, and **por** are used without **de**) and put the subordinate verb in the infinitive. This construction is preferred.

Usted estudiará antes que yo escriba, You will study before I write.
Yo estudiaré antes de escribir, I shall study before writing.

A. 1. Vivirá con su padre hasta que compre su propia casa. 2. Vivirá en casa de su padre hasta comprar su propria casa. 3. Estudian tanto como su hermana porque son muy diligentes. 4. Estudian más que su hermana para que ella no tenga mejores notas que ellos. 5. Por difíciles que sean las lecciones, él las aprende. 6. Sin que yo juzgue mal de él, puedo decir que nadie le quiere a él. 7. En caso de que no me muestre cómo trabaja, no compraré las plumas para él. 8. Aunque los rubíes que me enseñe sean muy caros, los compraré si me gustan. 9. Antes de que lo impidiéramos, se escapó. 10. A pesar de que tengan mucho que hacer, estarán temprano en casa. 11. He perdido mi sombrero, de manera que tengo (*result clause, hence indicative*) que comprar otro. 12. Preparó la comida de manera que nosotros tuviéramos que comer con él. 13. Es imposible que viajemos todo el tiempo hasta que volvamos a la escuela. 14. Nos es imposible viajar todo el tiempo hasta volver a la escuela. 15. No fué necesario tocar el piano. 16. En caso de que no nos (*from us*) compre el piano, lo venderemos a su tío. 17. Aunque no quieran decirme la verdad, encontraré quién me la diga (someone to tell me it). 18. Siempre que se acuerden de ello, se escriben la una a la otra.

AA. 1. We shall work until we finish this lesson. 2. However large he may be, a big man is not always strong. 3. Although we may judge ill of him, this is sure—he is a good student. 4. Without their having to study much (Without that they have to study much), they always have good marks. 5. As soon as they return to the house, they will not want (**desearán**) to study. 6. Unless she prepares (the) dinner, she will not want to eat it. 7. We shall not write again until you finish doing that. 8. I shall buy the piano for him in order that he may play it in his own house. 9. We have studied well in order that we may have good marks. 10. We study hard so that we may have very good marks. 11. I shall have to play the piano until they wish to do it. 12. Whenever he wants to play, he calls the other little children in his house. 13. We played until our parents entered the room. 14. In case they wish to see them, we shall go away (*use form of* **irse**). 15. In spite of the fact that he studied all night, he did not learn his lessons well. 16. We wish to prepare the meal before we eat because they do not feel well and can't cook. 17. I shall drink the coffee unless it is bad, for I like coffee. 18. In case they buy that house from their uncle, he will ask them eighty-five hundred dollars for it.

LESSON LIV

Review Appendix C.

1. Subjunctive in Main Clauses. The subjunctive is used in independent clauses but rarely. But cf. the examples below:

¡**Viva Chile!** Hurrah for Chile! (*lit.*, Long-live Chile!)
Quisiera hacerlo, I should like to do it.
¡**Quien supiera escribir!** If I could only write!

In such cases, the subjunctive may be understood as depending on some unexpressed verb.

2. The subjunctive is also used in the first person plural (without being introduced by **que**) and in the third person singular or plural (with or without **que**) to express a wish.

Estudiemos ahora, Let us study now.
(Que) estudien ahora si quieren, Let them study now if they wish.

Note: The first person plural often takes the form **vamos a** plus the infinitive.

Estudiemos ahora,
Vamos a estudiar ahora, } Let us study now.

If the third person (singular or plural) has an object pronoun, the pronoun precedes the verb if **que** is used or if the verb is negative; if **que** is not used and the verb is affirmative, the pronoun follows.

Que lo estudien si quieren, Let them study it if they wish.
Que no lo estudien si no quieren, They needn't study it if they don't want to.
Estúdienlo si quieren, Let them study it if they want to.

In the first person plural, when a subjunctive is affirmative, the pronoun object (1) follows and is joined to the verb; and (2) when that pronoun is reflexive **nos**, the verb form drops final -s.

Escribámoslo, Let us write it.
Sentémonos, Let us sit down (*for* sentemos *plus* nos).
But
No nos sentemos, Let us not sit down.

3. **Subjunctive in Adjective Clauses.** The subjunctive is used in adjective clauses which refer to a noun regarded as not yet definitely known. (Cf. the English: "I am looking for a man who can do this work," and "I am looking for the man who did this work.")

Busco al hombre que lo hizo, I am looking for the man who did it.
But
Busco un hombre que pueda hacerlo, I am looking for a man who can do it.

Es el mejor alumno que haya en el mundo, He is the best student in the world (*subjunctive because the statement is not literally true*).

VOCABULARY

la **Argentina,** Argentina
caro, -a, dear, expensive
gritar, to shout, to call out
gordo, -a, stout
hermoso, -a, beautiful, handsome
hizo, (he, she, it) did, made; you did, made
interesante, interesting
intitularse, to be called, to be entitled
marcharse, to march off, to go off
el **mundo,** world; **todo el mundo,** everybody
el **Perú,** Peru (*use definite article in Spanish*)
único, -a, only

A. 1. quisiéramos estar 2. que compren 3. un niño que prepare 4. vendamos 5. vamos a vender 6. no nos preocupemos más 7. una mujer que toca el piano 8. la mejor casa que hay en la calle 9. que pida 10. el niño más flojo que haya en el mundo 11. la alumna que toque el piano 12. han hallado al hombre que lo escribió 13. el hombre que vive aquí 14. comamos 15. que laven 16. ¡viva España! 17. quisiera verla 18. buscamos una niña que escriba bien 19. que se sienten 20. afeitémonos 21. no nos lavemos 22. vamos a lavarnos 23. que lo tenga 24. que no lo tenga 25. téngalo

AA. 1. let us remain 2. I wish I were there 3. I wish we were there 4. I wish I were there (*can the infinitive be used?*) 5. let us not shave 6. let him cook 7. hurrah for Argentina! 8. hurrah for Peru! 9. let him shave 10. we should like to study 11. let us bathe 12. a man who wrote 13. we want a girl who cooks well 14. he is the only Englishman who has a house in this street 15. let us write to each other (*express in two ways*) 16. let us write to one another (*express in two ways*)

B. 1. Todos los hombres gritaron: ¡Viva España! 2. ¡Viva el Rey! 3. Ya está caliente la comida; comámosla. 4. Queremos leer unos libros que sean muy interesantes. 5. No nos gustan los alumnos cuyas lecciones están muy mal preparadas. 6. Éstos son los únicos muchachos en esta clase. 7. Quisiera ser más flaco; me parece que soy demasiado gordo. 8. Levantémonos ahora, y afeitémonos, porque tenemos muchas cosas que hacer antes de irnos. 9. Deseo tener un hombre que me enseñe cómo se hizo este trabajo. 11. Quisiera leer esa poesía hermosa que se intitula: "¡Quién supiera escribir!" 12. Quedémonos aquí hasta que su hermano vuelva; si no, no le encontraremos después. 14. Buscamos al hombre que vive en esta casa. 15. Juan es el mejor hombre que haya vivido en esta ciudad.

BB. 1. I should like to call with the others: Hurrah for the King! but I don't like (the) kings. 2. Can you show me a man who cooks so well that everyone likes what he prepares? 3. His mother cooks well. 4. Yes, but there are no men who cook well. 5. Let us prepare the meal (in order) to see if you will like it. 6. Let us get up before we have breakfast. 7. I should like to see the man who did this work; it is very good. 8. If they intend (**piensan**) to go early, let them go to bed now. 9. Have you found the poem which is entitled: "If I could only read!" 10. Let them sell the cloth if they can (it); I don't want it—it isn't good. 11. Let's stay here until your uncle comes; if we leave the room before he comes-in, he won't find us. 12. John is the best man who ever taught here, I think. 13. Let us wash now, because afterwards we shall not have much time. 14. These are the most expensive pens they sell here; but they are bad nevertheless. 15. Let them stay here, if they wish; but if they don't study, let us not speak to them, either. 16. Let us look for a man who writes so well that he may work with us here.

LESSON LV
SUBJUNCTIVE IN NOUN CLAUSES

Review Appendix C.

1. The subjunctive is used in noun clauses after verbs meaning **to wish, to will, to desire, to forbid, to deny, to**

ask, to doubt, to fear, to hope, to be glad or **sorry,** and verbs with similar meanings.

> **Quiero que usted estudie,** I want you to study (I want that you study).
> **Desean que los visitemos,** They want us to visit them.
> **Espero que le guste,** I hope[1] he likes it.
> **Prohiben que ella lo pida,** They forbid her asking for it.
> **Temo que no lleguen a tiempo,** I am afraid they may not arrive on time.
> **Duda que ella esté aquí,** He doubts that she is here.

Note:

(a) A verb of doubting, when used negatively, no longer expresses doubt, and may, if it implies a fact, be followed by the indicative.

> **No duda que están aquí,** She doesn't doubt (the fact) that they are here.

Similarly, certain negative-interrogative expressions implying a fact are followed by the indicative.

> **¿No sabe que están aquí?** Doesn't she know that they are here?

(b) A few verbs may take the infinitive construction as well as the **que** construction, even where the subject of the main verb and that of the subjunctive are different. This construction may be used by **aconsejar,** *to advise;* **dejar,** *to leave, to let;* **mandar,** *to order, to command;* **permitir,** *to permit, to allow,* and **prohibir,** *to forbid.*

> **Me manda escribirle (Me manda que le escriba),** He bids me write her.
> **Me permite escribirle (Me permite que le escriba),** She permits my writing him.

2. Verbs meaning **to say, to think, to declare,** and verbs with similar meanings, take the indicative when affirmative (for then they state a fact); but the subjunctive when interrogative or negative (for then there may be doubt about the statement made).

---

[1] That may be omitted in English, but **que** is seldom omitted in Spanish (though **rogar, permitir** and a few others occasionally drop it).

Dice que estaba aquí, He says that he was here.
¿**Dice que estuviese aquí?** Does he say that he was here?
No dice que estuviese aquí, He does not say that he was here.
Note:
No dice si estuvo aquí, He doesn't say whether he was here
(**si** = *whether* takes only the indicative).

3. Impersonal verbs with a subjunctive noun clause are discussed in Lesson XLVI, 1 and 2.

VOCABULARY

aconsejar, to advise
alegrarse, to rejoice, to be glad
aprobar (ue), to approve
mandar, to bid, order, command, request
pasar, to pass; to go; to happen
permitir, to permit, to let, to allow
preferir (ie), to prefer
prohibir, to forbid, to prohibit
suceder, to happen

A. 1. dudamos que estén 2. aprueba que tengamos 3. prefirió que trabajáramos 4. mandó que quedásemos 5. prohibe que sea 6. aconseja que visitemos 7. quiere que estudie 8. teme que no sea 9. me permiten que me despida 10. me manda que pregunte 11. nos permiten despedirnos 12. le prohibí acabar 13. espero que coman 14. me mandó preguntar 15. les prohibí que acaben 16. nos ruega que visitemos 17. queremos que vosotras nos visitéis 18. me permite (que) diga 19. me permite decir 20. me aconseja venir 21. dudo que veamos 22. es preciso ver 23. es preciso que veamos 24. espero que veáis 25. les es preciso hallar 26. es lástima que no sean 27. es lástima que no trabajen 28. ¿No sabe que están aquí?

AA. 1. we must see 2. we doubt that there was 3. did he say? 4. it is necessary 5. we prefer that he be 6. they prohibit our remaining (that we remain) 7. they ordered us to write 8. they don't permit our working 9. they advise our seeing 10. he ordered us to say 11. it is time to visit 12. I hope you visit 13. they prohibit our saying 14. they advise our seeing 15. I am glad you see 16. he regrets (**siente**) we visited 17. they advise our seeing 18. we are sorry they had 19. they permit our having 20. I don't know that they said 21. don't you know that he said? 22. do you know if they saw? 23. do you know whether they saw? 24. it is a pity they didn't have 25. it is a pity not to have 26. I don't doubt they worked.

B. 1. Duda que toquen el piano tan bien como lo tocaban sus padres. 2. Aprobamos que no haya más casas en esta calle porque ya hay bastantes. 3. Niega que hubiera (*the sense calls for a past subjunctive after a present tense, contrary to the general rule*) mucha neblina ayer; dice que había mucho sol. 4. Es preciso que le preguntemos si estará aquí mañana. 5. Nos ruega que hallemos el billete de banco que perdieron. 6. Le prohibo que lo busque porque no creo que lo hayan perdido. 7. Es lástima que tenga tantos años; ya no puede trabajar. 8. Me permitió que acostase a los niños en su cama de él porque ya era muy tarde. 9. Me mandaron que limpiara toda la vajilla porque yo primero acabé de comer. 10. Fué tiempo que nos visitasen. 11. Es preciso preguntarle si estará aquí mañana. 12. Esperamos que ustedes puedan verlo antes que les escriba. 13. Aconsejó que escribiésemos una carta a nuestros tíos y otra a nuestros primos también. 14. Dudo que los rubíes que enseñó sean tan caros como los que V. tiene. 15. Aconsejó que acostásemos a los niños porque tan tarde era. 16. ¿No sabe usted si ya han llegado?

BB. 1. He doubted that we wrote to our parents every week. 2. It was a pity that we did not show them the rubies before they bought theirs. 3. I forbade their going to bed then because they still had much to do. 4. They allowed us to go home before them. 5. We advise them to play the piano an hour every day. 6. I doubt that there are not as many houses in that street as in this. 7. She does not know if there was much mist yesterday. 8. He advises me not to lose any more notes if I want to do the work well. 9. We don't permit the children to go to bed so early. 10. It was necessary for them to write a letter every four days (all the four days). 11. It is a pity that they did not arrive yesterday because today we have to go away. 12. I advised the window's being shut (that the window shut itself) because it was very windy. 13. They forbade our seeing them before writing them. 14. It is time for us to wash the dishes, for if not, we shall not be able to go out. 15. He hopes to arrive before us.

[Study Appendix D. This may be used for class room drill and test preparation.]

LESSON LVI
THE INFINITIVE

1. In English, the infinitive is almost always recognized by the word **to** before it. "I wish **to** go."

Rarely, the **to** is absent. "I can go (I am able to go)."

2. In Spanish, the infinitive is not preceded by the word for **to**, but may be recognized by the ending: **-ar, -er,** or **-ir**.

3. In Spanish, the infinitive is used (a) after another verb; or (b) as subject of a verb.

4. After another verb:

(a) Some verbs are followed directly by the infinitive without any preposition.

dejar, to let, to permit	pensar (ie), to intend
desear, to desire, to want	poder (ue), to be able, can
hacer, to make	querer (ie), to wish, want
importa, it matters, it is important	

No puedo hacerlo, I can't do it.
Me hace ver, He shows me (*lit.*, He makes me see).

(b) Some verbs are followed by the preposition **a** plus the infinitive.

aprender a, to learn to	oponerse a, to refuse to, to oppose
comenzar (ie) a, to begin to	ponerse, -a, to begin to
empezar (ie) a, to begin to	principiar a, to begin to
ir a, to go to	venir a, to happen to
negarse (ie) a, to refuse to	volver (ue) a, (to do a thing) again

Aprende a hablar francés, He is learning to speak French.

(c) Some verbs are followed by the preposition **de** plus the infinitive.

acabar de, (to have) just; to have finished
acordarse (ue) de, to remember
alegrarse de, to be glad
dejar de, to leave off, to cease
guardarse de, to refrain from
olvidarse de, to forget
tener ganas de, to be eager, to feel like
tratar de, to try to

Tenemos ganas de verle, We are eager to see him.

(d) A number of isolated verbs are found with various prepositions.

acordar (ue) en, to agree on
consistir en, to consist of
insistir en, to insist on
fijarse en, to notice carefully
tardar en, to be slow in
echar a, to begin to
echar de, to manage to
luchar por, to struggle to
estar para, to be about to
estar por, to be inclined to, to feel like

Lucharon por escaparse, They struggled to get loose.
Tardó en venir, He was late in coming.

(e) For **para** and **a**, see Lesson L, 2b.

5. Before an infinitive, **que** is used where **lo que** would be used before a finite form.

Me dijo qué hacer, He told me what to do. (*Cf.*, **Me dice lo que tenemos que hacer**, He is telling me what we have to do.)

VOCABULARY

contentarse con, to be satisfied with
descansar, to rest
necesitar, to need
puro, -a, pure; la pura verdad, the "plain" truth
recorrer, to traverse, to go over
tras, after

A. 1. iremos a verlo 2. se fijó 3. no echó de aprender 4. volvieron a trabajar 5. queremos lavarnos 6. se contentaron con visitar 7. aprendemos a escribir 8. trataron de escribir 9. consiste en hacer 10. acordaron en escribirse 11. se guardó de decirlo 12. pienso escribirle 13. eran 14. iban a visitar 15. vivimos para trabajar 16. echó a perder 17. me alegro de verlas 18. le perdió (he ruined him) 19. lo perdió (he lost it) 20. olvidaron de mandármelo 21. estoy por escribirle 22. está para escribirle 23. lucho por hacerlo 24. vienen a verme 25. tarda en venir 26. importa tenerlo

AA. 1. we forgot to write 2. they again wrote 3. we shall be satisfied with having 4. do you agree to give?

THE INFINITIVE 141

5. they refrained from 6. will you go and (*use a plus infinitive*) visit? 7. will he go and stay? 8. will he go in order to say? 9. he lived in order to work 10. they managed to find 11. he lived to eat 12. it consists in making 13. they are opposed to writing 14. they intend to visit 15. we didn't manage to send 16. we forgot to write 17. they are about to write 18. we feel like going 19. are they coming? 20. they were late speaking 21. they wish to find 22. she was learning to write 23. I was inclined to write

B. 1. Teníamos ganas de tocar el piano antes de entrar en el otro cuarto a hablar con nuestros padres. 2. Deseo comprar la casa si no piden demasiado. 3. Iré a sentarme en aquella silla a descansar porque estoy muy cansado. 4. Estamos por comprar el paño, pero no tenemos bastante dinero. 5. Volverá a jugar en vez de estudiar porque es muy flojo. 6. Luchaban por escaparse, pero no tenían bastantes fuerzas. 7. Se olvidan de comprar las cosas que necesitan, y así siempre tienen que pedir[lo] todo prestado. 8. Trataremos de ver la ciudad en vez de descansar esta tarde, porque estamos seguros que no tendríamos bastante tiempo para hacerlo en una sola carrera. 9. Estuvo por ver el caballo, pero se acordó de no tener dinero para comprarlo y así quedó en casa. 10. No nos contentamos con comprar lo que necesitamos, lo compramos todo (we buy everything). 11. Niega que volviesen a decir lo mismo—dice que dijeron la pura verdad. 12. No sabemos qué hacer. 13. Si queréis acordaros de lo que hallasteis, os acordaréis también de que es nuestro. 14. No echó de comprender lo que sucedía. 15. Echamos a correr tras ellos, y ellos también empezaron a correr. 16. Pensamos recorrer la ciudad en coche, porque no tenemos el tiempo de ir a pie. 17. No importa trabajar—importa trabajar bien. 18. Dejó de escribir y volvió a estudiar la lección.

BB. 1. I don't remember having seen the horse of which you are speaking. 2. We managed to buy the cloth, because we did not find any other that we liked. 3. I intend to sell him the cloth. 4. I intend to tell him what we think of him—and he will not like the truth. 5. I began to run, and they after me. 6. He finished eating, and then he began to wash the dishes. 7. They stopped writing to us, and then we didn't write to them. 8. They have just written it; and now they are studying again. 9. She had just written to her friends when they entered the room. 10. It is important to buy only good things. 11. I don't feel like playing instead of studying, because I have already played too much. 12. I feel like buying that cloth, but I haven't enough money. 13. We don't want to play the piano before they come, for we still have to dress. 14. They will go and (*use* a) buy the house if they have not where to live. 15. He said it again, for we didn't understand it when he said it first.

LESSON LVII

PRESENT PARTICIPLE AND INFINITIVE (*summary*)

Review Lesson LVI.

1. For the present participle in periphrastic tenses, see Lesson XXXVII, 3.

Está estudiando, He is studying.

Note also:

Sigue trabajando, He goes on working (*from* **seguir**).
Viene llegando, He is arriving (*from* **venir**).
venirse durmiendo, to be falling asleep
Anda filosofando, He goes ahead philosophizing (*from* **andar**).

2. The infinitive is sometimes used in Spanish where the English employs the form in **-ing**. This is the case after such verbs as **ver**, *to see*; **oír**, *to hear*; **entender**, *to hear*; **mandar**, *to order, to have*.

Me vió trabajar, He saw me working.

Note the passive sense with **mandar**.

Mandó hacerlo, He had it done (ordered it done).

PRESENT PARTICIPLE AND INFINITIVE

3. The infinitive is used as subject or object of a verb.

(El) leer es aprender, Reading is learning.
Saber es poder, Knowledge is power (To know is to be able).
Quiero leerlo, I want to read it.

4. Pronoun objects follow and are joined to either an infinitive or a present participle, thus forming one word (this may necessitate a written accent).

Estudiándolo mucho, lo aprendió, By studying it hard, he learned it.
Quiero escribírselo a ella, I want to write it to her.

(Forms like: **Se lo quiero escribir,** though found, should be avoided.)

5. **Formation of Adverbs.** Any adjective may be turned into the corresponding adverb by adding **-mente** to the feminine (cf. English **-ly** in **pretty, prettily**).

nueva mente nuevamente, newly, recently
traidoramente, treacherously
felizmente, happily

Of course, many adverbs are formed independently of adjectives.

aprisa, quickly   **bien,** well

For irregular adverbs, see Lesson XXIII, 3.

For the comparison of adverbs, see Lesson XXIII, 1.

VOCABULARY

andar, to go
aprisa, quickly
felizmente, happily
filosofar, to philosophize
haciendo, doing, making (*present participle*)
leer, to read
malamente, badly
nuevamente, newly, recently
oír, to hear
la paz, peace
seguir (i), to go on, to keep on, to continue
tratar, to treat; —— **de,** to try to
traidoramente, treacherously
vió, (he, she, it) saw; you saw

A. 1. habiéndolo estudiado (*note that in Spanish the pronoun object can not ever follow the* **past** *participle*) 2. habiéndomelo enseñado 3. habiéndolo lavado 4. habiéndonos lavado 5. están tratando 6. peor 7. me manda hacer (**me** *here can not follow* **hacer** *because it is the object of* **manda**) 8. mejor 9. le vió venir 10. menos 11. nuevamente 12. ver es creer 13. más 14. seguimos escribiendo 15. trabajando ganaron 16. más felizmente 17. estudiando aprenderá 18. puedo ver 19. puedo verlo 20. queriendo hacerlo 21. menos 22. queremos hallarlos 23. habiéndolo aprendido

AA. 1. more 2. less easily 3. having spoken to us 4. [by] working one learns 5. they heard us coming-in 6. with more difficulty 7. less 8. they have us do 9. better 10. having 11. they wanted to tell us 12. he has us say 13. they saw me run 14. they saw me running 15. he informs me (he makes me to know) 16. they keep-on writing 17. they go-on philosophizing 18. having spoken to them

B. 1. El no tener a nadie en su (one's) casa es mejor que tener a muchos. 2. Trabajando así, Juan será el mejor alumno de la escuela. 3. Lo oí (heard) hablar con su hermano, pero nada dijo de ti. 4. Trabaja tan holgazanamente que nunca tiene la casa limpia. 5. Siguen perdiendo. 6. Nos ven trabajar todos los días, así que no pueden decir que no estudiamos. 7. Vivían tan felizmente en aquella ciudad que fué lástima que tuviesen que vender su casa. 8. Mejor es vivir felizmente con poco que vivir infelizmente con mucho. 9. No puedo verlos ahora porque siguen hablando con su padre. 10. Tan malamente me trataron que nunca volví a visitarlos. 11. Bien trabajar es mejor que mucho trabajar. 12. Oían (They heard) jugar a los niños, así que los acostaron. 13. Vivió y murió infeliz. 14. ¡Ay de ella!

BB. 1. Having a poor piano is better than having none. 2. They work so diligently that they always have good marks. 3. Although they work now, they keep on asking their parents for money. 4. So badly did he treat them that they never visited him again. 5. On hearing the child play, the mother put him to bed. 6. It is better to live in peace than always at (en) war. 7. Knowledge is not always power. 8. Speaking to me thus, he told me all about him and his cousins. 9. Having showed it to him, he took his hat and left the house. 10. He lived very unhappily (**infeliz**) and finally died. 11. By studying in (the) school one does not learn (it does not learn itself) all there is to be learned (**hay que aprender**). 12. In (the) school alone does one learn well (does it learn itself well). 13. He heard (**oyó**) us speak and afterwards he repeated to his brother what we said (**dijimos**).

LESSON LVIII
ORTHOGRAPHIC CHANGES (*concluded*)

Review Lesson LI (see Appendix E).

(a) **-zar** verbs change z- to c- before -e (*apparently without need; compare* **-jar** *verbs*).

rezar, to pray (*stem* **rez-**, *sound* through)

preterite indicative: **recé**
present subjunctive:
rece, reces, rece; recemos, recéis, recen

(b) **-cer** and **-cir** verbs change c- to z- before -o or -a. (*The verbs treated here are consonant plus* **-cer**, **-cir**.)

vencer, to conquer, to overcome (*stem* **venc-**, *sound* through)

present indicative: **venzo**
present subjunctive:
venza, venzas, venza; venzamos, venzáis, venzan

esparcir, to scatter (*stem* **esparc-**, *sound* through)

present indicative: **esparzo**
present subjunctive:
esparza, esparzas, esparza; esparzamos, esparzáis, esparzan

Inceptives (*these verbs are vowel plus* **-cer**, **-cir**, *with a few exceptions, most prominent being* **cocer**, **decir**, *and* **hacer**).

conocer, to know, to be acquainted with (*stem* **conoc-**, *sound* **c-** as **th** in through)

present indicative		present subjunctive	
conozco	conocemos	conozca	conozcamos
conoces	conocéis	conozcas	conozcáis
conoce	conocen	conozca	conozcan

The inceptives (so-called) insert **-c-** between the orthographical **-z-** and the ending.

(c) Verbs which, during inflection, happen to have an unaccented **-i-** fall between two vowels, always change that **-i-** to **-y-**.

leer, to read (*stem* **le-**)

preterite indicative	past subjunctive		present participle
leí	leyese	leyera	leyendo
leíste	leyeses	leyeras	
leyó	leyese	leyera	
leímos	leyésemos	leyéramos	
leísteis	leyeseis	leyerais	
leyeron	leyesen	leyeran	

Note written accents in preterite.

(d) Verbs ending in **-iar** or **-uar**[1] may (1) accent the **-i-** or **-u-**; or (2) have it form a diphthong with the initial vowel of the ending. Verbs ending in **-guar** put a diaeresis over the **-ü-** when the ending begins with **-e**.

enviar, to send (*stem* **envi-**)

>present indicative:
>>**envío, envías, envía;** enviamos, enviáis, **envían**
>
>present subjunctive:
>>**envíe, envíes, envíe,** enviemos, enviéis, **envíen**
>
>imperative singular intimate:
>>**envía** (*Lesson LXII,* 1)

Like **enviar** are conjugated **variar,** *to vary;* **vaciar,** *to empty;* **enfriar,** *to chill;* **guiar,** *to guide;* **telegrafiar,** *to telegraph;* etc.

continuar, to continue (*stem* **continu-**)

>present indicative:
>>**continúo, continúas, continúa;** continuamos, continuáis, **continúan**

---

[1] Verbs like **limpiar,** to clean and **averiguar,** to ascertain, differ from **enviar** and **continuar** only in not having the accent mark in the forms in black type above.

present subjunctive:
continúe, continúes, continúe; continuemos, continuéis, continúen

imperative singular intimate:
continúa

Like **continuar** are conjugated **efectuar**, *to effect*; **acentuar**, *to accent, to accentuate*; **graduar**, *to graduate* (*as by a measure*); **situar**, *to situate*; etc.

Note that (a) and (b) each change in seven forms: all present subjunctive; and preterite indicative first singular for (a) and present indicative first singular for (b).

(c) changes in the present participle; the third singular and plural of the preterite indicative; and all the past subjunctive—fifteen forms.

(d) changes in all the singular present indicative and subjunctive, and third plural; also in the singular imperative intimate—nine forms.

VOCABULARY

(la) **agua**, water
  alzar, to raise
  cocer (ue), to cook
  convencer, to convince
la **página**, page
reducir, to reduce
tañer, to play (*a string instrument*)
verdadero, -a, true, real

A. 1. que cuezan 2. rezo 3. leyeron 4. que creyesen 5. continúo 6. envían 7. conduzco 8. que no venzan 9. limpiamos 10. que reduzcamos 11. esparzo 12. conozco 13. leyó 14. que tú reces 15. leyó 16. ¿no hacen? 17. efectúo 18. efectuó 19. que averigüe 20. que continuaran 21. continuó

AA. 1. that he prays 2. that we scatter 3. it fell 4. they read 5. he makes 6. I continue 7. that she is reading 8. it is getting cold (**enfriarse**) 8. she begins 9. I pray 10. you are sending 11. they believed 12. I effected 13. they will continue

B. 1. Continúan estudiando mucho aunque siempre

tengan las mejores notas de la clase. 2. Principiaron a leer, y leyeron hasta la página veinte. 3. Quiero que todos los pequeños aprendan a rezar, y que recen. 4. Es menester que uno no esparza sus fuerzas. 5. No conozco a ese hombre, pero sí conozco a su hermano. 6. Cuece la comida porque su madre está en casa de su tía Isabel. 7. Lo que hacen, hacen bien. 8. ¿Quiere usted que yo busque a mi primo? 9. El perro mordió los huesos que halló en la calle, porque tenía mucha hambre. 10. Envían un billete de banco de a diez dólares (a ten-dollar bill) todas las semanas a sus hijos. 11. Le han telegrafiado que estarían aquí mañana, ¿no es verdad? 12. Cuando el agua se enfríe, la beberá. 13. No quería que leyesen esos cuentos de soldados. 14. Si vencen todas aquellas dificultades, serán más que hombres. 15. ¿Quiere tu madre que tú cuezas la comida?

BB. 1. The dogs found a bone in the street, and bit it. 2. The mother wants the child to pray every night. 3. We are cooking the dinner. 4. He continued studying although his eyes were sore. 5. I doubt that he knows our cousin, for he never lived in that city. 6. I should like to have this boy overcome his difficulties, for he is really (*form the adverb from* **verdadero**) intelligent, is he not? 7. Don't they send any money to their children at school? 8. I know that man, but I have never visited him at his home. 9. That night they read no more. 10. I shall drink the tea after it gets cold. 11. He has but little (**No tiene sino poco**) money, for he buys things he really does not need. 12. They believed what he told them. 13. I wish they didn't believe everything they tell them. 14. They empty their glasses and then ask for more milk.

LESSON LIX
INDEFINITE AND DEFINITE ARTICLES

1. As compared with English, Spanish omits the indefinite article:

(a) when there is a noun in the predicate nominative.

Es capitán, He is a captain. **Es profesor,** He is a teacher.
Quiere hacerse sastre, He wishes to become a tailor.

In this construction, the noun is treated as an adjective.

(b) before **otro,** (an)other; **cierto,** a certain; **ciento,** a hundred; and **mil,** thousand.

otro vaso de agua, another glass of water
Cierto hombre me lo dijo, A certain man told me so.
cien soldados, a hundred soldiers

2. As compared with English, Spanish often omits the definite article in apposition. The indefinite article is also sometimes dropped before a noun in apposition.

Buenos Aires, centro de la industria ganadera de Sud-América ..,
B. A., the center of the cattle industry of South America, ...

3. The definite article is used more widely in Spanish than in English. Note the distributive and possessive uses below.

El niño tiene la cara sucia, The child's face is dirty (The child has the face dirty).
Tiene los ojos azules, His eyes are blue.
Tiene la mano rota, His hand is broken.
Todos levantaron la mano derecha, All raised their right hands.
(*lit.*, All raised the right hand—*the Spanish view the matter not as plural hands, but as each having one right hand.*)

VOCABULARY

Alfonso, Alphonsus
azul, blue
el carpintero, carpenter
hacerse, to become
la industria, industry, business
el ingeniero, engineer
Jorge, George
nacer, to be born

la persona, person; (*plural*, people)
el ojo, eye
puesto, -a (put) on (*irregular past participle of* poner)
tal, such; un tal, such a; a certain (*with proper noun*)
tales ... tales, some ... others

A. 1. se limpian los dientes (to themselves they clean the = they clean their) 2. es sastre 3. Juan, el más grande (*why is the definite article kept with this noun in apposition? Translate:* "John, the largest") 4. Washington, presidente de los Estados Unidos 5. todos los niños perdieron el sombrero 6. J. R., capitán de ... 7. otra ciudad 8. la escribí 9. Jorge, rey de Inglaterra 10. con lápiz 11. tales corren ... tales gritan ... tales lloran 12. con pluma y tinta 13. cien casas 14. un tal X. me lo dijo 15. tienen los pies grandes 16. **es carpintero** 17. no hace nunca tales cosas 18. un tal Jorge me lo dijo

AA. 1. Alphonsus, the king of Spain 2. he never does such things 3. Albany, the capital of New York (**capital de N. Y.**) 4. they broke their right legs 5. another pen 6. her eyes are blue 7. they are not teachers 8. McKinley, president of the United States 9. one hundred thirty-seven 10. such a thing 11. is he an engineer? 12. some are studying, some are writing 13. Poincaré, the president of France 14. Alessandri, the president of Chile 15. they are writing with pen and ink

B. 1. Los niños se limpiaron los dientes, tomaron el sombrero, y salieron de la casa. 2. Jorge IV, rey de Inglaterra, nació en mil setecientos sesenta y dos, y murió en mil ochocientos treinta. 3. Cierto hombre me dijo que al que cuece no le gusta la comida. 4. En cierta calle de esta ciudad hay cien casas con sólo tres personas en cada una. 5. Nueva York, centro de muchas grandes industrias, está en los Estados Unidos. 6. Quiero otro vaso de agua; éste no está lleno. 7. El niño tiene la cara muy sucia; es preciso que la lave. 8. Él mismo es sastre, pero su hermano es capitán. 9. Jorge, también capitán, es su primo. 10. Los dos estudian para ser ingeniero. 11. **Encontré a** cierto hombre que me dijo que había hallado un reloj de oro. 12. Aquél no es ni soldado ni capitán, es sastre. 13. Tal (Such a one) habla un poco de todo que no entiende mucho de nada. 14. Todos tenían un libro en español, y otro en **inglés.**

BB. 1. Their eyes are blue, and their hair is black.
2. Alphonsus XII, the king of Spain, was born in 1857.
3. This man is an engineer and his brother is a captain.
4. The child cleaned his teeth, washed, had breakfast, and then left the house to go to school. 5. In a certain house on X . . . Street, live eighteen pupils from this school alone. 6. Buenos Aires, the center of the stock-raising industry of South America, has much more than a million people (inhabitants). 7. The little boy has a dirty face; he must wash it before he has supper. 8. Some were eating and some were drinking, and some were cooking. 9. A hundred people can easily live in this big house. 10. Don George is a Sevillian; doña Mary is also an inhabitant-of-Seville. 11. I never found such a thing. 12. A certain William X. told me so.

LESSON LX
DATES; WEATHER

Review Lessons XXVII and XXVIII.

1. For the days of the week, see Lesson XXXIV, 2.

2. The months, all masculine, and written with a small letter, are:

enero, January
febrero, February
marzo, March
abril, April
mayo, May
junio, June

julio, July
agosto, August
se(p)tiembre, September
octubre, October
noviembre, November
diciembre, December

a principios (mediados, fines or últimos) de marzo, at the beginning (middle, end) of March
¿A cuántos estamos del mes? What day of the month is it?

The first day of a month is usually **el primero**; but the other days are **el dos, el tres,** etc.

el primero (trece) de febrero, the first (thirteenth) of February
el veinte y uno de mayo, the twenty-first of May

3. The seasons are:

la primavera, spring
el verano, summer
el otoño, autumn
el invierno, winter

4. Note the expressions below (cf. the use of the article in Spanish):

la semana que viene (próximo), next week
el mes pasado, el año pasado, last month, last year
el tres próximo pasado, (on) the third of last month

5. Expressions of time are made on the models below:

es la una, it is one o'clock
son las dos, it is two o'clock
es la una y media, it is half past one
son las tres y cuarto, it is a quarter past three
son las tres y media, it is half past three
son las cinco menos cinco, it is five minutes of five
son las seis menos cuarto, it is a quarter of six
faltan quince (minutos) para las ocho, it is fifteen minutes of eight
son las cinco y diez, it is ten minutes past five
¿Qué hora es? What time is it? (*Also:* ¿Qué horas son?)
a las ocho, at eight o'clock
de la mañana, a. m., in the morning; por la mañana, during the morning
de la tarde, p. m., in the afternoon; por la tarde, during the afternoon
de la noche, p. m., in the night; por la noche, de noche, (in) during the night

6. Review Lesson XXVIII, 4. Note also:

hace buen tiempo, it is good weather
hace frío, it is cold

The difference between **hay** and **hace** is that conditions of weather *seen* rather than *felt* are expressed by **hay**; those felt rather than seen, by **hace**. Hay sol and hace sol, however, are both correct. All these expressions are impersonal.

Note that the subject is personal in:

El tiempo es bueno, The weather is good.

DATES; WEATHER

VOCABULARY

anteayer, day before yesterday
atrasar, to be slow (*used of a watch*)
avanzar, to advance
pasado mañana, day after tomorrow
el calor, warmth; **hace calor,** it is warm (*used only of weather*)
hábil, clever, skilful, apt
día hábil (útil), work day, week day
la lluvia, rain

A. 1. hay viento 2. viernes el siete de marzo de mil novecientos 3. el cinco de octubre 4. la semana pasada 5. el dos próximo pasado 6. ¿hace frío? 7. el año que viene 8. hay neblina 9. son las cinco veinte y tres de la mañana 10. son las ocho 11. eran las once y cuarto 12. hace buen tiempo 13. el tiempo es bueno 14. el veinte y cinco de noviembre de mil novecientos veinte y cuatro 15. jueves 16. el viernes que viene 17. a las siete diez y ocho 18. ¿qué hora es? 19. ¿qué horas son? 20. ¿a cuántos del mes estamos? 21. a mediados de julio 22. el domingo (on Sunday) 23. los jueves (on Thursdays)

AA. 1. it is half past eight 2. what time is it? 3. [on]=(the) Thursday 4. on June eighteenth, 1920 5. the first of December, 1902 6. it was eighteen minutes past four in the morning 7. last Thursday 8. next Monday 9. it is cold 10. it is very cold 11. it is foggy 12. the past month 13. it is fine weather (*two ways*) 14. it is ten minutes of ten 15. on Friday next 16. Sundays (*16 and 17 are both:* the Sundays) 17. on Sundays 18. at eighteen minutes past eight in the evening 19. at a quarter of eleven 20. at a quarter of six 21. it is a quarter past one 22. it was rainy

B. 1. ¿Cuánto azúcar compró usted anteayer? 2. ¿Qué libros estudiasteis en vuestra clase de español el año pasado? 3. El primero de octubre empezamos a leer un libro de Scott y el quince de diciembre empezamos otro de Shakespeare. 4. ¿Irá usted hoy?—No, hay lluvia y hace frío, y me siento un poco enfermo. 5. A las cinco menos cuarto estudiábamos todavía; a las seis, dormíamos; y a las ocho menos cuarto, acabamos de dormir. 6. Para mañana tenemos que escribir en español los meses, que son: abril, noviembre, agosto, julio, enero, mayo, junio, diciembre, febrero, marzo, setiembre, octubre. 7. ¿Estará escribiendo ahora tu hermana?—Sí, está escribiendo los días de la semana, que son: sábado, miércoles, domingo, martes, viernes, lunes, jueves. 8. El domingo no estudiaba nunca. 9. A las cinco veinte y dos de la tarde murió. 10. La semana que viene se terminarán las clases, y nosotros viajaremos durante todas las vacaciones. 11. ¿Qué hora es en su reloj (by your watch)?—Son las diez menos veinte y dos, pero mi reloj atrasa. 12. No estaré en ésa hasta fines de febrero. 13. Cuando llegamos a Madrid, había mucho viento y no hallamos la calle en donde vivía nuestro amigo. 14. ¿Cuántos años tendrá tu hermano el veintidós del mes que viene? 15. A las cuatro menos cuarto llegó el señor S. con su hermano menor (Mr. S. with . . .).

BB. 1. The day after tomorrow we shall have to prepare for the Spanish class the book we were to read. 2. These are the books you asked-for. 3. The twenty-first of March, I bought a book entitled: "Los cuatro jinetes del Apocalipsis," in English, "The Four Horsemen of the Apocalypse," which my friend told me to read. 4. And on the twenty-first of April I finished reading it. 5. It is a quarter of four, and there is yet much to be done. 6. At the beginning of August they arrived in this city, but they are not in the city now. 7. What time is it by your watch? (*see B, 11*) 8. Isn't it nine o'clock yet?—Yes, it is eleven minutes past nine. 9. What books can they be reading? you did not show me them. 10. At half past two we began to study; at eighteen minutes of five we were still studying; at a quarter past six we ate supper; and at a quarter of nine we had not yet finished working. 11. Monday begins the week—it is a work day. 12. How old was your brother last Thursday, the eighteenth of November? 13. Who came the day before yesterday? 14. It is very windy today, and yesterday it was so sunny—

it is never good weather. 15. Next month, school (classes) will be over (**terminarse**), and the long vacations will be here. 16. It is neither rainy nor cold, but I do not like the weather when it is so misty. 17. The days of the week are: Monday, Sunday, Wednesday, Friday, Thursday, Tuesday, and Saturday. 18. The months are: October, February, November, March, June, August, July, May, January, December, September, and April.

LESSON LXI
USES OF DEFINITE ARTICLE

Review Lesson LIX.

1. As contrasted with English, Spanish shows the following peculiarities:

(a) The definite article is used before abstract or generic nouns.[1]

El hombre es mortal, Man is mortal.
La vida es corta, Life is short.
La nieve es blanca, Snow is white.

(b) In speaking of persons, the definite article is always placed before any title of address.

el capitán García, Captain García
El profesor Soler no está, Professor Soler is-not-here.
El señor Gutiérrez no está, Mr. Gutiérrez is-not-here.

Adjectives, sometimes nouns, are put in the same construction.

la pequeña Isabel, little Elizabeth
el primo Juan, Cousin John

Note that the article is not used in speaking to a person.

¿**Señor Blanco, puede usted decirme . . . ?** Mr. B., can you tell me . . . ?

[1] See Appendix F.

(c) The definite article is always used with adjectives of nationality employed as nouns, except directly after **hablar** or **en**.

Aprendió el francés, He learned French.
But
Aquí se habla inglés, English is spoken here.
Habla inglés, She speaks English.
en alemán, in German

If some expression intervenes, then the article is retained.

Habla muy bien el inglés, He speaks English very well.

The article is always used with **castellano**, (Castilian) Spanish.

Habla el castellano, He speaks Spanish.

(d) The definite article is used with certain countries and cities, and with any country modified.

en el Canadá, in Canada	**el Paraguay**, Paraguay
del Perú, of Peru	**el Japón**, Japan
el Cairo, Cairo	**el Callao**, Callao
la dulce Francia, fair France	
la pintoresca España, Spain the picturesque	

2. For the definite article with expressions of time, see Lesson LX, 4 and 5.

3. Note that the definite article is not repeated with a second noun if both nouns refer to the same person.

el tío y profesor, the uncle and teacher (*same person*)

VOCABULARY

corto, -a, short	**servir (i)**, to serve; to be good for
dulce, sweet, fair, gentle	
latino, -a, Latin	**siguiente**, following
mortal, mortal	**el sobrino**, nephew; **la sobrina**, niece
la nieve, snow	
pintoresco, -a, picturesque	**la vida**, life

A. 1. los hombres 2. las madres son buenas 3. el Canadá 4. el Cairo 5. el señor X. 6. aprenden el francés 7. la mujer 8. el tío Guillermo 9. escribe muy bien el alemán 10. el profesor B. 11. los alumnos estudian, los padres trabajan 12. la semana que viene 13. en español

14. la América española 15. el Japón 16. hablan inglés
17. el lunes próximo 18. mi profesor y amigo 19. su
señora esposa 20. en alemán

AA. 1. Latin America 2. men are mortal 3. pupils
study 4. in English 5. your uncle 6. do they speak
French? 7. in German 8. Japan 9. do they speak
German? 10. Callao 11. next year 12. we are learning
Spanish 13. men work 14. next Sunday 15. Mr. S.
16. Paraguay 17. Captain García 18. my nephew and
pupil, Mr. González 19. they speak French well 20. fair
France

B. 1. No me gusta estudiar el español todo el tiempo.
2. Los perros muerden los huesos. 3. Los caballos son muy
ligeros, pero los automóviles son aun más ligeros. 4. El
capitán Cienfuegos tiene un caballo que costó mil doscientos dólares. 5. Un amigo mío, el señor Moreno, me
dijo que tiene tres hijos en aquella escuela. 6. La semana
pasada, escribí una carta a mi primo. 7. No estoy escribiendo al señor Sanfuentes, sino al señor Chaparro.
8. El Canadá está cerca de los Estados Unidos. 9. Cuando
estaremos en Francia, estudiaremos el francés. 10. Mi
prima, la pequeña Isabel, llegará el martes próximo.
11. La pintoresca España y la dulce Francia—yo quisiera
ver estos dos países tan interesantes (very interesting
countries). 12. El año que viene estaremos en el Paraguay
porque entonces pienso hablar muy bien el español, que
vamos aprendiendo ahora. 13. El profesor preguntó al
alumno: ¿Dónde está el Callao? y el alumno contestó: en
el Perú. 14. El castellano se habla en España. 15. Habla
inglés, pero sólo lee el español. 16. Los hombres tienen
dos manos y dos pies. 17. Quiero presentarle a mi amigo
y profesor, el señor Gutiérrez. 18. Ahora no vive en el
Japón.

BB. 1. Are (**Van**) horses or automobiles faster?—I like
automobiles better than horses. 2. Which is larger—
Canada or the United States? 3. Dogs like bones. 4. Professor Sánchez asked a pupil where Cairo is, and the pupil

did not answer. 5. When we were in Spain, we studied Spanish all the time. 6. Do you like to study only Spanish all the time? 7. My dear Friend: that week we were in Spain, this week we are in France, and the latter part of next month we intend to be in Japan. 9. He speaks Spanish very well, but he doesn't read French. 10. We should very much like to see the fair France of which we are to read in the "Chanson de Roland." 11. Aren't they writing to Captain Moreno today? 12. They received a letter from him last month. 13. How much did Captain Dávila pay for his horse? 14. An uncle of mine, Professor Uribe, teaches in our school. 15. Men are mortal. 16. Little Mary visited us last week with her mother.

LESSON LXII
IMPERATIVE

1. In Spanish, there are special forms for the imperative only in the **intimate affirmative**.

habla (tú), speak	**hablad (vosotros)**, speak
bebe (tú), drink	**bebed (vosotros)**, drink
escribe (tú), write	**escribid (vosotros)**, write

Except for very marked emphasis, the pronoun subjects are not used.

2. In all other imperative forms, the subjunctive is used.

(a) **negative imperative** (intimate)

no hables (tú), do not speak
no habléis (vosotros), do not speak

no bebas (tú), do not drink
no bebáis (vosotros), do not drink

no escribas (tú), do not write
no escribáis (vosotros), do not write

(b) **formal, affirmative or negative**

(no) hable V., (do not) speak
(no) hablen VV., (do not) speak

IMPERATIVE

(no) beba V., (do not) drink
(no) beban VV., (do not) drink
(no) escriba V., (do not) write
(no) escriban VV., (do not) write

Note that the formal imperative must express the pronoun subject **usted, ustedes** (*see Lesson XIII, 6*).

3. The imperatives of the first person plural and third singular and plural (there is no imperative of the first singular) are given in Lesson LIV, 2.

4. Distinguish carefully "Let him do it (if he likes)" and "Let him do it," (i. e., don't stop him from doing it).

The first uses (**que** plus) the subjunctive; the second uses the imperative of **permitir** or **dejar** plus the subjunctive or infinitive.

Que lo haga si quiere, Let him do it if he likes.
Permítale Vd. que lo haga,
Permítale Vd. hacerlo, } Let (Permit) him (to) do it.
Déjele Vd. hacerlo,

5. Learn the intimate imperatives below (the other forms of these verbs are of course from the subjunctive):

tener:	ten (tú)	tened (vosotros)
haber:	he	habed
ser:	sé	sed
estar:	está	estad
decir:	di	decid
ver:	ve	ved

A. 1. bebe 2. decid 3. conjuga 4. vivid 5. vive (tú) 6. habla 7. bebe (tú) 8. temed 9. no seas 10. laven ustedes 11. coma usted 12. estad 13. no tenga usted 14. venda Vd. 15. tengan ustedes 16. no aburras 17. lee 18. no leas 19. estén ustedes 20. no vendáis 21. busca 22. no tengáis 23. ten 24. escriba V. 25. ved 26. no tengas 27. escribamos 28. tenga Vd. 29. no venda Ud. 30. no tengan ustedes 31. no vendas 32. no busques 33. no busque V. 34. cierre Vd. 35. no yerre Ud. 36. cierra 37. cuenta 38. almuerza 39. vuelve 40. repitan Vds. 41. no cuente Vd. 42. no repitas 43. no almorcéis 44. no vuelvan ustedes 45. que tengan 46. que coman 47. que diga

AA. 1. have 2. play 3. don't have 4. have 5. count 6. say 7. let us play 8. be 9. look-for 10. see 11. return 12. be 13. don't return 14. do not be 15. don't look-for 16. say 17. tell 18. don't fear 19. wash 20. have-breakfast 21. read 22. don't eat 23. don't look-for 24. sell 25. repeat 26. do not count 27. count 28. drink 29. don't be 30. be 31. say 32. don't conjugate 33. let him be 34. don't work 35. study 36. let us study 37. let them study 38. let them drink 39. let her eat

B. 1. Trabaja en América, donde hay buen trabajo. 2. Vende las pizarras que has hallado. 3. No comáis la comida que él preparó; no cocina bien. 4. Leed este libro, y os alegraréis de haberlo leído (*past participle of* **leer**). 5. Sed alumnas diligentes y todas tendréis buenas notas. 6. Acueste Ud. al niño, Señora, porque se ve (it is evident; *lit.*, it sees itself) que tiene sueño. 7. No venda usted su casa a aquel hombre; nunca puede pagar. 8. Di a tu padre todo lo que te dijeron a ti. 9. Quédese Vd. aquí, pues yo tengo que irme. 10. Vd. tendrá que quedarse aquí hasta que llegue mi hermano. 11. Siga usted buscando a su hermano porque bien pronto le hallará. 12. Ten la verdad como la mejor cosa del mundo. 13. No digas eso a tu padre. 14. No compren Vds. una casa en aquella calle; es la calle más sucia del mundo. 15. Halle usted sus libros antes que vuelva. 16. Escriban Vds. a sus padres todas las semanas hasta que vuelvan a casa. 17. No cuente usted el dinero. 18. Repita usted a estos señores lo que nos dijo ayer. 19. Que lo tengan si tanto les gusta. 20. Busque usted sus libros; si no los busca, no los hallará.

BB. 1. Don't work in Spain—there isn't much work there. 2. Write to your parents every day while you are at (the) school. 3. Don't look for your books; I have found them already. 4. Put your children to bed, Mrs. Smith; they are tired. 5. Don't stay here any longer,

John, for I shall be here until they arrive. 6. Don't sell your automobile until you are sure that you can buy another. 7. Don't be so lazy; study sometimes. 8. Keep on studying, and you will soon have good marks, as your sister has (them). 9. Read these books, Mr. García; you will find in them much that is interesting. 10. Don't sell the things you found—you may (can) find the [one] who lost them. 11. Don't count your money, John, until you earn it. 12. Always tell the truth. 13. Don't sell your house until you have another for yourself. 14. Buy that house if they want to sell it; it is the best one in the city. 15. Don't tell your father what they said, for they did not tell the truth. 16. Find your books when you reach home (to the house) today; for without them you are not to come back to school. 17. Don't buy a piano unless you play the piano.

LESSON LXIII

IMPERATIVE WITH PRONOUN OBJECTS

Review Lessons XXI; XXXVIII; LIV, 2; LVII, 4; and LXII.

1. With the negative imperatives, the pronoun objects always precede the verb.

No lo enseñes, Don't show it.

But with an affirmative imperative,[1] they follow and are joined to it.

Enséñalo, Juan, Show it, John.
Enséñelo usted, señor García, Show it, Mr. G.
Enseñadlo, Show it (*intimate plural*).
Enséñemelo Vd., Show it to me.

Note that the stress remains on the original syllable of the verb when pronouns are added; and that this may necessitate a written accent mark.

[1] In all, three cases have the pronoun object follow the verb: present participle, (teniéndolo); infinitive (tenerlo); and affirmative imperative (téngalo Vd.).

In the third persons singular and plural, the pronouns precede even in the affirmative, provided **que** is used.

Que lo digan (ellos) si quieren, Let them say it if they like.
But,
Díganlo (ellos) si quieren, Let them say it if they like.

2. Reflexive pronouns follow exactly the same rules as the ordinary direct and indirect pronouns.

acuéstate, go to bed; **no te acuestes,** don't go to bed

Usted, as usual, takes everything in the third person.

acuéstese V., go to bed; **no se acuesten Vds.,** don't go to bed

3. The affirmative second person plural and first person plural drop final **-d** and **-s** respectively of the verb when adding the reflexive pronouns (**os, nos**). Cf. Lesson LIV, 2, Note, par. 3.

acostaos, go to bed (*for* **acostad** *plus* **os**)
acostémonos, let us go to bed (*for* **acostemos** *plus* **nos**)

Such contraction occurs nowhere else than in the two cases above. It never occurs, for instance, in the negative.

no nos afeitemos, let us not shave

VOCABULARY

ajeno, -a, strange, foreign; that of another
arrimarse, to approach, to come close
enteramente, entirely
el maestro, la maestra, teacher
la vista, sight; view

A. 1. lávate 2. bébalo Vd. 3. siéntate 4. escribámonos uno a otro 5. no os escribáis más de dos veces 6. léalo Vd. 7. pídeselo 8. págueselo Vd. 9. peinaos 10. límpialo 11. pídanselo Vds. 12. que sentemos 13. preséntese Vd. a ella 14. siéntense ustedes 15. lavaos 16. enséñaselo a él 17. pídanselo Vds. a ella 18. que se escriban unos a otros 19. lávese Vd. 20. acuérdese V. de . . . 21. péinate 22. no lo peines 23. ¡no lo pienses! 24. pídanselo ustedes a ellas 25. enséñeselo Vd. a él 26. felicítense ustedes, señores 27. llégate (approach) 28. diríjase usted 29. sentaos 30. no llegue usted 31. dirígete 32. acuérdate 33. créame Vd. 34. ¡sálvate! 35. créeme

AA. 1. I sit down 2. get washed 3. cook it 4. pay

IMPERATIVE WITH PRONOUN OBJECTS

them 5. comb yourself 6. ask them for it 7. wash them 8. introduce them to her 9. let him ask them 10. comb him 11. congratulate yourself 12. ask him for them 13. show them 14. write to each other 15. ask it of them 16. I don't think so 17. don't think so (it)! 18. clean them 19. approach 20. come here (**llegarse**) 21. remember 22. sit down 23. rejoice 24. follow him 25. let us write to one another 26. bathe 27. sit down 28. make your way 29. let us sit down 30. take a bath 31. introduce them to them 32. shave 33. show them to them 34. pay them for it 35. read it 36. run-off 37. believe us 38. let us remember

B. 1. Acordaos unos de otros más tarde. 2. Tenlo (Consider it) por seguro que no te enseñaré lo que he hallado. 3. Si quieren vender su casa, cómprela usted. 4. Escribaos uno a otro de manera que no os perdáis enteramente de vista. 5. No se lo pida usted nada a su tío, porque él no tiene nada que darle. 6. Díganles ustedes que no estaré en su casa hoy. 7. Véanse Uds. en el espejo lo (how) sucios que están. 8. Entrégueles usted el dinero que tiene para ellos. 9. Sed siempre buenos, y seréis felices. 10. Enséñale a tu padre lo que has hallado. 11. Permítame Vd. que le enseñe la lección de su hijo. 12. Felicítense ustedes de tener niños tan buenos. 13. Conténtate con lo que tienes; no busques lo ajeno. 14. Ya sabe Ud. por qué trabajamos así. 15. Envíales una carta, porque no les escribimos la semana pasada. 16. Siéntate ahí y quédate hasta que acabemos de hablar. 17. Léalo usted porque muy interesante es. 18. Hállalo antes de llegar a la casa, porque si no, no te dejará entrar tu papá. 19. Dígalo V. a su padre, porque muy contento estará él al oírlo. 20. Cómprame aquel piano, porque de muy buenas ganas aprendería yo a tocarlo.

BB. 1. Put the child to bed, madam, because the little [one] must be very tired. 2. Buy me some pencils, John, I haven't any; and buy some (**los**) good [ones]. 3. Repeat it, because I did not hear what you said. 4. Look-for them until you find them. 5. Give him the money you found, because it is not yours. 6. Permit me to show you what they wrote yesterday in my book. 7. Now you know what work they want to do. 8. Look at yourself in the glass—aren't you dirty! (¡**lo sucio que estás!**) 9. Congratulate yourself on having such good marks—it is evident that you study well. 10. Read the books I bought—they are the most interesting I have ever read. 11. Let us be satisfied with what we have; let us not seek what-others-have (**lo ajeno**). 12. Let us sit down here and talk. 13. Find it before you return home. 14. Send them a letter. Let us both write them letters. 15. Ask me for nothing—I have nothing to give you. 16. Let us write each other every week so that we may have sure news of each other. 17. Buy them for him. 18. Let him cook the dinner. 19. Don't let those books get lost (Let those books not lose themselves). 20. Always try to be happy. 21. And be good; with that, you will always be happy.

LESSON LXIV

1. Spanish Present for English Perfect. In Spanish, the present tense is used to denote an action begun in the past and continued to the present. In English, the perfect is used.

Está aquí desde hace tres días, } He has been here for three days.
Hace tres días que está aquí, }

Similarly, the imperfect denotes an action begun far in the past and continued to some nearer time.

Estaba aquí desde hacía tres días, } He had been here for three
Hacía tres días que estaba aquí, } days.

This construction is not found in the negative.

Hace un año que no ha estado aquí, He hasn't been here for a year.

2. The conjunction **e** for **y** and **u** for **o**. Before a noun beginning with **i** (**hi-**) the conjunction **y** becomes **e**; and before a noun beginning with **o-** (**ho-**) the conjunction **o** becomes **u**. This is to prevent two **i**'s or two **o**'s coming together.

Gómez e hijo, Gomez and Son
uno u otro, one or another, either

But **y** is retained before **y-** or **hie-**.

verdad y yerro, truth and error
agua y hielo, water and ice

3. **Por** and **Para**. **Para** denotes purpose, destination.

taza para te, teacup
el lápiz es para él, the pencil is for him

Por means **on account of, in exchange for, by means of.**

Me da su pluma por mi lápiz, He gives me his pen for my pencil.
Viajan por automóvil, They travel by automobile.
Lo hace por mí, He does it for me (on my account).

For **por** (**de**) to denote the agent with the passive, see Lesson XVI, 3.

4. Distinguish between the following verbs:

conocer, to know (to be acquainted with, to know through having seen, heard, *etc.*)
saber, to know (to be aware of, to have as part of one's mental knowledge; to know how)

¿**Conoce usted al señor Herrera?** Do you know Mr. Herrera?
Sabemos que Vd. le conoce, We know that you are acquainted with him.

saber, can (to know how to, to be mentally able)
poder, can (to be physically able)

Sabe leer, She can (knows how to) read.
Puede levantarlo, He can lift it.

5. **saber a,** to taste of

La comida sabe a cebollas, The dinner tastes of onions.

VOCABULARY

el año, year
el árbol, tree
  asistir, to be present
la cebolla, onion
  desde, since
  europeo, -a, European
  excelente, excellent
  hace tres días, three days ago
la hacienda, country estate
  indio, -a, Indian
el instinto, instinct
  luchar, to struggle, to wrestle
  mientras, while
  nadar, to swim
  ordinario, -a, ordinary
el pensamiento, thought
  pensar (ie), to think
  pensar (ie) en, to think of (*to occupy the mind with*)
  pensar (ie) de, to think of (*to have an opinion of*)
  respectado, -a, respected
  siempre, always
la taza, cup
  taza para te, teacup
  taza de te, cup of tea
el yerro, error, mistake

A. 1. es para él 2. hace dos días 3. flojo u ocupado 4. hace ocho días (a week, *as the Spanish reckon the first day*) que estoy aquí 5. nos conoce 6. no sabemos leer el castellano 7. saben que estaremos 8. sabe a 9. saben nadar 10. estaba enfermo, pero ahora puede nadar 11. para ella 12. por él 13. felices e infelices 14. libro para principiar 15. ordinaria o excelente 16. no podemos levantarlos 17. infelices y felices 18. por la mañana 19. le conocemos sólo desde hace quince días 20. ¿no lo conocéis de vista? 21. flojo u ocupado 22. es conocido de todos 23. por ciento treinta dólares 24. para su padre 25. la vajilla fué lavada por la niña

AA. 1. they have been working here for twelve weeks 2. we know that you know him 3. it is for them 4. Europeans and Indians 5. coming and going (**venirse e irse**) 6. one or another 7. we know Madrid well 8. he can write English 9. he can wrestle with his brother 10. I write it for him 11. can he wrestle? 12. a teacup 13. do you know them? 14. it tastes of 15. Indians and Europeans 16. do you know it? 17. they knew him 18. they are known by all 19. for three dollars 20. it was read by my brother 21. lazy or busy students

B. 1. Hacía tres días que estaban allí, y todavía no habían principiado a trabajar. 2. Saben que hemos hallado el reloj que perdieron. 3. Gómez e hijo ya no están en Madrid; están en Sevilla y tienen una hacienda cerca de allí. 4. Todos los soldados perdieron sus armas mientras dormían. 5. No sabemos lo que usted dice. 6. Este niño no sabe leer, ni siquiera sabe escribir. 7. Yo no puedo leer más—estoy enfermo y no tengo más fuerzas. 8. No quiero comer—toda la comida sabe a cebollas. 9. Flojo u ocupado, feliz e infeliz, excelente u ordinario—en este mundo hay [de] todo. 10. Compré este libro para mi hermano, porque él sabe leer—tiene ocho años. 11. Hace tres años que vivimos en esta casa, y mucho nos gusta esta calle. 12. Por la tarde cayó (he fell) y ahora tiene el brazo enfermo. 13. Europeos e indios—unos y otros son hombres—y los hombres son todos mortales, todos tienen alma. 14. Sabemos que usted no conoce a mi hermano; quiero presentarle a usted. 15. Yo quería decirle lo que pensaba de él. 16. No piense usted en esas cosas. 17. La compró por el señor X., el cual la dió a su hija. 18. Conocemos a un hombre que sabe lo que hay en este libro—lo escribió él mismo. 19. Deseo comprar la casa—es la mejor de aquella calle. 20. Estos lápices son para tu hermana. 21. Yo soy; él es.

BB. 1. Didn't the soldiers find their arms? Are they lost? 2. Do you know that they found the axe they lost? 3. He works from six in the afternoon to two a. m. 4. He is so diligent and industrious that he always gets good marks. 5. They know we met him last year in Madrid. 6. That smells of onions—I don't like onions—I won't eat it. 7. Happy and unhappy, excellent and commonplace (ordinary), there are all sort[s] of students in my class. 8. They have been working here for eighteen years, and they will be working here for ever. 9. He is always thinking of such things—truth, the soul, and so on. 10. He is philosophizing. 11. They have been visiting us once a year (**al año**) for thirteen years. 12. We wished to buy the piano, when we were told that it cost too much. 13. I bought your uncle's books for my brother. 14. Fernández and Son are no longer (**más**) in that street. 15. His arm is hurt. 16. It is they. 17. Can't this child read? 18. How old is he? 19. He doesn't know how to wrestle. 20. Europeans and Indians do not live happily together.

LESSON LXV

1. Irregular Past Participles. Seven verbs in Spanish have an irregular past participle, though regular in all other forms.

   abrir, to open; **abierto**, opened
   cubrir, to cover; **cubierto**, covered
   escribir, to write; **escrito**, written
   imprimir, to print; **impreso**, printed, imprinted
   morir (ue), to die; **muerto**, died, dead; (*transitively*) killed
   volver (ue), to return; **vuelto**, returned
   solver (ue) to solve; **suelto**, loose, loosened; solved

2. Four regular Spanish verbs have an irregular past participle in addition to the regular past participle.

   oprimir, to oppress; **oprimido**, **opreso** (*rare*), oppressed
   suprimir, to suppress; **suprimido**, **supreso** (*rare*), suppressed
   prender, to catch; **prendido** (*used for perfect tenses*), **preso** (*adjectival*)
   romper, to break, to tear; **rompido** (*used for perfect tenses*), **roto** (*adjectival*)

3. Verbs in **-ducir** belong to the so-called inceptive verbs. For the present tense, see Lesson LVIII, (b).

   conducir, to drive, to conduct, to take (*stem inceptive*)

preterite indicative	past subjunctive	
conduje	condujese	condujera
condujiste	condujeses	condujeras
condujo	condujese	condujera
condujimos	condujésemos	condujéramos
condujisteis	condujeseis	condujerais
condujeron	condujesen	condujeran

Note that the first and third singular of the preterite indicative do not stress the ending; also that the third singular and plural, as well as the first singular, do not have the usual preterite endings of **-ir** verbs.

IRREGULAR PAST PARTICIPLES

Note -j- in the stem; and no diphthongs in the endings.

VOCABULARY

la cantidad, quantity, amount
deducir, to deduce
la hoja, leaf, page
el juez, judge
reducir, to reduce
tener a, to hold

A. *Give the past participles of:* 1. to write 2. to imprint 3. to come 4. to loose (to solve) 5. to return 6. to print 7. to return 8. to die 9. to solve

AA. 1. han muerto 2. conducimos 3. ha escrito 4. conduce 5. que deduzcan 6. habían conducido 7. reducir 8. estaba escrito 9. queda escrito 10. han vuelto 11. lo condujimos 12. ha muerto 13. se ha muerto 14. está todo impreso 15. ¿está abierto? 16. está abierta 17. fué abierto 18. que conduzcamos 19. que condujeses 20. está escrito 21. hojas sueltas 22. fué impreso 23. que haya reducido

AAA. 1. that we deduce 2. is it opened? 3. she died 4. did he return? 5. he led 6. printed 7. I reduced 8. I conducted 9. that you are leading 10. it is written 11. you conducted 12. that he deduced 13. that she has led 14. by whom was it opened? 15. has she written? 16. they reduced 17. covered 18. oppressed 19. captive (**preso**) 20. loose 21. imprinted 22. they have suppressed 23. suppressed

B. 1. Tiene su libro abierto y está leyendo (is reading). 2. ¿Qué deduce usted de todo eso? 3. Dígale V. que conduzca al niño a mi padre. 4. Condujeron al hombre, al que tenía por el brazo, al juez. 5. Dos jueces han muerto la semana pasada. 6. Han vuelto a hacer la misma cosa. 7. Nunca escribió un libro; ha escrito, sí, unas hojas sueltas (occasional)—nada más. 8. No se han escrito una a otra desde que la mayor dejó la ciudad. 9. Después de sacar una cantidad de dinero al tío, le dejaron solo y sin familia. 10. ¡Pobre niña! está muerta—y ¡qué infeliz era! 11. Han impreso el libro del señor Gutiérrez, pero yo no creo que sea tan bueno como el primero que escribió. 12. Quitaron a mi hermano todo lo que tenía y lo dejaron así. 13. Han cubierto la mesa con libros y papeles. 14. Tienen el hombre preso.

BB. 1. Who printed the book your brother wrote? 2. It isn't written yet. 3. He will never write a book; he has written some occasional pages, but that is all. 4. They have written me that they will visit us next Wednesday. 5. He has again bought a house in that city and intends to remain there for ever. 6. His book is open, but he is not studying. 7. Poor dog! He is dead now. 8. They took from the little boy all the things he had, and then they ran away. 9. Tell them to bring the child here—I shall see what is the matter with him. 10. They told me that Mr. X. died last week. 11. I want them to bring the man they found (who was) robbing the child. 12. They have done-away-with (**suprimir**) examinations this year. 13. The soldiers found the man.

LESSON LXVI

PRINCIPAL PARTS OF VERBS; IRREGULAR VERBS

1. The various forms of Spanish verbs are made up on five fundamental parts—the so-called principal parts: (1) first person singular present indicative; (2) infinitive; (3) present participle; (4) past participle; (5) third person plural preterite indicative.

hablar, to speak (*stem* **habl-**)

From (1), **hablo**, are formed:

(a) present indicative: habl-o, -as, -a; amos, -áis, -an
(b) present subjunctive: habl-e, -es, -e; -emos, -éis, -en
(c) imperative, intimate affirmative: habl-a; -ad
(d) imperfect indicative: habl-aba, -abas, -aba; -ábamos, -abais, -aban

The other imperatives come from the corresponding forms of the present subjunctive.

From (2), **hablar**, are formed:

(a) future indicative: hablar-é, -ás, -á; -emos, -éis, -án
(b) conditional: hablar-ía, -ías, -ía; -íamos, -íais, -ían

From (3), **hablando**, are formed:

the progressive tenses with **estar, seguir, andar, venir**, *etc.*
estoy hablando, sigue escribiendo, *etc.*

From (4), **hablado**, are formed:

(a) the perfect tenses: he hablado, habré hablado, que haya hablado, *etc.*
(b) the passive voice: está escrito, fué escrito, *etc.*

From (5) **hablaron**[1] are formed:

(a) the preterite indicative: habl-é, -aste, -ó; -amos, -asteis, -aron
(b) the past subjunctive: habl-ase, -ases, -ase; -ásemos, -aseis, -asen
habl-ara, -aras, -ara; -áramos, -arais, -aran
(c) the future subjunctive: habl-are, -ares, -are; -áremos, -areis, -aren

The future subjunctive, which is discussed briefly in Lesson LXXVII, need not be learned here (but note similarity with forms of past -ra subjunctive).

2. Of irregular verbs below, note that nearly all irregularities are due to changes in the stem. Of the endings, the future and conditional are always regular.

Some verbs with an irregular first person singular indicative form the entire present subjunctive on the stem of that form. Of the verbs already given, **ser, decir, tener** go by this rule. Note that **haber** is an exception to this rule.

3. **Salir**, to go out

(1) **salgo**[2]
  (a) **salgo**, sales, sale; salimos, salís, salen
  (b) **salga, salgas, salga; salgamos, salgáis, salgan**
  (c)   **sal**   salid
  (d) salía, salías, salía; salíamos, salíais, salían
(2) salir (*contracted to* **saldr-**)
  (a) **saldré, saldrás, saldrá; saldremos, saldréis, saldrán**
  (b) **saldría, saldrías, saldría; saldríamos, saldríais, saldrían**
(3) saliendo
  está saliendo, *etc.*

---

[1] Strictly, the first and second persons singular and plural of many verbs are to be connected with the forms in (1); but for convenience, all verbs are given as **hablar** above.
[2] Forms in boldface have some irregularity.

(4) salido
    (a) he salido, *etc.*   (b) *no passive*
(5) salieron
    (a) salí, saliste, *etc.*
    (b) saliese, salieses, *etc.* saliera, salieras, *etc.*
    (c) saliere, salieres, *etc.*

4. **Traer**, to bring, to fetch

(1) traigo
    (a) **traigo, traes, trae; traemos, traéis, traen**
    (b) **traiga, traigas, traiga; traigamos, traigáis, traigan**
    (c)   trae   traed
    (d) traía, traías, *etc.*
(2) traer
    (a) traeré, traerás, *etc.*   (b) traería, traerías, *etc.*
(3) trayendo
    está trayendo, *etc.*
(4) traído
    (a) he traído, *etc.*   (b) fué traído, *etc.*
(5) trajeron
    (a) **traje, trajiste, trajo; trajimos, trajisteis, trajeron**
    (b) **trajese, trajeses, trajese; trajésemos, trajeseis, trajesen**
        trajera, trajeras, trajera; trajéramos, trajerais, trajeran
    (c) **trajere, trajeres, trajere; trajéremos, trajereis, trajeren**

5. **Valer**, to be worth

(1) valgo
    (a) **valgo, vales, vale; valemos, valéis, valen**
    (b) **valga, valgas, valga; valgamos, valgáis, valgan**
    (c)   **val** *or* **vale**   valed
    (d) valía, valías, *etc.*
(2) valer (*contracted to* **valdr-**)
    (a) **valdré, valdrás**, *etc.*   (b) **valdría, valdrías**, *etc.*
(3) valiendo
(4) valido
    (a) ha valido, *etc.*   (b) *no passive*
(5) valieron
    (a) valí, valiste, *etc.*
    (b) valiese, valieses, *etc.*   valiera, valieras, *etc.*
    (c) valiere, valieres, *etc.*

VOCABULARY

copiar, to copy   pasearse, to take a walk, to go out

A. *Give the principal parts of:* 1. vivir 2. conjugar 3. beber 4. estar 5. comer 6. tener 7. rezar 8. haber 9. ser.

AA. 1. *Form the tenses from each part of the above verbs.*

AAA. 1. valí 2. traigo 3. salir 4. valgo 5. traer 6. trajeron 7. hemos salido 8. habían traído 9. he valido 10. trayendo 11. salgo 12. valiendo 13. valí 14. salieron 15. valieron 16. valdrán 17. que valga 18. traigo 19. traje 20. tráeme 21. traeréis 22. que salgamos 23. que salieran 24. salgamos 25. valían 26. trayéndome 27. no salgan ustedes 28. que valiese

AAAA. 1. it was worth 2. I bring 3. we shan't go 4. he is going out 5. they brought 6. that we are worth 7. going out 8. to go out 9. they went out 10. let us bring 11. that they brought 12. to bring 13. going out 14. let us go out 15. weren't you going out? 16. that they might be worth 17. they will bring 18. that they went out 19. it can be brought 20. it will be worth 21. bringing 22. were they bringing?

B. 1. ¿Ha hablado usted todavía a su padre de los libros que trajo consigo? 2. De cuanto dinero con que salió, nada tiene ahora. 3. No vale nada—ni siquiera sabe trabajar. 4. Y ¿qué quiere usted que valga? 5. No puede salir hoy el niño—está enfermo. 6. En aquella esquina hay una casa blanca, de donde salieron los dos hombres a quienes usted busca. 7. Y si escribe el ejercicio, ¿qué valdrá tal trabajo escrito? 8. Han deseado que nosotros saliéramos con ellos, pero no hemos tenido mucho tiempo para pasearnos. 9. No acabó de hablar cuando volvió a salir el primo. 10. Salíamos de la casa cuando entró nuestro primo don Jorge. 11. No puede jugar ahora porque saldrá dentro de poco. 12. Tráeme un libro, no tengo nada que leer ahora. 13. No valiendo nada hoy, es posible que valga algo mañana. 14. ¿Qué te trajeron tus tíos? 15. Sal ahora mismo; no quiero que quedes más tiempo aquí. 16. No salgan ustedes, porque nos queda todavía mucho que hacer con ustedes. 17. Tráigame Vd. otro vaso de leche—éste no es muy grande.

BB. 1. Let us leave (go out) before they return. 2. Tell them to bring me some (a little of) dinner; I haven't eaten all day. 3. Did you show me the book that you brought to your father? 4. Does it look (**parece**) good to him? 5. A certain friend of mine told me that they brought him the book of which you were speaking to me; can you tell me what (how) is-its-title? 6. They didn't prepare the exercises they brought, but they copied them; and so these exercises are worth nothing. 7. Where are the books they brought with them? 8. Don't go-out, Henry, for they haven't come yet, and I should like to talk with you till they come. 9. He had just said that they were coming, when they arrived, bringing all kind[s] of things with them. 10. They haven't any (Nothing remains to them) of all the money they took with them. 11. Bring me some bread and a glass of milk. 12. If the book of which you were speaking is worth ten dollars, that one would be worth a hundred. 13. Can't John go out today? 14. No, he is too ill. 15. It was necessary for us to go out with her. 16. I'll go out with you after my father reaches home.

LESSON LXVII
ORDINALS

1. The ordinals to **tenth** are:

primero, first	**sexto,** sixth
segundo, second	**sé(p)timo,** seventh
tercero, third	**octavo,** eighth
cuarto, fourth	**noveno,** ninth
quinto, fifth	**décimo,** tenth

For the ordinals from **eleventh** on, see Appendix G.

For **primero**, **tercero**, and **noveno**, there are also the shorter forms **primo**, **tercio**, and **nono**, which are used in the compounds. **Sexto** may be written **sesto** (as it is usually pronounced).

2. Ordinals are regularly inflected like any other adjective.

   la primera lección, the first lesson

3. Beyond **tenth**, the ordinals, as they are rarely used, need not be memorized.

4. For the ordinals in dates, see Lesson LX, 2.

5. In titles, ordinals are used to **tenth**; from **eleventh** on, the cardinals are used. In other expressions, the cardinals are used with the one exception of **primero**.

   Carlos quinto, Charles the Fifth (*note the absence of the definite article*)
   Enrique tercero, Henry the Third
   Luis catorce, Louis the Fourteenth
   el primer tomo, the first volume   *But* **tomo dos,** volume two (the second volume)

6. For the apocopation of **primero, tercero**, see Lesson XIX, 1.

7. Fractions are formed up to *tenth* by using a cardinal as numerator and an ordinal as denominator. **Tercio,** *third*, is used in fractions instead of **tercero**. From *eleventh* on, add **-avo** to the cardinal for the denominator, first dropping the final vowel.

   dos octavos, two eighths
   ocho trezavos, eight thirteenths

Seventeenth, eighteenth, and **nineteenth** keep **-e, -o,** and **-e** respectively.

   diecisieteavo   dieciochoavo   diecinueveavo

VOCABULARY

ayudar, to aid, to help
el capítulo, chapter
Carlos, Charles
cero, zero
dividir (por), to divide by
el jefe, chief, leader, head
la manzana, apple
más, more; plus
medio, -a, half (*adjective*)
menos, less; minus
la mitad, half (*noun*)
la parte, part
el quebrado, fraction
el tomo, tome, volume (*of a series*)

A. *Count the ordinals as rapidly as you can from* **first** *to* **tenth**.

AA. 1. *Count the ordinals from* twenty-first *to* twenty-ninth, *using the text.* 2. *Count the ordinals from* thirtieth *to* ninetieth, *using the text.*

AAA. 1. centésimo 2. milésimo 3. millonésimo 4. Carlos quinto 5. primera página 6. capítulo diez y ocho 7. Luis trece 8. Enrique cuarto 9. Alfonso trece 10. la mitad 11. dos tercios 12. tres cuartos 13. cuatro quintos 14. cinco sextos 15. siete octavos 16. siete décimos 17. diez onzavos 18. siete dozavos 19. ocho trezavos 20. nueve catorzavos 21. dos quinzavos 22. tres dieciseisavos 23. ocho veintavos 24. nueve veintiunavos 25. un niño 26. por centésima vez. 27. el primero de enero de mil ochocientos noventa y dos 28. tercer libro 29. el dos de mayo de mil novecientos veinte y tres 30. el cuatro de julio de mil setecientos setenta y seis 31. la mitad del camino 32. un dólar y medio 33. un dólar cincuenta

AAAA. 1. Alphonsus XIII. 2. (the) half (of) my apple 3. Charles V. 4. (*Count from* first *to* tenth; eleventh *to* twentieth; *decimals from* thirtieth *through* ninetieth); hundredth; thousandth 5. John the Second 6. millionth 7. an apple and a half 8. one half; two thirds 9. one quarter 10. two fifths 11. one sixth 12. two sevenths 13. three eighths 14. four ninths 15. three tenths 16. four elevenths 17. five twelfths 18. six thirteenths 19. seven fifteenths 20. eight fourteenths 21. nine twenty-thirds 22. one hundredth 23. a millionth

B. 1. No tenemos que ocuparnos de dos tercios, tres cuartos, etcétera, porque no pensamos tener (keep) libros en español. 2. Por centésima vez te digo que no puedo ayudarte ahora; vuelve más tarde y ya (then) hablaremos. 3. El cinco de mayo de mil novecientos murió aquel gran presidente, aquel jefe de una gran nación. 4. ¿Cuánto es dos más tres dividido por cinco más uno menos cero? 5. Carlos quinto, uno de los reyes más grandes que ha tenido España, murió en mil quinientos cincuenta y ocho. 6. En la página diez y ocho hallará usted las noticias que busca. 7. No me basta la mitad de una manzana; quiero una manzana y media. 8. La tercera parte de su libro no contiene nada que valga. 9. Luis catorce de Francia no fué tan bueno como grande. 10. Más vale ser bueno que grande. 11. Sin embargo, la mitad del mundo quiere ser grande y la otra mitad no puede ser buena. 12. Tres onzavos de veinte y dos son seis. 13. Todavía no he leído el tomo tres.

BB. 1. I don't care-about (**No me ocupo de**) thirds, fourths, and sixths. 2. We do not have to bother-with (**preocuparnos de**) such things in our school, for no one intends (**piensa**) to keep books. 3. Can you say in Spanish: sixteenth, seventeenth, eighteenth, nineteenth, twentieth, hundredth? 4. Have you read the first volume yet? Then you do not intend to read the second. 5. (The) Half (of) the boys in the city go to my school. 6. He has to be told a thing for [the] hundredth time (*see B, 2*) before he begins to do it. 7. On what page can I find that? 8. It begins on the twenty-eighth page. 9. Louis the Thirteenth of France died in the year 1643. 10. There are no more apples; but there is still (the) half (of) an orange (**una naranja**)—eat it if you wish. 11. Who was Charles V.? 12. He says it would be better to be good than great. 13. How do you say in Spanish: 2/3; 5/6; 5/17?

LESSON LXVIII

Review Lesson LXVI.

1. **Andar,** to go

(1) ando
   (a) ando, andas, *etc.*
   (b) ande, andes, *etc.*
   (c) .   anda   andad
   (d) andaba, andabas, *etc.*
(2) andar
   (a) andaré, andarás, *etc.*   (b) andaría, andarías, *etc.*
(3) andando
   está andando

(4) andado
    (a) he andado, *etc.*   (b) *no passive*
(5) anduvieron
    (a) anduve, anduviste, anduvo; anduvimos, anduvisteis, anduvieron
    (b) anduviese, anduvieses, *etc.*   anduviera, anduvieras, *etc.*
    (c) anduviere, anduvieres, *etc.*

Andar means **to go**, with the idea of personal locomotion.
Anda ligero, He goes (walks) lightly, (he has a light gait).
Andemos, Let's be off.

2. Estar, to be

(1) estoy
    (a) estoy, estás, está; estamos, estáis, están
    (b) esté, estés, esté; estemos, estéis, estén
    (c)   está   estad
    (d) estaba, estabas, *etc.*
(2) estar
    (a) estaré, estarás, *etc.*   (b) estaría, estarías, *etc.*
(3) estando
(4) estado
    (a) he estado, *etc.*   (b) *no passive*
(5) estuvieron
    (a) estuve, estuviste, estuvo; estuvimos, estuvisteis, estuvieron
    (b) estuviese, estuvieses, *etc.*   estuviera, estuvieras, *etc.*
    (c) estuviere, estuvieres, *etc.*

For the difference in meaning between **estar** and **ser**, see Lessons XIV and XV.

3. Caer, to fall [1]

(1) caigo
    (a) caigo, caes, cae; caemos, caéis, caen
    (b) caiga, caigas, caiga; caigamos, caigáis, caigan
    (c)   cae   caed
    (d) caía, caías, *etc.*
(2) caer
    (a) caeré, caerás, *etc.*   (b) caería, caerías, *etc.*
(3) cayendo
    está cayendo
(4) caído
    (a) ha caído, *etc.*   (b) *no passive*
(5) cayeron
    (a) caí, caíste, cayó; caímos, caísteis, cayeron
    (b) cayese, cayeses, *etc.*   cayera, cayeras, *etc.*
    (c) cayere, cayeres, *etc.*

---

[1] For the change to -y-, see Lesson LVIII, (c).

Note that **caer**, like other verbs ending in a strong vowel, requires an accent on an initial stressed **-i** of an ending.

4. **Huir,** to flee [1]
(1) **huyo**
    (a) **huyo, huyes, huye;** huimos, huis, **huyen**
    (b) **huya, huyas, huya; huyamos, huyáis huyan**
    (c)   **huye**   huid
    (d) **huía, huías,** *etc.*
(2) huir
    (a) **huiré,** huirás, *etc.*   (b) huiría, huirías, *etc.*
(3) **huyendo**
    está huyendo
(4) huido
    (a) ha huido, *etc.*   (b) *no passive*
(5) **huyeron**
    (a) **huí,** huiste, **huyó;** huimos, huisteis, **huyeron**
    (b) **huyese, huyeses,** *etc.*   huyera, huyeras, *etc.*
    (c) **huyere, huyeres,** *etc.*

Where **-ui-** occur together, they are considered as forming two syllables, whether or not an accent is written.

Argüir writes a diaeresis over the **-u-** except where **-y** follows: **arguyo, arguyes, arguye;** but **argüimos, argüis.** (Do not confuse **argüir,** where the **-u** is sounded and is a separate syllable, with verbs like **seguir,** where the **-u** is silent and serves merely to indicate the (good) sound of **g** before **-i-**; see Lesson I, 8.)

5. **Oír,** to hear.
(1) **oigo**
    (a) **oigo, oyes, oye;** oímos, oís, **oyen**
    (b) **oiga, oigas, oiga; oigamos, oigáis, oigan**
    (c)   **oye**   oíd
    (d) oía, oías, *etc.*
(2) oír (oir-)
    (a) oiré, oirás, *etc.*   (b) oiría, oirías, *etc.*
(3) **oyendo**
    está oyendo, *etc.*
(4) oído
    (a) he oído, *etc.*   (b) fué oído, *etc.*

---

[1] Note the change to -y- here too; the -y- is also inserted between u followed by -a, -e, or -o, the so-called strong vowels.

(5) oyeron
  (a) oí, oíste, oyó; oímos, oísteis, oyeron
  (b) oyese, oyeses, etc.   oyera, oyeras, etc.
  (c) oyere, oyeres, etc.

Note that unstressed -i- before a vowel is changed to -y-. The present subjunctive, on the model of the first singular present indicative, has irregular -g-. In the second and third singular and third plural indicative, and second singular imperative, -y- is inserted before -e.

6. **Reír**, to laugh (*R-ch. III*)
(1) río
  (a) río, ríes, ríe; reímos, reís, ríen
  (b) ría, rías, ría; riamos, riáis, rían
  (c)   ríe   reíd
  (d) reía, reías, etc.
(2) reír (reir-)
  (a) reiré, reirás, etc.   (b) reiría, reirías, etc.
(3) riendo
  está riendo, etc.
(4) reído
  (a) ha reído, etc.   (b) *no passive*
(5) rieron
  (a) reí, reíste, rió; reímos, reísteis, rieron
  (b) riese, rieses, etc.   riera, rieras, etc.
  (c) riere, rieres, etc.

The irregular forms of the preterite indicative and past subjunctive may be explained as the radical-changed -i- of the stem combining with an initial i- of the ending to form a single -i-. The stem, however, forms a separate syllable, whether there is an accent or not on either it or the following vowel. Thus, **reír**, **río**, and **rió** have two syllables each; **reiré** has three.

VOCABULARY

al fin, finally
argüir, to argue
el cuidado, care
  tener cuidado, to be careful, to take care
  ¡cuidado! look out! ¡cuidado con . . . ! look out for
freír, to fry; frito, fried (*irregular past participle*)
influir, to influence
(la) Norte América (América del Norte), North America
la piedra, stone
no poder menos; no puedo menos de . . . , I can't help
seguramente, surely
sonreír, to smile
el suelo, ground, floor
tirar, to throw
de vez en cuando, from time to time

IRREGULAR VERBS

A. 1. huimos 2. que andemos 3. que huyan 4. caí 5. argüí 6. caerán 7. arguyo 8. cayó 9. caigo 10. que oigan 11. anda 12. está 13. no oyó 14. huyo 15. estando 16. sonrió 17. no han estado 18. freíamos 19. rieron 20. huirán 21. argüían 22. oiríamos 23. huid 24. que esté 25. cayó 26. hemos caído 27. oiré 28. ¿andáis? 29. estoy 30. que caigamos 31. huí 32. huye 33. huyes 34. que cayese 35. caían 36. oían 37. oyó 38. que sonriésemos 39. reiremos 40. oirían 41. freiré 42. que huyésemos 43. anduvieron 44. estábamos 45. que cayeran 46. que anduviera 47. que oyésemos 48. arguyo.

AA. 1. I am going 2. I hear 3. being 4. he fell 5. will they fall? 6. they will flee 7. I shall go 8. they hear 9. they were going 10. that they argue 11. that you hear 12. listen (hear) 13. to be 14. he was falling 15. I argue 16. going 17. be 18. I fled 19. that she goes 20. were they arguing? 21. flee 22. they fled 23. they argue 24. they were fleeing 25. they are falling 26. they have gone 27. did you hear? 28. I am frying 29. they will hear 30. that she is 31. I fell 32. that we hear 33. were they? 34. he fled 35. I hear 36. that they flee 37. that you smiled 38. frying 39. I shall influence 40. they influenced 41. he was influencing 42. that he smiled 43. he will fry 44. they influence 45. fried.

B. 1. Oí lo que dijeron tus hermanos, pero ellos no sabían que yo lo oí. 2. No deseaba que yo la oyese. 3. Oye, Juan, tráeme un vaso de leche—tengo mucha sed. 4. Así andábamos mucho tiempo, no hablando nunca y al fin llegamos a la casa, donde nos lavamos la cara y las manos e hicimos (had) una buena comida. 5. No estando él allí, seguramente habría ido yo hasta Madrid. 6. Cayó el niño al suelo y se rompió dos dedos. 7. Huyamos antes de que nos vean y nos cojan. 8. No huiré; ni tengo por qué ni puedo. 9. He oído su hermano hablar de los indios de Norte América; parece que son muy interesantes. 10. No es preciso que ande tanto su hermano; mejor sería que descanse un poco. 11. Usted arguye tanto y si bien que no podemos menos de creer lo que nos dice. 12. No quiero que caigas tanto, Juan; ¡cuidado con lo que haces y dónde andas! 13. Tiró el niño una piedra y entonces huyó.

BB. 1. The little girl fell to the ground and broke her arm. 2. That boy threw the stone—I saw him run away. 3. They do not go far, for they are soon tired. 4. Was it necessary for them to go so much? 5. They did not want him to hear it—but he did hear it. 6. Listen, boy, take these dishes and give them to the girl to wash. 7. I wish this child would not fall so much. 8. They are always arguing—they are forever speaking, but they never work. 9. If you were there, I should visit them next week. 10. They hear us speak of that story, which they think very interesting. 11. They fled before they heard what we were going to say to them. 12. Look out for what you say; and don't tell all you hear. 13. Will they be here tomorrow? 14. Who is going around (**por**) here, hearing all these things?

LESSON LXIX
EXCLAMATIONS AND INTERJECTIONS

1. Exclamatory expressions are very common in Spanish. As these are often highly idiomatic, they are best learned by experience. Do not follow the literal meaning of Spanish interjections, as they are much weaker in sense than the English.

2. Following are some common expressions, with suggestions of English equivalents.

¡**ay**! oh! ah! (*cf. also A, 2 below*)
¡**ea**! hi! hurray!
¡**diablo**! the deuce!
¡**mil diablos**! the deuce! (*stronger than* ¡**diablo**!)
¡**válgame Dios**! good heavens!
¡**oiga**! (¡**oye**!) listen! see here!
¡**mire**! (¡**mira**!) see here! listen here!
¡**vamos**! come! come!
¡**vamos a ver**! come, let's see
¡**Jesús mil veces**! good gracious!

EXCLAMATIONS AND INTERJECTIONS

¡canastos! gee whiz! good gracious!
¡Jesús, José, y María! goodness gracious!
¡Dios mío! dear me! heavens! gracious!
¡toma! well! I declare!
¡Juan de mi alma! Why, my dear John!

3. **Tan** or **más** = very.

¡Qué niño más grande! What a big child! (*Lit.*, What a child more large!)
¡Qué hombre tan estúpido! What a very stupid man!
¡Qué bueno es! How good he is!
Y ¡cómo he de hacerlo! And how am I to do it!

4. Note the use of **que** where there is a full or partial ellipsis of a main clause (*cf. with* **Creo que no**).

Y ¡cómo que no hay otro modo de decirlo! And how (do you mean) that there is no other way of saying it!

VOCABULARY

agradecer, to thank
Guillermo, William
embustero, cheat
estúpido, -a, stupid
por allí, over there

A. 1. ¡canastos! 2. ¡ay de vosotros! 3. ¡qué niña más floja! 4. ¡Jesús mil veces! 5. ¡oiga! 6. ¡vamos a ver! 7. ¡diablo! 8. ¡mira, Juan! 9. ¡Oh! ¡sí! 10. y ¡cómo han de hallarlo si no lo han perdido? 11. ¡válgame Dios! 12. ¡Dios mío! 13. ¡oye! 14. ¡mire! ¡Qué niño más estúpido! 16. ¡ay!

AA. 1. listen here! 2. Oh, no! 3. and how should he study? 4. the deuce! 5. goodness gracious! 6. poor George! 7. let's see! 8. ah! 9. oh! 10. I declare! 11. gee whiz! 12. the deuce! 13. good gracious! 14. What a cheat (¡**Qué hombre más embustero**!) 15. let's eat!

B. 1. Vamos a ver. ¿Quiere usted trabajar aquí?— ¡Aquí! ¡Jamás! 2. Y ¡cómo ha de estudiar cuando tú estás todavía aquí! 3. He perdido mis libros y todavía no los he encontrado. 4. Vamos a ver, María. ¿Cuántos años tienes? 5. ¡Jesús, José, y María! ¿Es verdad lo que usted dice? 6. ¡Qué buenos son ustedes! ¿Qué puedo hacer para decirles lo agradecido que quedo? 7. ¡Canastos! cuanto más la niña lava los vasos, tanto más sucios están.

8. ¡Diablo! y ¿qué se imagina usted, entonces? 9. ¡Vamos! ¿Quiere usted saber una cosa? ¡Es usted una gran embustera! 10. ¡Por Dios! ¡Guillermo! ¡no le dejes entrar! 11. ¡Toma! ¡que no hay otro remedio (there is no help for it)! 12. ¿Le diste el dinero a él? (Did you give....) 13. ¡Canastos! ¿Y te lo dará él? 14. ¡Ya lo creo (I should say) que me lo dará! 15. ¡Dios mío! ¡qué enfermo me siento! 16. Vamos a comer. ¿Que no tienes hambre? 17. Parece que los tema.

BB. 1. Poor John! Everything he does comes out (**salir**) badly. 2. Gee whiz! George! don't you ever study? 3. Hurry! Go out quickly! See what is over there! 4. Come! Let's eat! I'm very hungry. 5. The deuce! When will he get here? 6. How is he to come if they didn't tell him you are waiting for him? What a lazy boy you are! Why don't you do something from time to time? 8. Good heavens! Does he imagine we can wait all night? 9. Well! the more he studies, the less he knows. 10. Dear me! I am so ill and I can't eat anything. 11. Goodness, Henry, don't let them come in now; we haven't eaten yet! 12. Let's see, mother; how old will I be tomorrow? 13. Listen, Henry; will you lend me a pencil? 14. You lost your money! Heavens! How did you do that! 15. How well that child studies! How old can he be? 16. He is fifteen years old. 17. Goodness! I should say so! (*see B, 14*)

LESSON LXX
HABER, to have

1. **Haber,** to have
(1) **he**
  (a) **he, has, ha; hemos,** habéis, **han**
  (b) **haya, hayas, haya; hayamos, hayáis, hayan**
  (c)   **he**   habed
  (d) **había, habías,** *etc.*
(2) haber (*contracted to* **habr-**)
  (a) **habré, habrás,** *etc.*   (b) **habría, habrías,** *etc.*

(3) habiendo
   no periphrastic tenses
(4) habido
   (a) ha habido, *etc.* (b) *no passive*
(5) hubieron
   (a) **hube, hubiste, hubo; hubimos, hubisteis, hubieron**
   (b) **hubiese, hubieses,** *etc.*   **hubiera, hubieras,** *etc.*
   (c) **hubiere, hubieres,** *etc.*

For the distinction between **haber** and **tener**, see Lessons XXVII, XXVIII and XXIX. For the various tenses of **hay**, see XXVIII, 3.

The imperative singular **he** means usually: *behold*; **he aquí,** *behold.*

2. **Saber,** to know; to know how; can

(1) **sé**
   (a) **sé, sabes, sabe; sabemos, sabéis, saben**
   (b) **sepa, sepas, sepa; sepamos, sepáis, sepan**
   (c)   sabe   sabed
   (d) **sabía, sabías,** *etc.*
(2) saber (*contracted to stem* sabr-)
   (a) **sabré, sabrás,** *etc.*   (b) **sabría, sabrías,** *etc.*
(3) sabiendo
(4) sabido
   (a) ha sabido, *etc.*   (b) fué sabido, *etc.*
(5) **supieron**
   (a) **supe, supiste, supo; supimos, supisteis, supieron**
   (b) **supiese, supieses,** *etc.*   **supiera, supieras,** *etc.*
   (c) **supiere, supieres,** *etc.*

For meanings, see Lesson LXIV, 4 and 5.

3. **Ser,** to be

(1) **soy**
   (a) **soy, eres, es; somos, sois, son**
   (b) **sea, seas, sea; seamos, seáis, sean**
   (c)   sé   sed
   (d) **era, eras, era; éramos, erais, eran**[1]

[1] **Ser** and **ir** are the only two Spanish verbs with irregular imperfect indicative.

(2) ser
   (a) seré, serás, *etc.*   (b) sería, serías, *etc.*
(3) siendo
(4) sido
   (a) ha sido   (b) *no passive*
(5) fueron [1]
   (a) fuí, fuiste, fué; fuimos, fuisteis, fueron
   (b) fuese, fueses, *etc.*   fuera, fueras, *etc.*
   (c) fuere, fueres, *etc.*

For the differences in the use of **estar** and **ser**, see Lessons XIV and XV.

4. Caber, to be contained

(1) quepo
   (a) quepo, cabes, cabe; cabemos, cabéis, caben
   (b) quepa, quepas, quepa; quepamos, quepáis, quepan
   (c)   cabe   cabed
   (d) cabía, cabías, *etc.*
(2) caber (*stem contracted to* cabr-)
   (a) cabré, cabrás, *etc.*   (b) cabría, cabrías, *etc.*
(3) cabiendo
(4) cabido
   (a) ha cabido, *etc.*   (b) *no passive*
(5) cupieron
   (a) cupe, cupiste, cupo; cupimos cupisteis, cupieron
   (b) cupiese, cupieses, *etc.*   cupiera, cupieras, *etc.*
   (c) cupiere, cupieres, *etc.*

Note the construction with **caber**.

Cuatro sillas caben en esta pieza, This room holds only four chairs (Four chairs are-contained in this room).
No cabe duda, There is no doubt.

5. Ir, to go

(1) voy
   (a) voy, vas, va; vamos, vais, van
   (b) vaya, vayas, vaya; vayamos, vayáis, vayan
   (c)   ve   id
   (d) iba, ibas, iba; íbamos, ibais, iban
(2) ir
   (a) iré, irás, *etc.*   (b) iría, irías, *etc.*

---

[1] The preterite indicative and past subjunctives of **ir** have the same forms as those of **ser**. Note that **fué, fueron** omit the -i-, as do also all past subjunctives. Verbs in -ducir; decir; ir; and traer are in the same class as regards the third singular and plural preterite indicative and all past subjunctives.
Strong preterites (as **anduvo, hubo, estuvo,** *etc.*) omit the -i- in the third person singular preterite indicative only.

(3) **yendo**
　　está yendo
(4) **ido**
　　(a) **ha ido,** *etc.*　　　　　　　(b) *no passive*
(5) **fueron**
　　(a) **fui, fuiste, fué; fuimos, fuisteis, fueron**
　　(b) **fuese, fueses,** *etc.*　　　　**fuera, fueras,** *etc.*
　　(c) **fuere, fueres,** *etc.*

For the meaning of **ir**, compare also Lesson LXVIII, 1. **Ir** means **go** in the most general sense of the word. **Voy a Nueva York,** I am going to New York (how, is not indicated).

Ir is also used as a sort of future auxiliary. **Voy a visitarle,** *I am going to (I shall) visit him.*

The form **vamos** is confined to the imperative first plural use in main clauses only: **Vamos a entrar,** *Let us go in.* In subordinate clauses calling for the subjunctive, the regular subjunctive form is used, introduced by **que**. **Quiere que vayamos,** *He wants us to go.*

VOCABULARY

el campo, field
　en el campo, in the country
el diario, newspaper
la duda, doubt
el escritorio, writing desk
el estante, bookshelf, set of shelves
hacemos, we do, we make
la llave, key
la madera, wood
el papel secante, blotting paper
la plumafuente, fountain pen
supe, *etc.*, I learned (of) (*a special meaning of preterite of* **saber**)

A. 1. iba. 2. he 3. sé 4. que sepa 5. que vayamos 6. soy 8. que sean 9. que quepa 10. iban 11. no cabían 12. habría 13. puede haber 14. que supiesen 15. ¿cupo? 16. que haya 17. que hayan 18. habríamos 19. id 20. idos 21. vámonos 22. iremos 23. sed 24. seremos 25. eran 26. cabrán 27. que sepan 28. sabrán 29. supieron 30. vamos 31. que cupiesen 32. supisteis 33. sé 34. helo aquí 35. sería 36. que hubiera 37. iré 38. había 39. sabríamos 40. que estuvieran 41. voy 42. voy a ir 43. fuisteis 44. que vayamos

AA. 1. that we know 2. I have 3. I know 4. going

5. I knew 6. there is room 7. they will be 8. I can go
9. did they learn? 10. I am 11. I've learned 12. that
there is room 13. we shall go 14. they have gone 15. have
16. there is 17. that I know 18. we shall have 19. they
were going 20. that they went 21. they will know 22.
containing 23. they are going to write 24. behold
25. there-will-be-room 26. did you know? 27. there-was-
room 28. that you had 29. there were 30. there will be
31. I am going

B. 1. Supe ayer que van a visitarnos. 2. Cien personas
caben en este cuarto. 3. Voy a comprar una plumafuente,
un estante de madera, y papel secante. 4. No hay mucho
que decir; tenemos que comprarlos hoy mismo. 5. No cerró
la puerta con llave (He did not lock) porque perdió la
llave y no sabe dónde encontrar otra. 6. Quiero que seáis
tan diligentes como sea posible. 7. ¿Cabrá otro escritorio
en esta pieza? 8. Yo creo que no. 9. Iremos a la ciudad
mañana, hoy hemos de quedarnos aquí en el campo. 10. Es
sastre, pero no trabaja. 11. Lo habrán perdido, porque
están buscando algo ahora. 12. No sabrán lo que hacemos
a menos que usted se lo diga. 13. ¿Habrá alguien allí que
me enseñe lo que he de hacer? 14. Puede haber mucho
dinero allí; pero no me importa, porque no es mío. 15. Y
¿cómo ha de ser tuyo si nunca trabajas? 16. Juan, ¿por
qué quieren ellos que nosotros nos vayamos? 17. Leían el
diario.

BB. 1. There cannot be room for eighty-five persons in
these two rooms. 2. There have been many men in this
city who have liked very much to live here. 3. Did they
learn who came to visit them when they were at our house?
4. As I was going to tell it to them, they left. 5. There
cannot be so many pupils in your school—it is too small.
6. How many houses are there now on your street, John?
7. Let us go; we have not much time now. 8. There will
be many persons there, I think. 9. They will know it before long (little time). 10. They want us to go before the

children are too tired. 11. If they knew that, we should have to tell them all we heard. 12. I know that you know it, but I don't know when you met (**conocer**) him. 13. We are to see them tomorrow. 14. No doubt of it.

LESSON LXXI
VOWELS

Review Lesson II.

1. Note the following distinctions in the vowels **o** and **e**.

(a) stressed **o** when it is followed by a single consonant or comes at the end of a word is pronounced much as in hope.

poco **ocho** **habló**

Followed by two consonants (only one at the end of a word), or in the diphthong **oi** (**oy**), it is pronounced as in English lock.

donde **hombre** **ron** (rum) **hoy**

(b) **e** when followed by a single consonant, at the end of a word, or followed by **n** or **s** plus a consonant, is pronounced much as in rake.

pero **hablé** **entrar** **bestia**

In the diphthong **ei** (**ey**), followed by two consonants (only one at the end of a word), or by **rr** or **j**, it is pronounced as in English met.

ley **excepto** **ver** **perro** **deja**

2. **Diphthongs and Triphthongs.** For the sake of convenience, vowels are divided into two classes—the strong (**a, o, e**) and the weak (**i, u**).

A diphthong is a combination of two vowels coming together and pronounced as a single vowel sound; the two vowels therefore form one syllable.¹ A triphthong is a similar combination of three vowels.

3. (a) One weak and one strong vowel coming together form a diphthong, and so one syllable. If there is a written accent over a diphthong, it can come only on the strong vowel.

ai	el aire, air		ia	la Gloria, (*girl's name*)
au	el aula, auditorium		ua	la aduana, customs (house)
ei	el aceite, oil		ie	el hielo, ice; yerro, error
eu	la deuda, debt		ue	el abuelo, grandfather
oi	hoy, today		io	el yodo, iodine; **nación**
ou	Cousiño, (*proper name*)		uo	el cuociente, quotient

(b) Two weak vowels coming together form a diphthong, whether or not the i has a written accent.²

ui el cuidado, care; muy, very; el juicio, judgment, opinion; lingüistico, linguistic
iu la ciudad, city

4. Two weak vowels and one strong vowel coming together form a triphthong, making a single syllable. An accent, if written, must come on the strong vowel. There are four triphthongs in Spanish.

iei limpiéis, (that) you clean
uai acentuáis, you accent
iai limpiáis, you clean
uei acentuéis, (that) you accent

5. (a) Two strong vowels coming together are considered as forming two separate syllables, that is, they never form a diphthong but are pronounced separately.

cre er (creer), to believe   ro er (roer), to gnaw

(b) A strong and weak vowel coming together, *with an accent written on the weak vowel,* are considered in two

---

[1] For general purposes, we may note that each syllable is formed on one vowel sound—single vowel, diphthong, or triphthong. In combinations like gui-, gue-, qui-, que-, the u- need be considered as neither vowel nor consonant—it serves merely to indicate the pronunciation of q- or g-.

[2] But verbs in -uir, as huir, argüir, whether or not an accent is written, show two syllables: hu ir, argü ir. Similar are words like flúido, where the fl- at the beginning of the words have to be supported by the full vowel force of -u-. (But in lingüistico, the -ui- form one syllable.)

separate syllables; that is, they do not form a diphthong but are pronounced separately.

el ma íz (maíz), corn
o ír (oír), to hear
acentú o (acentúo), I accentuate

A. *Tell whether the single vowels below are strong or weak; and where two or three vowels occur together, whether they form diphthongs or triphthongs, or are in separate syllables.* 1. farmacéutico (pharmaceutical) 2. fué 3. nación 4. averiguáis 5. juicio 6. flúido 7. guía (*diphthong or triphthong?—why is the* -u- *here?—is the* -u- *pronounced?*) 8. leáis (*diphthong or triphthong?—are there two weak vowels? how many syllables are there?*) 9. acentúas 10. acentuáis 11. acentuaré 12. varía 13. variará 14. buey 15. tiene 16. tenéis 17. rey 18. vacío 19. vuelvo 20. volváis 21. volvió 22. volvéis 23. vaivén (fluctuation) 24. jabalíes 25. genio (temper) 26. invierno 27. acción (share of stock) 28. ley 29. leyes

AA. *Pronounce the words in A.*

AAA. *Learn the new words in A.*

AAAA. *Compose sentences containing one or more words in A. Can you make these sentences without first writing an English model for each?*

LESSON LXXII

1. **Dar,** to give

(1) **doy**
   (a) **doy,** das, da; damos, dais, dan
   (b) **dé,** des, **dé;** demos, deis, den
   (c)   da   dad
   (d) daba, dabas, *etc.*
(2) dar
   (a) daré, darás, *etc.*   (b) daría, darías, *etc.*
(3) dando
   está dando, *etc.*
(4) dado
   (a) he dado, *etc.*   (b) fué dado, *etc.*

(5) dieron
   (a) di, diste, dió; dimos, disteis, dieron
   (b) diese, dieses, *etc.*   diera, dieras, *etc.*
   (c) diere, dieres, *etc.*

   asco me da, it disgusts me   dar las dos, to strike two o'clock
   dar a la calle, to face the street   darse por, to act as if
   dar en la trampa, to fall into the trap
   dar con, to come across

2. Ver, to see (*stems* ve- *and* v-)

(1) veo
   (a) veo, ves, ve; vemos, veis, ven (*from both stems*)
   (b) vea, veas, *etc.*
   (c)   ve   ved
   (d) veía, veías, *etc.*
(2) ver
   (a) veré, verás, *etc.*   (b) vería, verías, *etc.*
(3) viendo
   está viendo
(4) visto
   (a) he visto, *etc.*   (b) fué visto, *etc.*
(5) vieron
   (a) vi, viste, vió; vimos, *etc.*
   (b) viese, vieses, *etc.*   viera, vieras, *etc.*
   (c) viere, vieres, *etc.*

Besides the past participle, **ver** is irregular in having two stems (**ve-** being found in the first singular present indicative, all present subjunctive, and all imperfect indicative).

   no ver la(s) hora(s) de, to be very anxious to
   es de ver, it is worth seeing, you ought to see

3. Poder (*R-ch. I*), to be able, can

(1) puedo
   (a) puedo, puedes, *etc.*
   (b) pueda, puedas, *etc.*
   (c)   *no imperative*
   (d) podía, podías, *etc.*
(2) poder (*contracted to* **podr-**)
   (a) podré, podrás, *etc.*   (b) podría, podrías, *etc.*
(3) **pudiendo** (*note the* u *of the stem*)
(4) podido
   (a) ha podido, *etc.*   (b) *no passive*
(5) **pudieron**
   (a) **pude, pudiste, pudo; pudimos, pudisteis, pudieron**

(b) **pudiese, pudieses,** *etc.*   **pudiera, pudieras,** *etc.*
(c) **pudiere, pudieres,** *etc.*
a más no poder, with all one's might
no poder más, to be exhausted
no poder menos de, can't help

4. Querer (*R-ch. I*), to wish, to want; to love

(1) quiero
   (a) quiero, quieres, *etc.*
   (b) quiera, quieras, *etc.*
   (c)   quiere   quered
   (d) quería, querías, *etc.*
(2) querer (*contracted to stem* **querr-**)
   (a) **querré, querrás,** *etc.*   (b) **querría, querrías,** *etc.*
(3) queriendo
(4) querido
   (a) ha querido, *etc.*   (b) es querido, *etc.*
(5) **quisieron**
   (a) **quise, quisiste, quiso; quisimos, quisisteis, quisieron**
   (b) **quisiese, quisieses,** *etc.*   **quisiera, quisieras,** *etc.*
   (c) **quisiere, quisieres,** *etc.*
querido, -a, beloved, dear
como usted quiera, as you like
¿Qué quiere decir . . . ? What does . . . mean?

VOCABULARY

acontecer, to happen
amable, nice, amiable, kind
el asco, disgust
avisado, -a, prudent, clever
la bendición, blessing
la calle, street
el consejo, advice
gracias, thanks
por lo menos, at least
la prisa, haste
tener prisa, to be in a hurry

A. *Give parts and conjugate each tense of* **querer, ver, dar, poder.**

AA. 1. he querido 2. fué dado 3. querremos 4. quería 5. podré 6. dieron 7. demos 8. ¿visteis? 9. da 10. dad 11. que quieran 12. darán 13. que dieran 14. que veamos 15. ve 16. veré 17. que vea 18. daban 19. que dé 20. quise 21. dad 22. que pueda 23. dábamos 24. podríais 25. disteis 26. pudiendo 27. daremos 28. ved 29. ve 30. verán 31. que pudierais 32. podían 33. pudiste 34. que quisiéramos 35. querían 36. dad 37. que diese 38. que viésemos 39. no puede

AAA. 1. I give 2. can you? 3. they saw 4. that you can 5. we wish 6. you would not give 7. you have 8. see 9. you were able 10. that they could 11. you will wish 12. that I want 13. give 14. I saw 15. that he was able 16. that she gives 17. that they saw 18. were you giving? 19. they wished 20. we should see 21. you saw 22. that you gave 23. I was able 24. you could 25. you would want 26. he used to give 27. we shall give 28. that I may see 29. shall we be able? 30. that we wanted

B. 1. Quieren mucho a sus padres porque son niños muy amables. 2. Esta casa no da a la calle X., sino a la calle A. 3. No pude menos de decir cuanto aconteció. 4. No dieron en la trampa—les había dicho (said) mi hermano lo que iba a suceder. 5. Mi querido Juan: Ya hace ocho días que quiero escribirte, y hasta hoy no he escrito. 6. Si damos con el niño que robó los lápices, podremos decirle algo. 7. No ven las horas de visitar a sus abuelos porque éstos les dan muchos regalos de año nuevo. 8. Dice que no podría hacerlo. 9. No ha podido hacerlo. 10. No pudimos examinar el paño porque no teníamos mucho tiempo. 11. Sin embargo puedo decirle que no me gusta de ninguna manera. 12. No habrían podido hacerlo. 13. Él no querrá acompañarme si vamos antes de lunes. 14. ¿Qué te dió tu tío? 15. Nada me dió ni me dará nada, si no es un buen consejo y su bendición. 16. El hombre no quiso conducir el automóvil por no saber cómo conducirlo. 17. Quisimos que ellos nos acompañasen, pero ellos no pudieron venir. 18. ¿Han visto ustedes a la niña que lavó la vajilla? 19. No era una niña, sino mi hermano Juan. 20. Es imposible que den en la trampa—saben demasiado. 21. No vi al hombre que vino a verme. 22. Después de que hube visto aquello, me fuí sin decir nada.

BB. 1. Children ought (**debieran**) to do as their parents tell them. 2. I came across a man who showed me the street where my uncle and aunt lived. 3. They are very anxious to return to Seville, for they don't like Madrid.

4. They did not fall into the trap. 5. My cousins live on X. Street, which is the longest street in the city. 6. They wanted to visit us today before going to New York (Nueva York). 7. We shall be able to do it, but we shall not want to do it. 8. They wanted us to see their new house, but we had to go away the same day, and so we did not have enough time. 9. Dear Henry, This letter can not be very long, because I am in a hurry. 10. He could have done it if he had wanted to. 11. Did he want to drive the auto? (**Conducir, guiar,** *or* **manejar** *may be used.*) 12. No, he was too ill. 13. Did they see the book you wrote? 14. They couldn't do that—it was impossible. 15. It was necessary for us to study at least six hours a day. 16. They won't give you anything for that—it is no good. 17. Give me the books—give me them, I tell you. 18. See here; aren't you sick? 19. Then how can you swim? 20. I did not see my father today—he had to go away before I woke-up. 21. Do as you like.

LESSON LXXIII
CONSONANTS

Review Lessons LI and LVIII; Lesson I.

This lesson takes up in more detail some consonants omitted or discussed but briefly in Lesson I.

1. There are no consonants written doubled in Spanish, as in the English words pretty, supper.[1] ll and rr are not doubled—they are special sounds, ll being sounded approximately as li- in million, and rr being trilled twice as long as single r, which itself is pronounced with a single tap of the tongue. cc, as in **lección**, are two separate sounds.

rr is written so within a word, but only single at the

---

[1] Beware of writing **philósopho** for **filósofo**; **assistencia** for **asistencia**; **mathemáticas** for **matemáticas**; **arithmética** for **aritmética**; **annuario** for **anuario**; **innocente** for **inocente**; **sumptuoso** for **suntuoso**; *etc.*

beginning; the **r-** of **rosa** is pronounced the same as **-rr-** in **perro.**

The double **nn** in such words as **innoble,** *ignoble*; **ennoblecer,** *to ennoble, to embellish;* **ennegrecer,** *to blacken,* are too infrequent to merit more than passing attention.

x is pronounced as **ks**. But when a consonant follows, it has the sound **s**.

    eximio, eminent, famous   **excepto,** except (*pronounce* escepto)

2. The following sounds and spellings are to be carefully noted.

ce, ci, z, which in Spain are pronounced **the, thi** (*as in English* through), are pronounced **se, si** (*as in English* so) in all South America and much of southern Spain.

    cero   **cirio**   **zambullir**

d between vowels or at the end of a word is pronounced like **th** in **them.**

    ciudad

d at the beginning of a sentence, or after **l** or **n** in a phrase or word, is pronounced like English **d** (in **do**).

    dar   **en donde**   **andar**   **al dar**   **aldea,** village

h, although usually silent, is faintly pronounced with initial **hue-.**

    hueso

k is not an original Spanish letter, and is therefore found only in words of foreign origin.

    kilómetro, kilometer   **kiosco,** news stand (*also written* **quiosco**)

ll (*see above*) is by many Spaniards pronounced as **y** in English **yes.**

    hallar

The pronunciation of **b** and **v** is explained in Lesson I, 3. Note further that at the beginning of a phrase, or after **m** or **n,** one must pronounce **b** or **v** like English **b** (either **m** or **n** is here pronounced **m**).

¡va! well! really! en vez de, instead of
enviar, to send embestir (i), to attack
el baile, dance

A. *Review the pronunciation of all the letters of the alphabet.*

AA. *Learn the new words above.*

AAA. *Pronounce and translate:*

1. No escribía más de cinco ejercicios todas las tardes. 2. Compraron sus zapatos ayer. 3. ¿Has hallado el libro rojo? 4. Sus primas y las de su tío son muy diligentes. 5. ¿Están aquí los García? 6. ¿Por qué no repite V. lo que has oído? 7. Llamaba a su perro. 8. Aún dudo si están aquí. 9. Están en vacaciones. 10. Viven en la misma aldea. 11. Le cogí por el brazo. 12. En verdad, no lo oí. 13. Todos, excepto él. 14. Lo compré al hombre que tiene el kiosco. 15. No estudiamos matemáticas. 16. Este camino (road) tiene tres kilómetros. 17. Busque usted sus libros. 18. No viven en la misma ciudad. 19. Ellas en vez de ellos. 20. ¡Va! 21. Es difícil que lo encuentres.

LESSON LXXIV

1. **Decir** (*R-ch. III*), to say

(1) **digo**
  (a) **digo, dices, dice; decimos, decís, dicen**
  (b) **diga, digas, diga; digamos, digáis, digan**
  (c)   **di**   decid
  (d) decía, decías, *etc.*

(2) decir (*contracted to stem* dir-)
  (a) **diré, dirás,** *etc.*   (b) **diría, dirías,** *etc.*

(3) **diciendo**
  está diciendo

(4) **dicho**
  (a) **he dicho,** *etc.*   (b) **queda dicho,** *etc.*

(5) **dijeron**
  (a) **dije, dijiste, dijo; dijimos, dijisteis, dijeron**
  (b) **dijese, dijeses,** *etc.*   **dijera, dijeras,** *etc.*
  (c) **dijere, dijeres,** *etc.*

The compounds **bendecir,** *to bless*, and **maldecir,** *to curse*, are both regular in the future and conditional, and imperative singular. Note past participles, **bendito, maldito.**

bendeciré, bendice, maldecirán, maldecirían

2. Venir (*R-ch. II*), to come

(1) **vengo**
   (a) **vengo,** vienes, viene; venimos, venís, vienen
   (b) **venga, vengas, venga; vengamos, vengáis, vengan**
   (c)   **ven**   venid
   (d) venía, venías, *etc.*
(2) venir (*contracted to stem* **vendr-**)
   (a) **vendré, vendrás,** *etc.*   (b) **vendría, vendrías,** *etc.*
(3) viniendo
   está viniendo
(4) venido
   (a) ha venido   (b) *no passive*
(5) **vinieron**
   (a) **vine, viniste, vino; vinimos, vinisteis, vinieron**
   (b) **viniese, vinieses,** *etc.*   **viniera, vinieras,** *etc.*
   (c) **viniere, vinieres,** *etc.*

Este traje no me viene, This suit does not become me.
¿A qué viene eso? What is the good of that? What does that lead to?
convenir en, to agree to; (*3rd. sing. as impersonal*) it suits; Me conviene, That suits me.
Convengo en ello, I agree to it.

3. Hacer, to do, to make

(1) **hago**
   (a) **hago,** haces, hace; hacemos, hacéis, hacen
   (b) **haga, hagas, haga; hagamos, hagáis, hagan**
   (c)   **haz**[1]   haced
   (d) hacía, hacías, *etc.*
(2) hacer (*contracted to stem* **har-**)
   (a) **haré, harás,** *etc.*   (b) **haría, harías,** *etc.*
(3) haciendo
   está haciendo
(4) **hecho**
   (a) ha hecho, *etc.*   (b) está hecho, *etc.*
(5) **hicieron**
   (a) **hice, hiciste hizo**[1]**; hicimos, hicisteis, hicieron**

---

[1] c of the stem is here changed to z to indicate the th sound (as in through).

(b) hiciese, hicieses, *etc.*   hiciera, hicieras, *etc.*
(c) hiciere, hicieres, *etc.*

hacer caso de, pay attention to; **No haga Vd. caso de eso,** Don't pay attention to that.
hacer de, to act like
hacerse, to become, to make oneself; **se hace tarde,** it is becoming late; **se hace noche,** night is drawing on

4. Poner, to put, to place

(1) **pongo**
  (a) **pongo,** pones, pone; ponemos, ponéis, ponen
  (b) **ponga, pongas, ponga; pongamos, pongáis, pongan**
  (c)   **pon**   poned
  (d) **ponía, ponías,** *etc.*

(2) poner (*contracted to stem* **pondr-**)
  (a) **pondré, pondrás,** *etc.*   (b) **pondría, pondrías,** *etc.*

(3) poniendo
  está poniendo

(4) **puesto**
  (a) he puesto, *etc.*   (b) fué puesto, *etc.*

(5) **pusieron**
  (a) **puse, pusiste, puso; pusimos, pusisteis, pusieron**
  (b) **pusiese, pusieses,** *etc.*   pusiera, pusieras, *etc.*
  (c) **pusiere, pusieres,** *etc.*

ponerse, to become
ponerse a, to set about, to begin

5. Tener (*R-ch. I*), to have, to hold

(1) **tengo**
  (a) **tengo,** tienes, tiene; tenemos, tenéis, tienen
  (b) **tenga, tengas, tenga; tengamos, tengáis, tengan**
  (c)   **ten**   tened
  (d) **tenía, tenías,** *etc.*

(2) tener (*contracted to stem* **tendr-**)
  (a) **tendré, tendrás,** *etc.*   (b) **tendría, tendrías,** *etc.*

(3) teniendo
  está teniendo

(4) **tenido**
  (a) he tenido, *etc.*   (b) fué tenido, *etc.*

(5) **tuvieron**
  (a) **tuve, tuviste, tuvo; tuvimos, tuvisteis, tuvieron**
  (b) **tuviese, tuvieses,** *etc.*   tuviera, tuvieras, *etc.*
  (c) **tuviere, tuvieres,** *etc.*

For idioms with **tener,** see Lessons XXVII, 3, 4, 5; XXIX, 1; LVI, 4c.

no tener nada que ver con, to have nothing to do with
tener razón, to be right
detenerse, to stop, to halt

VOCABULARY

el centavo, cent
doler (ue), to pain, to ache
  le duele la cabeza, he has a headache
la fonda, inn
  gastar, to spend
la pelota, ball
un rato, a while
el resfriado, cold (*the sickness*)
el remedio, remedy
  no hay remedio, there is no help for it

A. *Give the principal parts and conjugate every tense of* **hacer, decir, poner, venir,** and **tener.**

AA. 1. vendrán 2. haz 3. que hiciéramos 4. pondremos 5. dirá 6. pon 7. pongan ustedes 8. digo 9. ven 10. puse 11. poníais 12. hacíamos 13. pondré 14. que ponga 15. dijisteis 16. tenga usted 17. teníamos 18. dijeron 19. que viniésemos 20. que venga 21. ponía 22. que tengamos 23. tuve 24. di 25. vine 26. tengamos 27. que haga 28. decías 29. no hagas 30. tendré 31. que pusieran 32. que digamos 33. venid 34. hagamos 35. tuvimos 36. tiene 37. pusieron 38. decid 39. ¿veníais? 40. harán 41. pongamos 42. que tengan

AAA. 1. they were putting 2. I make 3. I put 4. I say 5. they put 6. that I made 7. we shall make 8. they have 9. that he has 10. would he say? 11. I shall place 12. let us do 13. let us put 14. let her say 15. we come 16. they will come 17. was she doing? 18. let us have 19. would they have? 20. let him put 21. do it 22. that I place 23. he did it 24. would he put? 25. had he? 26. have 27. say 28. that she says 29. would they put? 30. I've made 31. that she made 32. that I had 33. I shall say 34. he was saying 35. that they said 36. they wouldn't come 37. that we came 38. that we come 39. come

B. Detente, mi hija, quiero hablar contigo. 2. Nunca tiene razón; siempre está hablando de cosas con que no tiene nada que ver. 3. Se detuvo en una fonda al lado del camino y no volvimos a verlo. 4. Me hace mal el brazo derecho; no sé lo que tendré. 5. Tengo ganas de ver lo que han comprado; no veo las horas de visitarlos. 6. Se puso muy serio; después de un rato nos habló como sigue. 7. A los veinte y cuatro años, se hizo médico. 8. Vinieron a vernos la semana pasada, pero no estuvimos en casa, y así no pudimos hablar con ellos. 9. Hace diez años, no tenía ni un centavo; hoy es el hombre más rico de la ciudad. 10. Se puso entonces a trabajar con todas sus fuerzas. 11. Vino a su casa después de las tres y media. 12. Tiene ganas de ponerse el sombrero y salir, pero todavía está demasiado enfermo. 13. Di, ¿qué quieres más? ¿ir a la escuela o jugar a la pelota? 14. Hagámoslo, que (for) tenemos que hacerlo; después saldremos. 15. Hacía tres horas que teníamos el dinero—y después de otra hora más, lo habíamos todo gastado. 16. Ven mañana—allá veremos (we'll see about it then). 17. Me dijeron que yo no se lo dijese a usted—pero no hay remedio, usted tiene que saberlo.

BB. 1. They have lived in this house for ten years, but they don't like it. 2. Probably they will sell it and buy another. 3. Do you feel like setting about studying to be a doctor? 4. Did you say that this child can't read? 5. What they told me, it is not necessary for me to say over again to you. 6. Tell it to them—I'd like to have them hear it. 7. Tell me what you read and I'll tell you what you are. 8. Please come here at once. 9. Stop. Now tell me what you were doing. 10. My head hurts me very much. 11. You were right. It was his uncle, not (**que no**) his father, who bought the house. 12. I have a headache. 13. He is becoming more industrious; I think he will do his work well this year. 14. We felt like buying the house, but we are afraid they are asking too much for it. 15. They stopped at X. Street, where the father of one of the boys lives. 16. Will you come and (**a**) see us next week if you have time? 17. I haven't seen them for four years. 18. They stopped near the corner, and talked [for] fifteen minutes. 19. He has a cold.

LESSON LXXV
STRESS AND ACCENT; DIVISION INTO SYLLABLES

Review Lesson III, 1, 2, 3.

1. Accents are occasionally used, not to denote irregular stress, but to break two adjacent vowels into two syllables, (that is, prevent them from forming a diphthong, which would make one syllable only). The stress of the word may be regular.

    maíz   tío

Note that in both these words, the stress comes, in **maíz,** on the last syllable, as it should; in **tío,** on the next to the last, as it should. The accent merely shows the two vowels to form separate syllables, and not a dipthong.[1]

2. Accents are also used to distinguish an interrogative (direct or indirect) or exclamatory from a corresponding relative. Here the accent is written on the syllable normally bearing the stress, whether or not irregular.

    interrogative   relative
    ¿cuál? which?   cual, which
    ¿por qué? why?   porque, (*written as one word*) because

3. The general rules for division of words into syllables are:

(a) A single consonant goes with the following vowel.
    elegir, to choose; **e le gir**   **poner,** po ner
    afición, affection, tenderness; **a fi ción**

(b) **ch, ll, rr,** and **x** are considered as single consonants.
    borrar, to erase; **bo rrar**   **hallar, ha llar**   **mucho, mu cho**

(c) Two consonants are separated.
    atlético, athletic; **at lético**   **irlandés,** Irish; **ir lan dés**

Note 1. But if the second of two consonants is l or r, the two are considered as a single one (as above in 3b).
    hablar, ha blar   **abrir, a brir**

---

[1] Note that an accent is sometimes written over the strong vowel of a diphthong; nación, habéis. Here, of course, it indicates that the word is irregularly stressed.

Note 2. If the consonant before l is r or s or t; or if the consonant before the r is s, the two consonants are separated (as in 3c).

irlandés, ír landés **isla, island; is la**
atlético, at lético **israelita, Israelite; is raelita**

(d) A weak and a strong vowel together form a diphthong when (a) no accent is written at all; (b) an accent is written on the strong vowel. Similarly, two weak vowels and a strong vowel form a triphthong.

peinar, pei nar **habláis, ha bláis**
acentuáis, acen tuáis **buey, ox** (*one syllable*)

But when a strong and weak vowel occur together with an accent written on the weak vowel, they never form a diphthong but split into two separate syllables.

maíz, ma íz **tío, tí o**

Two strong vowels always separate into two distinct syllables.

leer, le er

Note also:

huir, hu ir **argüir, ar gü ir,** **flúido, flú i do** **cruel, cru el**

A. *In AAA in Lesson* LXXIII, (*1*) *divide every word into syllables;* (*2*) *indicate what words are regular, what irregular, in stress.*

LESSON LXXVI

1. **Antojarse,** to fancy (*impersonal*)

This verb is impersonal; that is, it is used only in the third person singular of the various tenses.

Se me antoja que . . . , I fancy that . . .
Se le antoja que . . . , He fancies . . .

The present, imperfect, and preterite are the only common tenses. These are formed regularly on the model of the first conjugation, and are used as in the examples above.

2. **Constar,** to be clear, to be evident

This verb is wholly regular in formation; but being impersonal, it is used only in the third person singular of the tense required.

3. **Placer,** to be pleased (*impersonal*)

(1) place
    (a) place   (b) **plegue,** *or* **plega,** *or* **plazga**   (c) *lacking*   (d) placía

(2) placer
    (a) placerá   (b) placería

(3) placiendo

(4) placido
    (a) ha placido, *etc.*   (b) *no passive*

(5) { **plugo,** *or* plació }   (b) { **pluguiese pluguiera,** *or* placiese placiera }

(c) { **pluguiere,** *or* placiere }

The compound **complacerse (en),** to be pleased to (with), is conjugated as are the inceptives.

4. **Asir,** to grasp, to seize

(1) **asgo**
    (a) **asgo,** ases, ase; asimos, asís, asen
    (b) **asga, asgas, asga; asgamos, asgáis, asgan**
    (c)   ase   asid
    (d) asía, asías, *etc.*

All other forms of **asir** are made up regularly.

5. **Soler** (*R-ch. I*), to be used, to be wont

(1) suelo
    (a) suelo, sueles, suele; solemos, soléis, suelen
    (b) solía, solías, *etc.*

Soler is used only in the present and imperfect indicative. Forms like **ha solido** are rarely found.

6. **Yacer,** to lie, to be lying down, to be prone

(1) { **yazco,** yaces, yace; yacemos, yacéis, yacen
(a)   **yazgo**
      yago

(b) {yazca, yazcas, *etc.*
yazga, yazgas, *etc.*
yaga, yagas, *etc.*
(c) {yace
yaz   yaced
(d) yacía, yacías, *etc.*

Other forms are made up regularly. This verb is quite rare.

7. Superlative Absolute. Besides the regular superlative of comparison, there is the so-called superlative absolute.

"It is **very** excellent, **most** excellent, **extremely** excellent, **quite** excellent" are English quivalents of the superlative absolute. In Spanish, this superlative absolute is formed by adding **-ísimo** to the stem of an adjective or adverb.

inteligente   inteligentísimo, most, very intelligent
ligero, swift   ligerísimo, swiftest
ligeramente, swiftly   ligerísimamente, most swiftly

Note that the original accent is retained in the new compound (see A 10 below)

8. Intensive (Emphatic) Prefixes. Re-, te-, que-, individually or two or three together, may be prefixed to an adjective or adverb to make it more emphatic.

¡qué bueno! how good!
¡qué rebueno! } how very good!
¡retequebueno! }

A word may be repeated for emphasis.

mucho mucho, very, very much

VOCABULARY

el alimento, food   emplear, to employ, to use
dulce, sweet   el helado, ice cream
los dulces, sweets, candy   tonto, -a, foolish

A. 1. solían trabajar 2. retonto 3. se le antoja 4. cerquísima (cerca) 5. que le plega o no 6. me complazco en decir 7. asgo 8. aquí yace 9. solía acontecer 10. facilísimo 11. dificilísimamente 12. que asgan 13. muchísimo 14. poquísimo (*from what word? why* **-qu-**?) 15. me place decirle

B. 1. Se le antoja ser soldado. 2. Solía acontecer que no había trabajo y entonces los pobres no tenían ni dinero ni alimento. 3. Hacían una carrera por la ciudad en coche muy rápidamente. 4. Aquellos niños son inteligentísimos— siempre saben sus lecciones. 5. Los verbos **placer, asir, y yacer** en esta lección no se usan mucho; en vez de ellos se emplean los verbos **agradar** o **gustar**; **agarrar** o **coger**; y **estar acostado** o **estar en el suelo**. 6. ¿Vive cerca de vosotros?—Sí, cerquísima. 7. Lo que tú dices es retequebueno. 8. Muchísimo me gusta. 9. La vida es dulce. 10. Facilísimo es trabajar, pero el no hacer nada cuesta (is hard). 11. Los helados eran riquísimos.

LESSON LXXVII
AUGMENTATIVES AND DIMINUTIVES

1. Certain endings are added to nouns, adjectives, and adverbs to give them various diminutive, affectionate, augmentative, or pejorative meanings. The beginner should never add these of his own initiative to any word, but should follow Spanish practice as he finds it.

2. The diminutive endings **-ito, -cito, -ecito** indicate smallness, affection, pity.

-illo, -cillo, -ecillo indicate smallness, or contempt, or indifference.

-uelo, -zuelo, -ezuelo indicate smallness or scorn.

3. The augmentative (or pejorative) endings **-ón, -erón, -etón, -azo** indicate bigness.

-acho, -achón, -arrón, -ejón, -ote, -ucho indicate bigness or scorn.

callado, quiet	calladito, very quiet, still as a mouse
cerca, near	cerquita, quite near

AUGMENTATIVES AND DIMINUTIVES 207

Serafina, Serafina	Finita, little Serafina
Juana, Jane	Juanita, little, dear Jane; "Janey"
hasta luego, good-by for a while	hasta lueguito, good-by for a short while
Luis, Louis	Luisito, little, dear Louis
papá, father, "dad"	papacito, dear father, "daddy"
Francisco, Francis	Paquito, "Frankie"
la buharda, garret window	la buhardilla, small garret
la campana, bell	la campanilla, small bell
la mujer, woman	la mujercilla, little woman, insignificant woman
la zorra, fox	la zorrilla, polecat, skunk
la casa, house	el caserón, ill-proportioned, big house
	la casucha, ugly old house
el viejo, old man	el vejote, repulsive old man

4. **Future (Hypothetical) Subjunctive.** In Spanish, there exists a future subjunctive, the forms of which are made by substituting -re etc. for the -ra past subjunctive.

hablare, hablares, hablare; habláremos, hablareis, hablaren
bebiere, bebieres, bebiere; bebiéremos, bebiereis, bebieren
viviere, vivieres, viviere; viviéremos, viviereis, vivieren

The future subjunctive is practically not found in modern Spanish, surviving only in some proverbs, legal language, and other stereotyped expressions.

venga lo que viniere, come what may
Primero. Que cada sección . . . y que si le fuere posible . . .
First. That each section . . . and that if it were possible for him. . . .
. . . en cuanto fuere posible . . . , in so far as may be possible . . .
pese a quien pesare, grieve whom it may (pesar, to grieve a person)

APPENDIX A
PERSON AND NUMBER

1. In English, a verb rarely changes in form. Thus **I speak, you speak, he speaks; we speak, they speak**—all these forms, with but one exception, are identical. People know just what we mean by the words **I, you, we,** and so on.

2. For convenience, we class the above forms according to **person** and **number**.

(a) By number we indicate whether we are speaking of one person or of several persons—of **I** or of **we**, of **he** or of **they.**

(b) By person we indicate whether we mean **I** (*first person*); **you** (*second person*); or **he, she, it** (*third person*) —these are all singular; or **we** (*first person*); **you** (*second person*); or **they** (*third person*)—these are all plural.

3. In Spanish, however, instead of always using the pronouns to indicate person and number, verbs add certain endings which are different for each person of the singular and plural. These endings are added to the stem (the stem of any Spanish verb may be obtained by dropping the ending of the infinitive, which is the form of the verb always given in vocabularies and corresponds to the English form of the verb with **to**—**to speak**).

Thus the Spanish verb **to speak** is **hablar.** Dropping the infinitive ending **-ar**, we have left the stem **habl-**, to which are added the various endings to give person and number (see Lesson IV).

APPENDIX B
IDIOMS

1. If one language could be translated into another merely by giving the equivalent of each word as it occurs,

language work would consist merely of learning the dictionary. But, aside from regular constructions, there are, in every language, certain expressions which can not be explained by the regular rules of the grammar of that language. As a general thing, these **idioms**, so-called, cannot be literally translated. Many of them, however, are easily understood.

2. **Gustar,** with a dative object, means literally **to please.**

La casa gusta a mi padre, The house pleases to my father; *better English*, My father likes the house.
Me gusta tocar el piano, To me it pleases to play the piano; *better English*, I like to play the piano.

Agradar and **alegrar** are used in the same sense.

No me agrada trabajar tanto, I don't like to work so much.

3. **Acabar de,** to have just (*used only in the present and imperfect*)

Acaba de trabajar, He has just worked (*literally*, He finishes from working).
Acabábamos de escribir, We had just written.

The preterite of this verb gives an idiom meaning **finished.**

Acabó de escribir, He finished writing.

4. **Volver a** (+ verb), again (*lit.*, **to return to.** . . .)

Volvió a hablar con mi tío, He spoke again with my uncle (*lit.*, He returned to speak with my uncle.)
Volvimos a escribir los ejercicios, We again wrote the exercises.

5. **Entrar en,** to enter, to go into (*In English, we say,* We enter a room; *but as* **enter** *cannot take a direct object, the Spanish says* **to enter into a room.**)

Entró en la pieza, She entered (into) the room.

6. Sometimes, the reverse of 5 is the case—the Spanish has not a preposition where the English has.

Busco un libro, I am looking-for a book.

7. **Tirar (de)**

Tiró una piedra, He threw a stone.
Tiró de la mesa, He pulled at the table.

8. Learn the above idiomatic expressions. There are innumerable expressions, some like, some different from, these. If the student once grasps the idea of the idiom, and learns the meaning and use of each as he comes to it, he will have no difficulty. The essential thing is to try to think in Spanish, as one does in English; to think in Spanish idiom.

APPENDIX C
THE SUBJUNCTIVE

1. The subjunctive mood, as a very important element of Spanish grammar, should be thoroughly understood in its main outlines before the student takes it up in detail. Though English possesses a few uses of the subjunctive, they are not numerous enough or close enough to the Spanish to be of much help in understanding the Spanish subjunctive.

2. The general purpose of the subjunctive is to lend to the verb a tinge of **doubt** or **uncertainty**. The subjunctive is thus found in **subordinate** clauses depending on a main verb expressing or implying doubt or uncertainty.

3. In the six instances below, the verb of the main clause casts doubt upon or expresses uncertainty about the subordinate clause. The subordinate clause is accordingly put in the subjunctive.

(**Note.** In Spanish, when a subordinate verb in a complex sentence has a different subject from that in the main clause, both verbs must be finite, and the second must be introduced by **que.**

Very rarely, **que** is found omitted, as after **impedir, solicitar,** and **permitir.** The beginner, however, should not omit **que.**

Sometimes, the infinitive is found even where the subject changes, chiefly after **aconsejar, permitir, prohibir,** and **mandar.**)

(1) **emotion, fear**

> I am afraid he **may come,** Temo que **venga.**

In all expressions of an emotion, as fear or joy, there is a desire to use the subjunctive as a less matter-of-fact mood.

(2) **doubt, uncertainty**

> Is it possible that they **may come?** Es posible que **vengan?**
> I doubt that she **will come.** Dudo que ella **venga.**

In neither case is the coming yet an actual fact—there is doubt, uncertainty—hence, the subjunctive.

(3) **command, request, forbidding**

> I ask him to give me the book (I ask him that he **give** me the book). Le pido que me **dé** el libro.

When a command is given, we never know whether it will be carried out—there is doubt, uncertainty; hence, the subjunctive.

(4) **conditions contrary to fact** (conditional sentences in which the if-clause states the contrary of the truth)

> If I **had stayed,** I should have seen him. Si **hubiese quedado,** le habría visto.

But it is not a fact that I stayed; hence, the subjunctive must be used to show that indefiniteness.

(5) in sentences where the subordinate clause, an **adjective clause** usually, describes somebody or something as yet not definitely known

> I want a gardener who **is** a good worker. Quiero un jardinero que **sea** un buen trabajador.

We do not really know just who that man may be; hence, the subjunctive must be used to indicate the uncertainty.

(6) in **adverbial clauses** not yet considered as actual facts, actual happenings

> I shall do it before he **comes** (*definite time of his coming not yet known*). Lo haré antes de que él **venga**.
> I wanted to do it before he **came** (*definite time of his coming not then known*). Quería hacerlo antes que él **viniese**.
> Even if he **does** it, it won't make matters better (*but there is still doubt as to whether he will do it*). Aunque lo **haga**, no servirá.
> I shall do it so that they **may recognize** my good intentions (*but we are not certain that they will*). Lo haré para que **reconozcan** mi buena voluntad.

APPENDIX D

SUMMARY OF SUBJUNCTIVE

Review Appendix C.

1. The subjunctive is the mood used in subordinate clauses (a few apparent exceptions are easily explained) to express doubt, uncertainty.

2. The endings of the first conjugation are:

present tense
-e, -es, -e; -emos, -éis, -en

past tense
{ **-ase, -ases, -ase; -ásemos, -aseis, -asen**
{ **-ara, -aras, -ara; -áramos, -arais, -aran**

(a) For practical purposes the beginner may use either the **-se** or **-ra** past subjunctive (but see contrary-to-fact conditions, Lesson XLV).

The form in **-se** is more common in Spain, and the form in **-ra** in parts of South America.

(b) The endings of the present subjunctive are the same as those of the present indicative save that **-e** is substituted for **-a** (**-o** in the first singular).

3. The endings of the second and third conjugations are:

present tense
-a, -as, -a; -amos, -áis, -an

past tense
{ -iese, -ieses, -iese; -iésemos, -ieseis, -iesen
{ -iera, -ieras, -iera; -iéramos, -ierais, -ieran

(a) The endings of the second and third conjugations are alike.

(b) In the present tense, substitute -a for -e of the endings of the present subjunctive of the first conjugation.

(c) In the past tense, substitute -ie- for -a- of the endings of the past subjunctive of the first conjugation.

4. The subjunctive is used:

(a) in contrary-to-fact conditions, with moods and tenses as follows:

Present contrary to fact

if-clause	result clause
si plus -se past subjunctive	-ra past subjunctive or conditional
si plus -ra past subjunctive	conditional

Si estuviese aquí, le hablaría
Si estuviese aquí, le hablara   } If he were here, I should speak to him.
Si estuviera aquí, le hablaría

Note also the substitutions:

Estuviera él aquí,
Estando él aquí,   } le hablaría, Were he here, I should speak to him.
A estar él aquí,

Past contrary to fact

si plus -se pluperfect subjunctive { -ra pluperfect subjunctive or conditional perfect
si plus -ra pluperfect subjunctive   conditional perfect

Si hubiese estado aquí, le habría hablado
Si hubiese estado aquí, le hubiera hablado } If he had been here, I should have spoken to him.
Si hubiera estado aquí, le habría hablado

Note also the substitutions:

Hubiese estado él aquí, le habría (hubiera) hablado
Habiendo estado él aquí, le habría (hubiera) hablado } Had he been here, I should have spoken to him.
A haber estado él aquí, le habría (hubiera) hablado

(b) in adverbial clauses of time, place, purpose, concession, manner, and other (adverbial) relations, if indefinite.

Le hablaré antes que ellos lleguen, I shall speak to him before they arrive.

Note:

Le hablaré antes de llegar (yo), I shall speak to him before (my) arriving.

(c) In adjective clauses, the antecedent of which is indefinite.

Busco un hombre que pueda hacerlo, I am looking for a man who can do it.

Note:

Busco al hombre que lo hizo, I am looking for the man who did it.

(d) in noun clauses, the indefinite subject or object of a verb: e. g., **it is necessary, it is time, it is possible;** verbs of wishing, willing, desiring, forbidding, denying, asking, doubting, fearing, hoping, to be glad or sorry.

Es preciso que estudie, He must study (It is necessary that he study).
Quiero que estudie, I want him to study (I want that he studies).

Note: where a real fact is stated, the indicative is used; so always after **si** = *whether*.

No dudo que están aquí, I don't doubt (this is a fact) that they are here.
No sabe si están aquí, He does not know whether they are here.

(e) in the first person plural and third person singular and plural, to express a hope (the so-called optative or hortatory use). Apparently these cases occur in independent clauses, as are a few other isolated instances; but these are explained on the ground of an understood main verb.

Estudiemos (Vamos a estudiar), Let us study.
Que lo digan (Díganlo), Let them tell it.
¡Viva el Paraguay! Hurrah for Paraguay!

APPENDIX E

Orthographic changes chart (cf. Lessons LI and LVIII)

-ar verbs change before e in all present subjunctive and first singular preterite indicative:

c becomes	qu:	sacar
g	gu:	llegar
gu	gü:	averiguar
z	c:	rezar
j	j:	(*not* g): dejar

(so also verbs like **crujir**)

-er, -ir verbs change before o in present indicative and a in all present subjunctive:

qu becomes	c:	delinquir
gu	g:	distinguir
c	z:	vencer; esparcir
g	j:	coger, elegir

Note also the changes below:

Verbs with a stem ending in ll and ñ drop initial i of endings **-ió** and **-ie-**: preterite third singular and plural; present participle; all past and future subjunctive; **bullir; teñir.**

Leer and other verbs in which an i becomes intervocalic change the -i- to -y-. This occurs in the same forms as in **bullir: leer; reír.**

Note special written accents in verbs like **reír.**

Verbs like **huir** introduce a y between the stem and ending in all forms where the ending begins with any vowel but i. This occurs in all forms as in **bullir**, and also in the present indicative all singular and third plural, all the present subjunctive, and in the affirmative imperative singular.

Distinguish verbs like **enviar, continuar,** which place a written accent on **-i-, -u-,** in all singular and third plural present indicative and subjunctive and intimate singular imperative; and verbs like **limpiar, averiguar,** which do not.

Like **enviar** are conjugated:

confiar to confide
desafiar, to challenge
desconfiar, to distrust
espiar, to spy
expiar, to expiate
fiar, to trust

guiar, to guide
porfiar, to persist
resfriar, to chill
telegrafiar, to telegraph
vaciar, to empty
variar, to vary; *etc.*

Like **continuar** are conjugated:

- **acentuar,** to accent
- **efectuar,** to effect
- **exceptuar,** to except
- **habituar,** to accustom
- **insinuar,** to insinuate
- **perpetuar,** to perpetuate
- **puntuar,** to punctuate
- **situar,** to situate
- **valuar,** to evaluate; *etc.*

Like **limpiar** are:

afiliar, to affiliate; **anunciar,** to announce; **diferenciar,** to differentiate; **estudiar,** to study; *etc.*

APPENDIX F

ABSTRACT AND GENERIC NOUNS

"Snow is white." We speak of the **whiteness** of snow, of the **mortality** of men. But we cannot see, touch, hear, etc. whiteness or mortality. These are simply ways of regarding snow or men. Nouns like **whiteness, mortality, truth, death, honesty,** etc., are **abstract** nouns — nouns which refer not to the thing itself but to a quality of that thing—its redness, truth, honesty, death, etc., something which has no reality detached from concrete nouns.

In a garden are: a birch, an oak, a maple. Each is a thing by itself, a special kind, a special unit. But when one wishes to refer to them all, one calls them "trees." "Trees" is a word which designates the class to which belong a certain group of units which possess certain qualities in common. So we speak of **men, quadrupeds, rodents, fauna, flora, mammals,** etc. Such nouns, referring to a class, are called **generic** nouns.

APPENDIX G
ORDINALS

primero, first
segundo, second
tercero, third
cuarto, fourth
quinto, fifth
sexto, sixth
sé(p)timo, seventh
octavo, eighth
noveno, ninth
décimo, tenth
undécimo, eleventh
duodécimo, twelfth
décimo tercio, thirteenth
décimo cuarto, fourteenth
décimo quinto, fifteenth
décimo sexto, sixteenth
décimo sé(p)timo, seventeenth
décimo octavo, eighteenth
décimo nono, nineteenth
vigésimo, twentieth
vigésimo primo, twenty-first
trigésimo, thirtieth

cuadragésimo, fortieth
quincuagésimo, fiftieth
sexagésimo, sixtieth
septuagésimo, seventieth
octogésimo, eightieth
nonagésimo, ninetieth
centésimo, hundredth
centésimo vigésimo, hundred twentieth
ducentésimo, two-hundredth
trecentésimo, three-hundredth
cuadragentésimo, four-hundredth
quingentésimo, five-hundredth
sescentésimo, six-hundredth
septengésimo, seven-hundredth
octogentésimo, eight-hundredth
nonagentésimo, nine-hundredth
milésimo, thousandth
dosmilésimo, two-thousandth
tresmilésimo, three-thousandth
millonésimo, millionth

See also Lesson LXVII.

APPENDIX H
IDIOMS AND TRANSLATION

Review Appendix B.

1. Idioms can not very well be classified, and so it is not practical to give rules for them. Idioms are learned best by noting individual cases in Spanish, and then practicing on them.

The exact use of idiom polishes translation and makes it natural.

The only rule of translation is: Translate (1) as closely as (2) idiomatic English permits (and vice-versa of course). (1) The English of the translation should be as rigorously close as the genius of either language permits. (2) The English translation should be English—**Not** English words in Spanish order or Spanish words in English order—but English words in English order; and so for the Spanish.

2. **Tiempo—hora—vez** give an obvious illustration. All are translated into English as **time**. But compare the three English sentences below.

(a) Art is long and time is fleeting. *Or*, I stayed a long **time**. Me quedé **mucho** tiempo.

(b) What **time** is it? ¿Qué **hora** es?

(c) I did it eight **times**. Lo hice ocho **veces**.

(a) is *time* in general, as men speak of "time and space." Spanish **tiempo**.

(b) is *time* specifically, measured by the clock, counted by the second, the minute, hour. Spanish **hora**.

(c) is *time* without reference to either of the above; it is time in the sense of *occasion*, single or multiple. I did it one **time**, on one occasion; I did it twenty **times**, on twenty occasions. Spanish **vez**.

To say (a) **Quedé mucha vez**, for **Quedé mucho tiempo**; or (b) **¿Qué tiempo es?** for **¿Qué hora es?**; or (c) **Lo hice ocho tiempos** or **horas** for **Lo hice ocho veces** would be meaningless or misleading. As well say in English: "What occasion is it?" for "What time is it?"

3. Compare the use of **gustar, acabar de, volver a, tener que, hay viento, ¡pobre de usted!, haber de, hay que,** the future of probability, the use of gender and mood—all these differ imperceptibly or markedly from the corresponding English.

4. Please!

sírvase (*plus the infinitive*) **Sírvase hacerlo,** Please do it.
tenga V. la bondad de (*plus the infinitive*) **Tenga V. la bondad de hacerlo,** Please do it.
hágame V. el favor de (*plus the infinitive*) **Hágame V. el favor de hacerlo,** Please do it.

Please = *Yes, please* is **Si me hace el favor.**

¿Quiere Ud. más agua?—Si me hace el favor, Do you want more water?—Yes, please.

5. If the student will take idioms at their face value, as something more or less different from the regular constructions, he will have no unusual trouble. The one thing is to remember that languages are different from each other, not merely in vocabulary, but in construction and expression. If the student will study structure and idiom rather than vocabulary, he will have little difficulty in giving smooth, natural translations; and ultimately, using a language without resort to translation at all.

LIST OF IRREGULAR VERBS

(Numbers and letters refer to lessons and subdivisions.)

acentuar, to accentuate 58
acordarse, to remember 39, 1(a); 52, 1
acostarse, to go to bed 39, 1(a); 52, 1
agradecer, to thank 58, (b)
almorzar, to lunch 39, 1(a); 52, 1; 58, (a)
alzar, to raise 58
andar, to go 68
aprobar, to approve 39, 1(a); 52, 1
argüir, to argue 68
asir, to grasp 76
avanzar, to advance 58, (a)
averiguar, to ascertain 51

bendecir, to bless 75
bullir, to boil 51
buscar, to look for 51, 1(a)

caber, to be contained in 70
caer, to fall 58, (c); 68
cerrar, to shut 39, 1(a); 52, 1
cocer, to cook 39, 1(a); 52, 1; 58, (b)
coger, to catch 51
comenzar, to commence 39, 1(a); 52, 1; 58, (a)
competir, to compete 39, 1(c); 52, 3
complacerse, to be pleased 76
conducir, to drive 58, (b)
confesar, to confess 39, 1(a); 52, 1
confiar, to confide App. E.
conjugar, to conjugate 51, 1(c)
conocer, to know 58
contar, to count 39, 1(a); 52, 1
continuar, to continue 58
convencer, to convince 58
convenir, to agree 74
costar, to cost 39, 1(a); 52, 1
creer, to believe 58, (c)
cubrir, to cover 65

dar, to give 72
decir, to say 74
deducir, to deduce 65

degollar, to behead 39, 1(a); 52, (*write* -güe- *where diphthon occurs*)
delinquir, to be delinquent 51
derretir, to melt 39, 1(c); 52, 3
desafiar, to challenge App. E.
desconfiar, to distrust App. E.
desosar, to bone 39, 1(a); 52, (*write* **deshueso,** *etc.*)
despedirse, to take leave 39, 1(c) 52, 3
despertar, to awaken 39, 1(a) 52, 1
detenerse, to halt 74
dirigirse, to go 51, 1(d)
distinguir, to distinguish 51
doler, to pain 39, 1(a); 52, 1
dormir, to sleep 39, 1(a); 52, 1

efectuar, to effect App. E.
elegir, to choose 39, 1(c); 52, 3 51, 1(d)
empezar, to begin 39, 1(a); 52, 1 58, (a)
encender, to kindle 39, 1(a); 52,
encerrar, to shut up 39, 1(a); 52,
encontrar, to meet 39, 1(a); 52,
enfriar, to grow cold 58
ennegrecer, to grow black 58, (b)
ennoblecer, to ennoble 58, (b)
entender, to understand 39, 1(a) 52, 1
entregar, to hand over 51
enviar, to send 58
equivocarse, to be mistaken 51 1(a)
erguir, to erect 39, 2 and 1(c) 51, 1(f)
errar, to err 39, 2
escribir, to write 65
esparcir, to scatter 58
espiar, to spy App. E.
estar, to be 68
exceptuar, to except App. E.
expiar, to expiate App. E.

fabricar, to manufacture 51
fiar, to trust App. E.
freír, to fry; *p.p.* frito 68

LIST OF IRREGULAR VERBS

guiar, to guide App. E.
gruñir, to grunt 51
guiar, to guide App. E.

haber, to have 70
habituar, to accustom App. E.
hacer, to do 74
holgarse, to loaf 39, 1(a); 52, 1; 51, 1(c)
huir, to flee 68

impedir, to prevent 39, 1(c); 52, 3
imprimir, to imprint 65
insinuar, to insinuate App. E.
ir, to go 70

jugar, to play 35; 39, 1(a); 52, 3; 51, 1(c)
juzgar, to judge 51, 1(c)

leer, to read 58

llegar, to arrive 51
llover, to rain 39, 1(a); 52, 1

menguar, to diminish 51, 1(e)
mentir, to lie 39, 1(b); 52, 2
merecer, to deserve 58, (b)
morder, to bite 39, 1(a); 52, 1
morir, to die 39, 1(b); 52, 2

nacer, to be born 58, (b)
negar, to deny 39, 1(a); 52, 1; 51, 1(c)
nevar, to snow 39, 1(a); 52, 1

oír, to hear 68
oler, to smell 39, 2
oponerse, to resist 71
oprimir, to oppress 65

parecer, to appear 58, (b)
pedir, to ask 39, 1(c); 52, 3
pensar, to think 39, 1(a); 52, 1
perder, to lose 39, 1(a); 52, 1
perpetuar, to perpetuate App. E.
placer, to please 76
poder, to be able 39, 1(a); 52, 1
poner, to put 74
porfiar, to persist App. E.
preferir, to prefer 39, 1(b); 52, 2

prender, to take 65
puntuar, to punctuate App. E.

querer, to wish 39, 1(a); 52, 1; 72

reír, to laugh 68
repetir, 39, 1(c); 52, 3
resfriar, to chill App. E.
rezar, to pray 58
roer, to gnaw 58
rogar, to ask 39, 1(a); 52, 1; 51, 1(c)
romper, to break 65, 2

saber, to know 70
sacar, to draw out 51
salir, to go out 66
seguir, to follow 39, 1(c); 52, 3; 51, 1(f)
sentarse, to sit down 39, 1(a); 52, 1
sentir, to feel 39, 1(b); 52, 2
ser, to be 70
servir, to serve 39, 1(c); 52, 3
situar, to situate App. E.
solver, to solve 39, 1(a); 52, 1; 65, 1
sonreír, to smile 68
suprimir, to suppress 65

telegrafiar, to telegraph 58
temblar, to tremble 39, 1(a); 52, 1
tener, to have 74
teñir, to stain 51
tocar, to touch 51, 1(a)
traer, to bring 66
tronar, to thunder 39, 1(a); 52, 1

vaciar, to empty 58
valer, to be worth 66
valuar, to evaluate App. E.
variar, to vary 58
vencer, to conquer 58
venir, to come 74
ver, to see 72
vestir, to clothe 39, 1(c); 52, 3
volver, to return 39, 1(a); 52, 1; 65

yacer, to lie 76

zambullirse, to dive 51, 2

VOCABULARY [1]

SPANISH—ENGLISH

A

a, to, at; (*conj. after verb of motion*), in order to 5; 50, 2 (b)

el abogado, lawyer 47

el abril, April 60

abrir, to open; *p. p.*, abierto 65

el abuelo, grandfather; **la abuela**, grandmother 71

aburrir, to bore, to weary, to tire 11

aburrirse, to be bored 48

acabar, to finish; acabar de . . , to have just (*see App. B*)

la acción, action; share (*of stock*) 71, A27

el aceite, oil (*used as food*) 71

acentuar, to accentuate 58; 71

acentúo, I stress, accent 3

el acero, steel 37

acompañar, to accompany, to go with 42

aconsejar, to advise 55

acontecer, to befall, to take place, to happen 72

acordar en (*R-ch. I*), to agree to 56

acordarse de (*R-ch. I*), to remind oneself of, to remember 48

(estar) acostado (*see* yacer) 76 B5

acostar (*R-ch. I*), to put to bed; (*reflexive*) to go to bed 35

acudir, to hasten, to come to 11

adelante (*adv.*), on, ahead 47

la aduana, customs, custom-house 71

afeitarse, to shave oneself 48

el afición, affection, fondness 75

a fin (de) que (*conj.*), in order that 53

agarrar, to grasp; to take (*a street car*) 76, B5

el agosto, August 60

agradar, to please; me agrada, it pleases me, I like it (*App. B*)

agradecer, to thank 69

(la) agua, water 2; 58

(la) águila, eagle 19

ahí (*adv.*), there 30

ahora (*adv.*), now 16

el aire, air; manner 71

¡ajá! (*interjec.*), aha! 3

ajeno, -a (*adj.*), strange, foreign, that of another 63

al (**a** *plus* **el**) *and infinitive* = on *and English present participle* 50

la aldea, village 73

alegrar, to please, rejoice; me alegra, it rejoices me, I like, I am glad of it (*App. B*); 55

alemán, -a (*adj.*), German 2

Alemania, Germany 15

al fin (*adv.*), finally 68

Alfonso, Alphonsus 59

alguno, -a (*adj. or pro.*), some; (*after noun*), none, no 19; 41

el alimento, food 76

al lado de (*prep.*), beside, at the side of 42

(la) alma, soul 19

¡ . . de mi alma! (*interjec.*), dear . . ! 69

almorzar (*R-ch. I*), to lunch 35

alojar, to lodge, to dwell 51

alumno, -a, pupil, student 5

alzar, to raise 58

allá veremos, we'll see about it (then) 74, B16

allí (*adv.*), there 11

---

[1] Numbers refer to lessons.

amable *(adj.)*, nice, amiable, kind 72
amar, to love 16
amarillo, -a *(adj.)*, yellow 41
a menudo *(adv.)*, frequently, often 48
a menos que *(conj.)*, unless 53
(la) América, America 4
americano, -a, American 14
amigo -a, friend 5
Ana, Anna 22
ancho, -a *(adj.)*, wide 41
andar, to go 57; 68
angosto, -a *(adj.)*, narrow 41
el animal, animal 51
anteayer *(adv.)*, day before yesterday 60
antes *(adv.)*, before 32
antes (de) que *(conj.)*, before 50
antiguo, -a *(adj.)*, ancient 25
antojarse; se le antoja, he fancies *(impersonal verb)* 49; 76
Apocalipsis, Apocalypse 60
el año, year 20
a pesar de que *(conj.)*, in spite of the fact that 53
aplicado, -a *(adj.)*, diligent, industrious 41
aprender, to learn 56
aprender, -a, to learn to 56
aprisa *(adv.)*, quickly 57
aprobar *(R-ch. I)*, to approve 55
la apuntación, note *(as, "to make a note of something")* 39
aquel, aquella; -os, -as, that; those *(adj.)*, 30
aquél, aquélla; -os, -as, that; those *(pro.)* 30
aquí *(adv.)*, here 11
el árbol, tree 64
la Argentina, Argentina 54
argüir, to argue 68
la aritmética, arithmetic 19
(la) arma, arm *(military term)* 51
arrimarse, to approach, to come (close) 63

el asco, disgust; asco me da, it disgusts me 72
asegurar, to assure
así *(adv.)*, so, and so 3
así que *(conj.)*, and so; so that 47
asir, to grasp, to seize 76
la asistencia, aid; presence, audience 73
asistir, to be present 64
la atención, attention 45
atlético, -a, athletic 3; 75
atrasar, to be behind; *(of a watch)*, to be slow 60
(la) aula, hall, lecture hall, auditorium 71
aun, even, still *(e. g., "that is still larger")* *(adv. of degree)*
aún, yet, as yet, still *(e. g., "he is still here")* *(adv. of time)* 3
aunque *(conj.)*, although 53
el automóvil, automobile 43
avanzar, to advance 60
averiguar, to ascertain 51
avisado, -a *(adj.)*, prudent, clever 72
ayer *(adv.)*, yesterday 11
ayudar, to aid, to help 67
el azahar, orange blossom 1
el azúcar, sugar 17
azul *(adj.)*, blue 3; 59

B

el baile, dance 73
bajar, to descend, to go down 31
bajo *(prep.)*, under 24
el bambú, bamboo 34
bañarse, to bathe oneself, to take a bath 48
barato, -a *(adj.)*, cheap, inexpensive 34
bastante *(adv. or adj.)*, enough 14
beber, to drink 10
bendecir, to bless 74
la bestia, beast 71
bien *(adv.)*, well 10, B7; 23

el billete de banco, bank note 37
blanco -a (*adj.*), white 6
el bolsillo, pocket 40
la bondad, kindness; tenga V. la
bondad de . . . , please . . .
(*App. H*)
bonito, -a (*adj.*), pretty 33
borrar, to erase, to efface 75
el brazo, arm 31
brillante (*adj.*), brilliant 39
brincar, to jump 51
bruñir, to polish 51
bueno, -a, good 10
Buenos Aires, Buenos Aires
(*capital of Argentina*) 59
el buey, ox 2
la buhardilla, small garret (*cf.*
buharda, garret window) 77
bullir, to boil 51
burlón, -a (*adj.*), humorous 33
buscar, to look for, to seek, to
fetch 12; 51

C

¡ca! (*interjec.*), not at all! 27
el caballo, horse 38
el cabello, hair; los cabellos, hair
(*singular collective noun in
English*) 31
caber, to be contained in, to
have room for 70
la cabeza, head 74
cada (*indecl. adj.*), each, every; cada uno *or* una (*pro.*),
each one, every one
caer, to fall 68
el café, coffee; café; (*pl.*) cafés
17; 34
Caín, Cain (*see Genesis in
Bible*)
el Cairo, Cairo (*city in Egypt*)
61
el calcetín, sock 16
caliente (*adj.*), hot 14
el calor, heat; tener (mucho)
calor, to be (very) warm
27; hace calor, it is warm
(*of weather*) 60
calzarse, to put on (shoes) 49
calladito, -a (*adj.*), very quiet
77

callado, -a (*adj.*), quiet 77
el Callao, Callao (*city in Peru*)
61
la calle, street 12
la cama, bed 1
cambiar, to change
el camino, way, road
la camisa, shirt 29
la campanilla, small bell (*cf.* la
campana, bell) 77
el campo, field; country; en el
campo, in the country (*as
opposed to the city*) 70
el Canadá, Canada 61
el canapé, couch 34
¡canastos! (*interjec.*), Gee
whiz! Good gracious! 69
cansado, -a (*adj.*), tired (*with
estar*) 15; tiring, annoying,
boring (*with ser*) 14
cantar, to sing 47
la cantidad, quantity, amount 65
la capital, capital (*of a country*)
59, AA3
el capitán, captain 14
el capítulo, chapter 67
la cara, face 8
Carlos, Charles 67
la carne, meat 17
caro, -a (*adj.*), dear, expensive 54
el carpintero, carpenter 59
la carta, letter 40
la carrera, circuit; race, trip 38
el carro, (street) car, trolley car
(*see* tranvía) 31
la casa, house 10
el caserón, big (*ill-proportioned*)
house 77
castaño, -a (*adj.*), chestnut-colored 31
el castellano, Castilian 61
castellano, -a (*adj.*), Castilian,
Spanish (*of the peninsula
Spain*) 61
la casucha, ugly old house 77
la cebolla, onion 39, BB5
el centavo, cent 74
la centinela, sentinel 33
el centro, center; el Centro, the

center of town, down town 59
cerca de (*prep.*), near 30
el cero, zero 67
cerquísima (*adv.*), very near 76
cerquita (*adv.*), quite close 77
cerrar (*R-ch. I*), to close, to lock, to shut 35
el cielo, sky, heaven 13
cierto, -a (*adj.*), certain, sure; (*for meaning before or after noun, see 33*)
el cilindro, cylinder 1
el cirio, wax candle 73
la ciudad, city 23
la clase, class; kind, sort 41
la cobardía, cowardice, act of cowardice 50
cocer (*R-ch. I*), to cook, to boil 58
cocinar, to cook 8
el coche, coach, carriage 38
coger, to catch, to seize, to take (g *to* j *before* a *or* o) 51
comenzar (*R-ch. I*), to begin 56
comer, to eat 10
el cometa, comet 33
la comida, meal, dinner 8
como (*conj.*), as; how 23
¿cómo? (*conj.*), how? 18
competir (*R-ch. III*), to compete 36
complacerse (en), to be pleased with 76
completo, -a (*adj.*), complete, perfect 39
comprar, to buy, to purchase 8
con (*prep.*), with 5
conducir, to lead; to drive (*as an auto*) 43
confesar (*R-ch. I*), to confess, to admit 35
la confianza, confidence
conjugar, to conjugate 16
conmigo, with me 42
conocer, to know, to be acquainted with, to be familiar with, to meet 58
considerar, to consider 32
consistir en, to consist of 56
constar (*impersonal*), to be clear, to be evident 76
contar (*R-ch. I*), to count; to relate, to recount 35
contentarse con, to be satisfied with 56
contento, -a (*adj.*), contented, glad, happy 7
contestar, to answer, to reply 36
contigo, with you, with thee 42
continuar, to continue 58
convencer, to convince 58
convencerse, to convince oneself, to be convinced 48
convenir, to agree; (*3rd sing. as impersonal*), it suits 74
copiar, to copy 66
el cortaplumas, penknife 34
cortar, to cut
corto, -a (*adj.*), short 61
correr, to run 42
la cosa, thing 10
costar (*R-ch. I*), to cost 39
Cousiño, Cousiño (*surname*) 2
creer, to believe; to think (*as,* "I think so") 23
cruel (*adj.*), cruel 71
crujir, to creak 51
el cuaderno, notebook 39
cuadrado, -a (*adj.*), square 33
cual (*rel. adj. or pro.*), which, what 24
¿cuál? (*inter. pro. or adj.*), which? what? 18
cuando (*conj.*), when
¿cuándo? when 18
cuanto, -a; -os, -as (*rel. adj. or pro.*), how much; how many; as much (many) as 23; 24
cuanto *or* mientras más . . . (tanto) más, the more . . . the more, 23
¿cuánto, -a; -os, -as? (*inter.*

SPANISH—ENGLISH VOCABULARY

adj. or pro.), how much? how many? 18

¿A cuántos estamos del mes? What day of the month is it? 60

el cuarto, fourth; quarter (*in telling time*) 60

el cuarto, room 49

cubrir, to cover; cubierto (*irreg. past. part.*), covered 65

la cuchara, spoon 18

la cucharita, spoon, teaspoon 18

el cuchillo, knife 18

el cuello, collar 29

el cuento, story; account 19

el cuidado, care; tener cuidado, to be careful, to take care; ¡Cuidado que . . . ! Look out that. . . . ! 68

cumplir (con), to fulfil, to complete 32

el cuociente, quotient 71

el cura, priest 1

cursi (*adj.*), cheap 34

cuyo, -a; -os, -as (*pos. adj. or pro.*), whose 24; ¿cúyo, -a; -os, -as? (*int.*) 18

CH

la chaqueta, jacket 29

chico, -a (*adj.*), little, small 33

el chubasco, squall 2

D

da, (he, she, it) gives 38

dado que (*conj.*), considering 53

dan, (they) give 38

dar, to give 16; 72

dar a la calle, to face the street 72

dar con, to come across 72

dar las dos (*etc.*), to strike two (o'clock) 72

dar las gracias, to thank 72

darse por, to act as if 72

darse por entendido, to appear to understand 72, B21

de (*prep.*), of, from; (*conj.*), than 5; 23

deber, ought, must; to owe 35

el deber, duty 32

decidirse (por), to decide (oneself), to make up one's mind 48; (*with verb*),——a

decir, to say, to tell 40; 74

el dedo, finger 31

deducir, to deduce 65

degollar (*R-ch. I*), to behead (List of Irreg. Verbs)

dejar, to let, to allow, to permit 62 (*transitive only*)

dejar de, to leave off (*doing a thing*); dejó de escribir, he stopped writing, he left off writing 50

delinquir, to be delinquent 51

de manera de (*or*) que (*conj.*), so that 50; 53

demasiado (*adv.*), too (*as*, too much) 46

de modo de (*or*) que (*conj.*), so that 53

de ninguna manera (*adv.*), in no way 41

un dentista, dentist 33

dentro de (*prep.*), within 40

el dependiente, clerk 43

derecho, -a (*adj.*), right; straight 31

el derecho, law 47

derretir (*R-ch. III*), to melt 36

desayunarse, to breakfast, to have breakfast 49

el desayuno, breakfast 50

descansar, to rest 56

descubridor, -a (*adj. or noun*), discoverer 2

desde (*prep.*), since; desde que (*conj.*), for (*Sp. present = Engl. perf.*) 64

desear, to desire, to want 15

desnudar(se), to undress (oneself), 49

desosar (*R-ch. I*), to bone (List of Irreg. Verbs)

despacio, -a (*adj.*), slow, leisurely 23

despacio (*adv.*), slowly 23
despedir (*R-ch. III*), to dismiss; (*refl.*), to take leave 36; 52
despertar (*R-ch. I*), to wake up (*transitive*); **despertarse**, to awaken, to wake up (*intransitive*) 49
después (*adv.*), after, afterwards 28
después de (*prep. of time*), after 25
después (de) que (*conj.*), after 50
detenerse, to stop, to halt (*intransitive*) 74
detenidamente (*adv.*), carefully 41
detrás de (*prep.*), behind 32
la **deuda**, debt 71
el **día**, day; **día hábil** (*or* **útil**), work day 33; 60
el **diablo**, devil; ¡**diablo**! the deuce! ¡**mil diablos**! the deuce! 69
el **diario**, newspaper 70
dice, (he, she, it) says, tells 24
dicen, (they) say, tell 24
el **diciembre**, December 60
el **diente**, tooth 8
dieron, (they) gave 36
difícil (*adj.*), difficult 10
la **dificultad**, difficulty 38
dijeron, (they) told, said 8, BB14
dijimos, we said
dijo, (he, she, it) said, told 3; 24
diligente (*adj.*), diligent, industrious 7
el **dinero**, money 19
dió, (he, she, it) gave; you gave 36
el **Dios**, God 27
¡**Dios mío**! (*interjec.*), Good heavens! 69
diré, dirás, *etc.*, I shall tell, you will tell, *etc.* 42

dirigirse, to make one's way (*toward*), to go 48
distinguir, to distinguish 51
dividir, to divide 67
el **dólar**, dollar 4
doler (*R-ch. I*), to pain, to ache; **le duele la cabeza**, he has a headache 74
el **domingo**, Sunday 34
don, Mr., master 20
donde (*conj.*), where 24
en donde (*conj.*), where, in which 73
¿**dónde**? (*int. conj.*), where? 21, B4
doña, Mrs., mistress, Miss 20
dormir (*R-ch. I*), to sleep 35
el **dormitorio**, bedroom 19
dos, two 2
la **duda**, doubt 70
dudar, to doubt 43
duele, it hurts; it grieves; **me duele este pie**, this foot hurts me 31
dulce (*adj.*), sweet; fair, gentle 61
durante (*prep.*), during 43
el **duro**, dollar (*coin used in Spain*) 1

E

e = **y**, and 64
¡**ea**! (*interjec.*), hi! hurray! 69
echar a, to begin to 56
echar de, to manage to 56
el **ejercicio**, exercise; practise 15
el, the (*def. art., masc. sing.*) 4
él (*disj. pro.*), him, (to) him 42; (*sub. pro.*), he 13
el (la) cual; los (las) cuales, (*rel. pro.*), who, whom 25
eléctrico, -a (*adj.*), electrical 30
elegir (*R-ch. III*), to elect, to choose 75
Elena, Helen 12
el mío (*pos. pro.*), mine; **el nuestro**, ours 40
el (la; los, las) que (*pers. pro.*), who, whom 25

el suyo (*pos. pro.*), his, hers, its; yours (*polite*), theirs 40
el tuyo (*pos. pro.*), yours; thine 40
(el) uno ... (el) otro, the one ... the other; each other; (*plural*), some ... others; one ... another 48
el vuestro (*pos. pro.*), yours 40
ella (*pers. and disj. pro.*), she; her, to her 13; 42
ellos, ellas (*pers. pro., disj. pro.*), they; them; to them 13; 42
embestir, to attack, to assail 73
embustero, -a (*adj. or noun*), cheat 69
empezar (*R-ch. I*), to begin 56
el empleado, clerk, employee 25
emplear, to employ, to use 76
en (*prep.*), in, on; **en su reloj**, by your watch 4; 60, B11
en casa (de) (*adv. or prep.*), at the house (of), at home 38
en caso (de) que (*conj.*), in case 53
encender (*R-ch. I*), to light, to kindle 35
encerrar (*R-ch. I*), to shut in, to lock up 35
encontrar (*R-ch. I*), to meet, to find, to come across 31
enemigo, -a (*adj. or noun*), enemy 16
el enero, January 60
enfermo, -a (*adj.*), sick, ill, sore 31
enfriar, to chill, to make cold 58
en lata (*adj.*), canned, tinned 41
ennegrecer, to blacken, to obscure 73
ennoblecer, to ennoble, to embellish 73
enorme (*adj.*), enormous 33
Enrique, Henry 12

en seguida (*adv.*), then, next, at once, immediately 43
enseñar, to show, to teach, to point out 24
entender (*R-ch. I*), to understand, to hear 35
entonces (*adv.*), then 33
entrar (en), to enter, to go into (*intransitive verb*) (*App. B*)
entregar, to hand over, to give (over) 51
el entresuelo, ground floor 19
el entusiasmo, enthusiasm 41
en vez de (*prep.*), instead of 45
enviar, to send 58
equivocarse, to be mistaken 52
erguir (*R-ch. II or III*), to erect (*see List of irreg. verbs*)
errar (*R-ch. I*), to err; to wander 39
es, (he, she, it) is; you (*polite*) are 6
escaparse, to escape, to run off 48
escocés, -a (*adj.*), Scotch(man) 33
escribir, to write 11
escrito (*irreg. past. part.*), written 16; 65
el escritorio, writing desk 70
la escuela, school 23
ese, esa; esos, esas (*adj.*), that; those 30
ése, ésa; ésos, ésas (*pro.*), that; those 30
(la) España, Spain 15
español, -a (*adj.*), Spanish 14
esparcir, to scatter 58
la especie, kind, sort, species, class 41
el espejo, mirror, looking-glass 48
esperar, to wait for, to hope
espía, spy 33
esposo, -a, spouse; husband; wife

la esquina, corner (*of a street*) 19
el estadista, statesman 16
(los) Estados Unidos, the United States 15
el estante, bookshelf, set of shelves 70
estar, to be (*see also* ser) 15; 68
estar para, to be about to 56
estar por, to be inclined to, to feel like 56
este, -a; -os, -as (*demonstr. adj.*), this; these 30
éste, -a; -os, -as (*demonstr. pro.*), this (one); these 30
el estudiante, student (*in college*) 30
estudiar, to study 13
estúpido, -a (*adj.*), stupid 69
etcétera, et cetera, and so forth 49
europeo, -a (*adj., noun*) European 64
el examen, examination 39
examinar, to examine 41
excelente (*adj.*), excellent 64
excepto (*prep.*), except 73
eximio, -a (*adj.*), eminent; famous 73
existir, to exist 24
el éxito, favorable result, outcome 39

F

fabricar, to manufacture; fabricarse, to be manufactured 49
fácil (*adj.*), easy 5
faltar, to be lacking; (*also used in expressions of time*; faltan cinco minutos para las ocho, it is five minutes of eight) 60
farmacéutico, -a (*adj.*), pharmaceutical 71
el favor, favor; hágame V. el favor de, please (*lit.*, do me the favor to . . .)
si me hace el favor, please (yes, please) (*App. H*)
el febrero, February 60
felicitarse, to congratulate oneself 48
feliz (*adj.*), happy, lucky 7
felizmente (*adv.*), happily 57
Fernández, Fernández (*surname*)
figurarse, to fancy, to imagine 49
fijarse en, to notice carefully 56
filosofar, to philosophize 57
el filósofo, philosopher 73
a fines de (*prep.*), at the end of (*a month*) 60
Finita, little Serafina 77
flaco, -a (*adj.*), thin, lean 8
flojo, -a (*adj.*), lazy 31
flúido, -a (*adj.*), fluent, liquid 71
el frac, (dress) coat 1
francés, -a (*adj.*), French 14
(la) Francia, France 15
freír, to fry; (*past part.*) frito 68
fresco, -a (*adj.*), fresh 15
frío, -a (*adj.*), cold 14
el frío, cold 27
fuerte (*adj.*), strong
la fuerza, strength; las fuerzas, strength, force (*singular noun in Eng.*)

G

Gabriel, Gabriel 12
ganadero, -a (*adj.*), herding, stock-raising 59
ganar, to gain, to earn 26
(las) ganas, desire(s); tener ganas de, to feel like 56
garboso, -a (*adj.*), graceful, elegant 1
gastar, to spend 74
el general, general 1
generalmente (*adv.*), generally 14
el genio, genius, character, temper

el giro, (bank) draft 1
la gloria, glory; (*also*) Gloria, Gloria (*a girl's name*) 71
Gómez, Gómez (*surname*) 64, B3
González, González (*surname*) 2
gordo, -a (*adj.*), stout 54
gracias (*adv.*), thanks 72
grande (*adj.*), large, big 6; 22
gritar, to shout, to call out 54
gruñir, to grunt 51
guardarse de ... , to refrain from ... 56
la guerra, war 1
el } guía, guide 33
la
guiar, to guide 58
Guillermo, William 69
guisar, to cook 1
gustar, to please; me gusta, it pleases me, I like (*App. B*)
el gusto, taste 49
Gutiérrez, Gutiérrez (*surname*)

H

haber, to have (*auxiliary for perfect tenses—cf. also* tener. *For idioms, see*) 28; 70
ha de, he is to ... 29
hay que, ought to ... ; you should ... 29
hábil (*adj.*), clever, skilful, apt
día hábil, work day 60
el } habitante, inhabitant 22
la
hablador, -a (*adj.*), talkative, garrulous 33
hablar, to speak, to talk 4
hace (he, she, it) makes, does 38; it is (*in expressions of weather*) 60; (*Sp. present for Eng. perfect*) 64
hacer, to do, to make 74
hacer saber, to let know, to inform 57, AA15
hacerse, to become, to make oneself 59; 74
hacia (*prep.*), towards 42

hacía, (he, she, it) was making, made; (*Sp. imp. for Eng. pluperf.*) 64
la hacienda, country estate 64
(la) hacha, axe (*for* el hacha) 19
hallar, to find 4
(la) hambre, hunger; **tener hambre**, to be hungry 27
haragán, -a (*adj.*), lazy 33
haré, harás, *etc.*, I shall do, you will do, *etc.* 42
hasta (*adv.*), as much as; (*conj.*), until 22, B7
hasta que (*conj.*), until 53
hasta luego (*adv.*), good-by, "so-long"; **hasta lueguito** (*adv.*), good-by, "so-long" 77
hay, there is, there are (*for other tenses, see* 28); (*for expressions of weather, see* 28, 4)
no hay remedio, there is no help for it 74
el helado, ice cream 39
el hermano, brother 6
hermoso, -a (*adj.*), beautiful, handsome 54
el hielo, ice 14
el hierro, iron 37
hinchado, -a (*adj.*), swollen 2
la hipótesis, hypothesis 34
hizo, (he, she, it) made, did 54
la hoja, leaf, page 39
holgarse (*R-ch. I*), to loaf, to have a good time 48
el hombre, man 9
el hombro, shoulder 40
la hora, hour; time; ¿Qué hora es? what time is it? 60
hoy (*adv.*), today 4
el hueso, bone 39
el huevo, egg 17
huir, to flee 68
el huracán, hurricane 2

I

igualmente (*adv.*), equally
imaginarse, to imagine, to

fancy (*also used impersonally*) 49
impedir (*R-ch. III*), to hinder, to prevent 36
importa, it matters, it is important 56
imposible (*adj.*), impossible; es — que (*takes subjunctive*) 43
imprimir, to imprint, to print; (*irreg. past part.*) impreso 65
indiferente (*adj.*), indifferent 41
indio, -a (*adj.*), Indian 64
la industria, industry, business 59
infeliz (*adj.*), unhappy; unlucky 29
¡infeliz de usted! unhappy you! woe to you! (*App. H, 3*)
el ingeniero, engineer 59
(la) Inglaterra, England 15
inglés, -a (*adj.*), English 14
innoble (*adj.*), ignoble 73
insistir (en), to insist (on) 56
el instinto, instinct 64
inteligente (*adj.*), intelligent 76
inteligentísimo, -a (*adj.*), intelligent, most (extremely) intelligent 76
interesante (*adj.*), interesting 38
intitularse, to be called, to have as title 54
el invierno, winter 60
ir, to go 56; 70
irlandés, -a (*adj. or noun*), Irish 75
irse, to go off, to go away 49
Isabel, Elizabeth 20
-ísimo, -a (*superlative absolute ending*) very, most, extremely 76
la isla, island 75
israelita (*adj. or noun*), Israelite 75
izquierdo, -a (*adj.*), left 31

J

el jabalí, wild boar
el jaguar, jaguar 1
jamás (*adv.*), never 41
el jamón, ham 19
el jefe, chief, leader, head 67
Jesús, Jesus; ¡Jesús mil veces! (*interjec.*), Good gracious! 69
el jinete, horseman
Jorge, George 59
José, Joseph; ¡Jesús, José, y María! (*interjec.*), Gracious! 69
la jota, jota (*name of the letter* j) 1
joven (*adj. or noun*), youth; young boy (girl) 35
Juan, John 12
Juana, Jane 77
Juanita, little (*or* dear) Jane 77
el jueves, Thursday 34
el juez, judge; (*pl.*) jueces 65
jugar (*R-ch. I*), to play 35
el juicio, judgment; sense, reason, opinion 71
el julio, July 60
el junio, June 60
juntos, -as (*adj.*), together 45
juzgar, to judge, to think, to consider 32

K

el kilómetro, kilometer 73
el kiosco (*also* quiosco), kiosk, news stand 73

L

el lado, side 42; al lado de (*prep.*), beside; a mi lado, beside me 42
la mía, mine 40
la nuestra, ours 40
el lápiz, pencil 5
largo, -a (*adj.*), long 33
las (*def. art. fem. plural*) 9
la lástima, pity; es lástima,

SPANISH—ENGLISH VOCABULARY

(*with subjunctive*), it is a pity 46
la suya, his, hers, its; yours (*polite*); theirs 40
latino, -a (*adj.*), Latin 61; el latín, (*the language*)
la tuya, yours, thine 40
lavar, to wash 16
la vuestra (*pro.*), yours 40
la lección, lesson 6
la leche, milk 17
leer, to read 58
lejos (*adv.*), far 48
levantar, to lift; (*refl.*), to get up 49
la ley, law 34
el libro, book 6
el liceo, high school 45
ligero, -a (*adj.*), swift, light, rapid 38
limpiar, to clean 8; 58
limpio, -a, (*adj.*), clean 15
lingüístico, -a (*adj.*), linguistic 71
listo, -a (*adj.*), ready 32
lo (*neuter adj. as adv.*), how 29, 2
el loro, parrot 2
los (*def. art., masc. pl.*), the 9
luchar (por), to struggle (to) 56; to wrestle 64
luego que (*conj.*), as soon as, when 53
Luis, Louis 67
Luisito, little Louis 77
el lunes, Monday 34
la luz, light; candle 30

LL

la llave, key 70
llegar (a), to arrive, to reach (*intransitive*) 32; 51
lleno, -a (*adj.*), full 15
llevar, to carry; (*refl.*), to carry off 49
llorar, to weep, to cry 27
llover (*R-ch. I*), to rain 35
la lluvia, rain; hay lluvia, it is rainy 60

M

la madera, wood 70
la madre, mother 6
madrileño, -a (*adj.*), (inhabitant) of Madrid 25
el maestro, (primary) school teacher 63
el maíz, maize, corn 3; 71
mal (*adv.*), badly 23
malamente (*adv.*), badly 57
maldecir, to curse 74
malo, -a (*adj.*), bad; ill, sick 14; 15
la mamá, mother, mamma 34
mandar, to order, to command, to send 44
la mano, hand 33
la mantequilla, butter 17
la manzana, apple 67
mañana (*adv.*), tomorrow; (*as noun, feminine*), morning 11
el maravedí, farthing; (*pl.*) maravedíes; *also*, maravedís, maravedises 34
marchar, to walk; (*refl.*), to go off 54
María, Mary 12; ¡Jesús, José, y María! Good gracious! 69
el martes, Thursday 34
el marzo, March 60
más (*adv.*), more 14; plus 67
las matemáticas, mathematics 73
el mayo, May 60
mayor (*adj.*), older 23; 33
me, me; myself; to me 21; 38; 48
la media, stocking 16
a mediados de (*prep.*), in the middle of (*a month*) 60
la medicina, medicine 47
el médico, doctor 47
la medida, measure, means 1
medio, -a (*adj.*), half (*see also* la mitad*) 60; 67
la mejilla, cheek 2
mejor (*adj.*), better 23
menester; es menester, it is necessary 51

menguar, to diminish (*see* **averiguar**)
menor (*adj.*), younger 23
menos (*adv.*), less 23; **por lo menos** (*adv.*), at least 72
mentir (*R-ch. II*), to lie, to tell a falsehood 35
merecer, to deserve (*see* **conocer**)
el **mes**, month 60
la **mesa**, table 7
meter, to put 40
mí (*disj. pro.*), me, to me; myself 42; 48
mi(s) (*pos. adj.*), my 17
el **miedo**, fear; **tener miedo**, to be afraid 27
mientras (*conj.*), while 64
el **miércoles**, Wednesday 34
la **mies**, grains; (*pl.*) **mieses** 34
mío, -a (*adj.*), my, mine 40
¡**mire**! see here! listen here! 69
mirar, to look (at) 50
mismo, -a (*adj.*), same; very, -self 24
la **mitad**, half (*see also* **medio**) 67
moderno, -a (*adj.*), modern 25
el **momento**, moment 40
la **Moneda**, the Mint; **Calle de la Moneda**, Treasury (Mint) Street 13
la **montaña**, mountain 25
morder (*R-ch. I*), to bite 39
moreno, -a (*adj.*), dark, brunette 14
morir (*R-ch. II*), to die 35; (*p.p. irreg.*) **muerto**, dead; killed (*trans.*) 65
mortal (*adj.*), mortal 61
la **mosca**, fly 24
el **mozo**, boy; servant, waiter 6; la **moza**, girl 6
el **muchacho**, boy; la **muchacha**, girl 8
mucho, -a; -os, -as (*adj. or pro.*) much; many 10

mucho (*adv.*), much, a great deal 10
la **mujer**, woman 5
la **mujercilla**, little, insignificant woman 77
el **mundo**, world; **todo el mundo**, everybody 54
mutuamente (*adv.*), mutually, each other, one another 48
muy (*adv.*), very 10

N

nacer, to be born; **nació**, (he, she) was born 59
la **nación**, nation 12
nada (*pro.*), nothing; (*adv.*), not at all 41
nadar, to swim 64
nadie (*pro.*), nobody 41
la **naranja**, orange 67, BB10
la **neblina**, mist, fog; **hay mucha neblina**, it is very misty 28
necesario, -a (*adj.*), necessary; **es necesario** (*takes subjunct.*) 43
necesitar, to need 56
negarse (*R-ch. I*), to refuse 56
el **negociante**, business man 47
los **negocios**, business
negro, -a (*adj.*), black 6
nevar (*R-ch. I*), to snow 35
ni (*conj.*), nor; **ni ... ni**, neither ... nor 7; 41
ni por mucho, not by a good deal 25
la **nieve**, snow 33
ninguno, -a (*adj. or pro.*), no, none, no one 19
la **niña**, girl 6
la **niñita**, little girl 77
el **niño**, boy 6
los **niños**, children 9
no (*adv.*), no; not 8; 41
¿**no**? isn't it true? isn't that so? won't he? didn't they? aren't you? *etc.* 35
no solamente ... sino que, not only ... but also 50
esta noche (*adv.*), tonight 46

¿no es verdad? (see ¿no? above) 35
no hay por qué, there is no reason for
no ... más (adv.), no more, no longer 41
no ... más que, only 23
(la) Norte América, North America; (also) América del Norte 68
no sea que (conj.), unless 53
nosotros, -as (pers. pro.), we; us 13; 42
la nota, mark (in school work) 39
las noticias, news 40
el noviembre, November 60
nuestro, -a (adj.), our, ours 40
(la) Nueva York, New York 59, B5
nuevamente (adv.), newly 57
nuevo, -a (adj.), new 57
nunca (adv.), never 41

O

o (conj.), or 7
el occidente, occident, west 1
el octubre, October 60
ocupado, -a (adj.), busy 48
ocuparse de, to busy oneself with, to bother about 48
¡oiga! (¡oye!), (interjec.), listen! see here! 69
oír, to hear 57; 68
el ojo, eye 59
oler (R-ch. I), to smell 39
olvidarse (de), to forget; se me olvida (impersonal), I forget 49
oponerse (a), to refuse, to oppose 56
oprimir, to oppress 65
ordinario, -a (adj.), ordinary, common, average 64
el otoño, autumn 60
otro, -a (adj. or pro.), other, another 13

P

el padre, father 6
pagar, to pay 51
la página, page 58
el país, country (nation) 61, B11
la paja, straw 33
la palabra, word, speech 16
el pan, bread; loaf 17
el paño, cloth 41
el papá, father, "dad"; (pl.), papás 34
el papacito, dear father 77
el papel, paper (in general; not a newspaper) 2
el papel secante, blotting paper 70
para (prep.) for; (conj.), in order to 5; 50
el Paraguay, Paraguay (country in South America) 61
parece, it seems; me parece, it seems to me; I think 30
la pared, wall
París, Paris 24, BB8
la parte, part 67
partir, to leave (intransitive), to depart 47
pasado (past. part. as adj.), past, last; el mes próximo pasado, last month; pasado mañana, day after tomorrow 60
pasar, to pass, to go; to happen 25
pasearse, to take a walk 66
la paz, peace 57
pedir (R-ch. III), to ask (a favor; dative of person, accusative of thing) 36
pedir prestado, to borrow 47
peinarse, to comb oneself 48
la pelota, ball 74
el pensamiento, thought; (a) thought 64
pensar (R-ch. I), to think; to intend 56; 65
pensar en, to think of (one's attention is centered on) 64

pensar de, to think of (*have an opinion of*) 64
peor (*adv.*), worse 23
pequeño, -a (*adj.*), small, little 5
perder (*R-ch. I*), to lose; to ruin 35; 56, A18
perezoso, -a (*adj.*), lazy, idle 7
permitir, to permit, to allow 55
pero (*conj.*), but 1
la persona, person 59
el Perú, Peru (*country in South America*) 61
el perro, dog 1
el pescado, fish (*out of water*) 41
el peso, dollar, peso (*South American coin; see also* **duro** *and* **peseta**); weight 20
el petróleo, kerosene 30
el pez, fish (*in water, not caught*) 41
el piano, piano 6
el pie, foot 19
la piedra, stone 68
la pieza, room 12
la pimienta, pepper 24
pintoresco, -a (*adj.*), picturesque 38
el piso, floor, story (*of a house*) 13; 19
el piso bajo *or* **los bajos,** ground floor (*of a two-story house*); **el piso alto** *or* **los altos,** upper floor (*of a two-story house*) 13
piso principal, main floor, second floor (*of a house of several stories*) 19
la pizarra, slate, blackboard 5
placer, to please 76
el planeta, planet 33
el plato, plate, dish, course 18
la playa, beach, shore 43
la pluma, pen; **plumafuente,** fountain pen 5
pobre, poor; ¡**pobre de él!** poor fellow! 14; 29
poco, -a; -os, -as (*adj.*), little; few 23

poco (*adv.*), little, but little 23
poder (*R-ch. I*), to be able, can 35
no poder más, to be exhausted 72
a más no poder, with all one's might 72
no poder menos de . . . , can't help (doing) 68
el poema, poem 33
la poesía, poem; poetry 54, B11
poner, to put; (*refl.*), to put on (*clothes*) 49; **ponerse,** to become; **ponerse a,** to set about, to begin to 56
poquísimo, -a (*adj.*), very little 76, A14
por, for, on account of, by, in exchange for, through, around 4; 68, BB14
por . . . que (*subjunct.*), however 53
por consiguiente (*adv.*), consequently 13
¡**Por Dios!** (*interjec.*), for Heaven's sake! 27
por lo común (*adv.*), generally 46
¿**por qué?** (*int. conj.*), why? 18
porque (*rel. conj.*), because 50
posible (*adj.*), possible; **es posible** (*subjunct.*), it is possible 43
postrero, -a (*adj.*), last (*of a series; see* **último**) 19
el precio, price 14
preciso; es preciso, it is necessary (*subjunct.*), 43
preferir (*R-ch. II*), to prefer 55
la pregunta, question 52
preguntar, to ask (*a question*) 24
prender, to catch; (*past. part.*) **preso, prendido** 65
preocuparse de, to be preoccupied with; to occupy oneself with 48
preparar, to prepare 8

presentar, to introduce, to present 42
el presidente; la presidenta, president 33
el preso, captive (*see* prender) 65
prestar, to lend, to pay (*with such words as* atención, attention) 45
la primavera, spring 60
primero, -a (*adj. or pro.*), first 19
el primo; la prima, cousin 6
principal (*adj.*), chief; piso principal, main floor, second floor 19
principiar (a), to begin (to) 56
a principios de (*prep.*), at the beginning of (*a month*) 60
la prisa, haste; tener prisa, to be in a hurry 72
probablemente (*adv.*), probably 32
el profesor, la profesora, teacher, professor 39
el programa, program 33
prohibir, forbid (*subjunct.*), 55
pronto (*adv.*), soon, quickly, at once, immediately 52
propio, -a (*adj.*), own 52
próximo, -a (*adj.*), next; near, nearest 60
la puerta, door 13
pues (*conj.*), for; (*adv.*), well 48
puesto (*adj.*), on, put on (*of clothes*) 59
puro, -a (*adj.*), pure; la pura verdad, the mere truth 56

Q

que (*conj.*), that, than 23; 30, 3
que (*expletive*) 69
que- (*prefix*) very (retequebueno) 76
que (*rel. pro.*), which, that, who, whom 10; 24
¿qué? (*int. pro.*), what? which? who? whom? 18

el quebrado, fraction 67
quedar, to remain, to stay 15
querer (*R-ch. I*), to wish; querer a, to love, to like (*a person*) 35
querer decir, to wish to say, to mean 72
como V. quiera, as you wish, as you like 72
querido, -a (*past. part. as adj.*), dear, beloved 72
¡quia! (*adv.*), not at all! (*see* ¡ca!) 27
¿quién? (*int. pro.*), who? whom? 18
¡Quién supiera . . . ! If I could only . . . ! 54
quien (*rel. pro.*), who, whom; he who, whoever 24; 25
quinto, fifth 67
quisiera, I should wish, I should like, I wish 44
quitar, to take away, to deprive of 47

R

rajar, to split, to cleave 51
rápidamente (*adv.*), rapidly, swiftly 38
raro, -a (*adj.*), rare, unusual 41
el rato, while 74
re- (*emphatic prefix*), very; rebueno, very good 76
recibir, to receive; to be passed (*in a class*) 39
recorrer, to traverse, to go over 56
redondo, -a (*adj.*), round 33
reducir, to reduce 58
reír, to laugh 68
reírse (de), to laugh at, to make fun of 48
el reloj, the watch, clock 12
el remedio, remedy, aid; no hay remedio, there is no help for it 74
repetir (*R-ch. III*), to repeat 36

el resfriado, cold (*a sickness*) 74
respectado, -a (*adj.*), respected 64
el rey, king 34
rezar, to pray 51
rico, -a (*adj.*), rich, excellent, sumptuous 14
ríen, they; you (*polite*) laugh 48
el rincón, corner (*inner corner*) 19
robar, to rob, to steal 47
roer, to gnaw; *see* leer, 58
rogar (*R-ch. I*), to beg, to ask, to request 51
rojo, -a (*adj.*), red 11
romper, to break; (*past part.*), roto 52; (*also*) rompido 65
ronco, -a (*adj.*), hoarse 33
la rosa, rose 73
el rubí, ruby 34
rubio, -a (*adj.*), blond, light 14

S

el sábado, Saturday 34
sabe a, it tastes of 64
saber, to know; to know how 46; 70
sacar, to pull out; to draw out 51
salir, to go out 11
la salud, health; ¡salud! your health! Greetings! 6
estar bueno (malo) de salud, to be in good (bad) health 43
salvarse, to save oneself, to run away 48
el santo, saint; holy 22
la sardina, sardine 41
el sastre, tailor 14
satisfactorio, -a (*adj.*), satisfactory 22
satisfecho, -a (*past. part. as adj.*), satisfied 10
se (*pers. pro.*), (to) himself, herself; yourself (*formal*); to him, to her; to you (*formal*) 38; 42; 48

la sed, thirst; tener sed, to be thirsty 17
la seda, silk 41
seguir (*R-ch. III*), to continue, to go on 57
según (*prep.*), according to 42
seguramente (*adv.*), surely, certainly 68
seguro, -a (*adj.*), sure, certain 49
la semana, week 34
el sendero, path 25
sentar (*R-ch. I*), to seat; (*refl.*) to sit down 35
sentir (*R-ch. II*), to feel; to be sorry 35
el señor, gentleman; sir; Mr. 13
la señora, lady; madam; Mrs. 13
la señorita, young lady; Miss 13
el septiembre, September (*also* setiembre) 60
ser, to be (*see also* estar) 14; 70
yo soy, *etc.*, it is I, *etc.* 18, BB1
Serafina, Serafina (*girl's name*) 77
servir (*R-ch. III*), to serve; to be good for; sírvase, please 36; (*App. H*)
sevillano, -a (*adj.*), (native) of Seville 25
si (*conj.*), if, whether 45
sí (*adv.*), yes 11; 30
sí (*disj. pro.*), himself, themselves; yourself, yourselves (*formal*) 48
siempre (*adv.*), always 64
siempre que (*conj.*), provided that 53
siguiente (*adj.*), following 49
la silla, chair 35
el sillón, big chair, armchair 2
sin embargo (*adv.*), nevertheless 38
sino (que), (*conj.*), but 41
sin que (*conj.*), without 53
sírvase V. (*and infinitive*), please (*App. H*)
sobresaliente (*adj.*), excellent 39

SPANISH—ENGLISH VOCABULARY

el sobrino, nephew; **la sobrina**, niece 61
socarrón, -a (*adj.*), sly; roguish 33
el sofá, sofa 45
el sol, sun; **hay mucho sol**, it is very sunny 28
el soldado, soldier 14
soler, to be wont, to be used to 76
solo, -a (*adj.*), alone, only 42
sólo (*adv.*), only 42
solver (*R-ch.* I), to solve; (*past part.*), **suelto**, solved, loosened; occasional 65
el sombrero, hat 4
son, (they) are 9, BB5
sonreír, to smile 68
su(s) (*pos. adj.*), his, her, its; their; your (*polite*) 17
suceder, to happen 55
sucio, -a (*adj.*), dirty, soiled 15
el suelo, ground, floor (*of a room*) 13
suelto (*see* solver) 39
el sueño, sleep; **tener (mucho) sueño**, to be (very) sleepy 27
suficiente (*adj.*), sufficient 14
suntuoso, -a (*adj.*), sumptuous 73
supiera; si supiera . . , if I knew how . . . 54
suprimir, to suppress; (*past part.*) **suprimido** *and* **supreso** 65
suyo, -a (*pos. adj.*), his, her, its; their; your (*polite*) 40

T

tal, such; **(un) tal**, such a; **tales** . . . **tales**, some . . . others 59
también (*adv.*), also 7
tampoco (*adv.*), either 10
tan (*adv.*), as; very 23; 69
tan (*adv. with adj. or adv.*) **como**, as (so) . . . as 50

tanto, -a (*adj.*), so much; (*pl.*) so many; **cuanto más** . . . **tanto menos**, the more . . . the less .23; 25
tanto (*adv.*), so much 25
tanto . . . **como**, so (as) much . . . as 50
tañer, to play (*a musical instrument*) 58
tardar en, to be slow in 56
tarde (*adv.*), late 35
la tarde, afternoon; **todas las tardes**, every afternoon 26
la taza, cup; **taza para te**, teacup; **taza de te**, cup of tea 64
-te- (*emphatic prefix*) very; **retequebueno**, very good 76
te (*pers. pro.*), (to) thee, you; yourself 21; 38; 48
el te, (*plural*, **tes**), tea 17
tejer, to weave 51
telegrafiar, to telegraph 58
el telegrama, telegram 33
temblar (*R-ch.* I), (**de** *and noun*), to tremble (with) 35
temer, to fear, to be afraid 10
temprano (*adv.*), early 45
el tenedor, fork 18
tener, to have 27; 74
tener a, to hold 67
tener ganas de, to feel like 56
tener hambre, to be hungry 27
no tener nada que ver con, to have nothing to do with 74
tener que, to have to, must 29
tener razón, to be right 74
tengo, I have 17
teñir (*R-ch.* III), to stain, to dye 51
tercero, -a (*adj. or pro.*), third 19
terminar, to finish 60, BB15
tesis, thesis 34
ti (*disj. pro.*), (to) thee; you; thyself, yourself 42; 48
la tía, aunt 6
tibio, -a (*adj.*), lukewarm, tepid 15

el tiempo, time; weather 35
  a tiempo (*adv.*), on time 46
  es tiempo de que, it is time for (to) (*with subjunct.*) 43
  tiene, (he, she, it) has; (you *polite*) have 11
  tienen, (they) have; (you *polite*) have 11
la tinta, ink 6
el tío, uncle 6
  tirar, to throw 68
  tirar de, to pull at (*App. B*)
la tiza, chalk 5
  tocar, to touch; to play (*a musical instrument*) 6; 16
  todavía (*adv.*), still, yet 34
  todo, -a (*adj.*), all; todos los ... every 14; 26
  ¡toma! (*interjec.*), well! I declare! 69
  tomar, to take 7
el tomo, tome, volume 67
  tonto, -a (*adj.*), foolish 76
  trabajar, to work 4
el trabajo, work 6
  traer, to bring 66
  traidor, -a (*adj. or noun*), treacherous, traitor 33
  traidoramente (*adv.*), treacherously 57
el traje, suit 49
la trampa, trap; dar en la trampa, to fall into the trap 72
  tranquilo, -a (*adj.*), tranquil, quiet, calm 49
el tranvía, street car, trolley car (*word used in Spain*) 31
  tras (*prep.*), after 56
  tratar de, to try to; tratar, to treat 56
  tronar (*R-ch. I*), to thunder 35
el trueno, thunder 33
  tú (*pers. pro.*), you; thou 13
  turco, -a (*adj. or noun*), Turkish, Turk 33
  tu(s) (*pos. adj.*), your; thy 17
  tuyo, -a (*pos. adj.*), thy, your 40

U

u = o, or 64
a últimos de (*prep.*), at the end of (*a month*) 60
un, una (*indef. art.*), a, one; unos, unas, some 9
único, -a (*adj.*), only 54
uno ... otro, the one ... the other; each other; (*pl.*) some ... others; one another 48
usar, to use, to wear 34
usted; (*pl.*), ustedes; V., Vd., Ud.; VV., Vds., Uds., you (*polite*) 13
útil (*adj.*), useful; día útil, work day 60

V

¡va! (*interjec.*), well! really! 73
las vacaciones, vacation 43
  vaciar, to empty 58
  vacío, -a (*adj.*), empty 15
el vaivén, fluctuation, alternating movement 2
la vajilla, kitchen utensils (*collective noun*) 16
  valer, to be worth 66
  ¡válgame Dios! Good heavens! 69
el valor, worth, value 33
  ¡vamos a ver! (*interjec.*), come! let's see! 69
  variar, to vary 58
el vaso, glass 15
  Vd. = usted, you (*polite form*) 13
  se ve, it is evident
  veinte (*num. adj.*), twenty 20
el vejote, (repulsive) old man 77
  vencer, to overcome, to conquer 58
  vender, to sell 10
  venir, to come 51; 74
  venir a, to happen to (*plus verb*) 56

SPANISH–ENGLISH VOCABULARY

la **ventana,** window 13
ver, to see 29; 72
  es de ver . . . , it is worth seeing . . . 72
  no ver las horas de . . . , to be very anxious to . . . 72
el **verano,** summer 60
el **verbo,** verb 16
la **verdad,** truth 6
  ¿**verdad?** (see ¿**no?** above)
  verdaderamente, truly, really, 58, BB6
  verdadero, -a (adj.), real, true 58
  vestir (R-ch. III), to dress; (refl.), to dress oneself, to dress 36
la **vez,** time (in series); **ocho veces,** eight times 12
  de vez en cuando, from time to time 68
  a veces (adv.), at times, sometimes 44
  viajar, to travel 43
  viene, (he, she, it) comes; you (polite) come 57
  la semana que viene, next week 60
el **viento,** wind; **hay viento,** it is windy 28
el **viernes,** Friday 34
  vino, (he, she, it) came; you (polite) came 50
el **vino,** wine 17
  Viña del Mar, Viña del Mar (lit., vineyard of the sea), name of a beach near Valparaiso, Chile 43

vió, (he, she, it) saw; you (polite) saw 57
la **virtud,** virtue 6
visitar, to visit 42
la **vista,** sight; view; **de vista,** by sight 63
¡**viva . . . !** hurrah for . . . ! 54
vivir, to live 11
volver (R-ch. I), to turn, to return; **volver a . . ,** to . . . again: **volvió a escribir,** he wrote again 35; (App. B); (irreg. past part.), **vuelto** 65
vosotros, -as (pers. pro.), you; yourselves 13; 42
la **voz,** voice 33
vuestro, -a (pos. adj.), your 17; 40

Y

y (conj.), and 5
ya (adv.), already, now; **ya no,** no longer 13
¡**ya lo creo!** I should say so! 69, B14
yacer, to lie 76
yo (pers. pro.), I · 13
el **yodo,** iodine 71

Z

zambullirse, to dive; see **bullir** 51
el **zapato,** shoe 29
la **zorra,** fox 1
la **zorrilla,** polecat, skunk 77
zumbar, to buzz 1

GENERAL VOCABULARY

ENGLISH—SPANISH

A

a, un, una (*indef. art.*) 9
to be able, poder (ue) 35
to be about to, estar para 56
to accentuate, acentuar; you accentuate, acentuáis 58; 71
to accompany, acompañar 42
according to, según (*prep.*) 42
account, el cuento 19
to ache, doler (ue); he has a headache, le duele la cabeza 74
to be acquainted with, conocer 58
action, la acción 71, A27
to admit, confesar (ie) 35
to advance, avanzar 60
to advise, aconsejar 55
affection, la afición 75
to be afraid, temer 10; tener miedo 27
after, después de (*prep. of time*) 25; después (*adv.*) 28; después (de) que (*conj.*) 50; tras (*prep.*) 56
afternoon, la tarde 26
afterwards, después (*adv.*) 28
again, volvió a . . . (*inf.*); he wrote again, volvió a escribir (*App. B*)
to agree, convenir 74
to agree to, acordar (ue) en 56
aha! ¡ajá! (*interjec.*) 3
ahead, adelante (*adv.*) 47
aid, la asistencia 73
to aid, ayudar 67
air, el aire 71
all, todo, -a (*adj.*) 14; 26
to allow, dejar 62; permitir 55
alone, solo, -a (*adj.*) 42
Alphonsus, Alfonso 59
already, ya (*adv.*) 13
also, también (*adv.*) 7
alternating movement, el vaivén 2
although, aunque (*conj.*) 53
always, siempre (*adv.*) 64
America, América 4

American, americano, -a (*adj. or noun*) 14
amiable, amable (*adj.*) 72
amount, la cantidad 65
ancient, antiguo, -a (*adj.*) 25
and, y (*conj.*) 5; e (*before initial* i *or* hi) 64
animal, el animal 51
Anna, Ana 22
annoying, cansado, -a (*with* ser; *used of persons*) 14
to answer, contestar 36
to be very anxious to, no ver las horas de 72
Apocalypse, Apocalipsis (*in the last book of New Testament*) 60
apple, la manzana 67
to approach, arrimarse 63
to approve, aprobar (ue) 55
April, abril 60
apt, hábil (*adj.*) 60
(they) are, son 9, BB5
aren't you? ¿no? ¿no es verdad? ¿verdad? 35
to argue, argüir 68
arithmetic, la aritmética 19
arm, (la) arma (*military term*) 51; (*of the body*) el brazo 31
around, por (*prep.*) 68, BB14
to arrive, llegar 32; 51
as, como (*conj.*) 23; as . . . as, tan (*adj. or adv.*) como 50
to ascertain, averiguar 51
to ask (*a favor*; *dative of person and accusative of thing*) pedir (i) 36 (*see* preguntar)
to ask (*a question*; *dative of person and accusative of thing*) preguntar 24 (*see* pedir)
to ask, rogar (ue) 51
as much (many) as, cuanto, -a; -os; -as 23; tanto (*noun*) como 50
as much as, hasta (*adv.*) 22, B7

242

as soon as, luego que (*conj.*) 53
to assail, embestir 73
at, a 5
athletic, atlético, -a (*adj.*) 3; 75
at once, en seguida (*adv.*) 43; pronto (*adv.*) 52
to attack, embestir 73
attention, atención 45
at the side of, al lado de (*prep.*) 42
audience, la asistencia 73
auditorium, (la) aula 71
August, el agosto 60
aunt, la tía 6
automobile, el automóvil 43
autumn, el otoño 60
to awaken, despertarse (ie) 49
axe, (la) hacha (*written and pronounced* el hacha—*see* 19)

B

bad, malo, -a (*with* ser) 14
badly, mal (*adv.*) 23; malamente (*adv.*) 57
ball, la pelota 74
bamboo, el bambú 34
bank note, el billete de banco 37
to bathe oneself, bañarse 48
to be, ser, estar 14; 15; 68; 70; it is I, *etc.*, soy yo, *etc.*
beach, la playa 43
beast, la bestia 71
beautiful, hermoso, -a (*adj.*) 54
because, porque (*rel. conj.*) 50
to become, hacerse 59; 74; ponerse 56
bed, la cama 1
bedroom, el dormitorio 19
to befall, acontecer 72
before, antes (*adv.*) 32; antes (de) que (*conj. of time*) 50
to beg, rogar (ue) 51
to begin, comenzar (ie) 56; to begin to, echar a 56; to begin, empezar (ie) 56; to begin (to), principiar (a) 56; to begin, ponerse a 56
at the beginning of (*a month*), a principios de 60
to behead, degollar (ue) (List of Irreg. Verbs)

behind, detrás de (*prep.*) 32
to be behind, atrasar; (*of a watch*) to be slow 60
to believe, creer 23
small bell, la campanilla (*from* campana, bell) 77
beside, al lado de (*prep.*) 42
better, mejor (*adj.*) 23
big, grande (*adj.*) 22.
to bite, morder (ue) 39
black, negro, -a (*adj.*) 6
blackboard, la pizarra 5
to blacken, ennegrecer 73
to bless, bendecir 74; (*past parts.*) bendito, bendecido
blond, rubio, -a (*adj.*) 14
blue, azul (*adj.*) 3; 59
(wild) boar, el jabalí
to boil, bullir 51; cocer (ue) 58
bone, el hueso 39
to bone, desosar (ue) (*List of irr. verbs*)
book, el libro 6
bookshelf, el estante 70
to bore, aburrir 11
to be bored, aburrirse 48
boring, cansado (*with* ser) 14
to be born, nacer; he was born, nació 59
to borrow, pedir (i) prestado 47
to bother about, ocuparse de 48
boy, el mozo; el muchacho; el niño; little boy, niñito 6; 8; 77
bread, el pan 17
to break, romper; (*irreg. past part.*), roto; (*also*) rompido 52; 65
breakfast, el desayuno 50
to breakfast, desayunarse 49
brilliant, brillante (*adj.*) 39
brother, el hermano 6
brunette, moreno, -a (*adj.*) 14
Buenos Aires, Buenos Aires (*capital of Argentina*) 59
to burnish, bruñir 51
business, los negocios; la industria 47; 59
business man, el negociante 47
busy, ocupado, -a (*adj.*) 48

to busy oneself with, ocuparse de 48
but, pero (*conj.*) 1; sino (que) 41
butter, la mantequilla 17
to buy, comprar 8
to buzz, zumbar 1
by, por 16; **by your watch**, en su reloj 60, B11

C

Cain, Caín (*see first book of Old Testament*)
Cairo, el Cairo (*city in Egypt*) 61
to call out, gritar 54
Callao, el Callao (*city in Peru*) 61
to be called, intitularse 54
calm, tranquilo, -a (*adj.*) 49
came, (he, she, it) **came**, vino; **you came** (*polite form*), vino 50
can, poder (ue) (*physically able*) 35; saber (*mentally able*) 70
Canada, el Canadá 61
candle, la luz 30
wax candle, el cirio 73
canned, en lata (*adj.*) 41
capital, la capital (*of a country*) 59, AA3
captain, el capitán 14
captive, el preso (*see* **prender**)
car, trolley car, el carro (*word used in South America*) 31; el tranvía (*word used in Spain*)
care, el cuidado 68; **to be careful**, tener cuidado 68
carefully (*adv.*), detenidamente 41
carpenter, el carpintero 59
carriage, el coche 38
to carry, llevar; **to carry off**, llevarse 49
Castilian, castellano, -a (*adj. or noun*) 61
to catch, coger 51; prender; (*past part.*), preso, prendido, **caught, captive** 65
cent, el centavo 74
center, el centro; (*also* **center of town, down town**) 59
certain, cierto, -a (*adj.*) 33; seguro, -a (*adj.*) 49
certainly, seguramente 68

chair, la silla 35; **arm chair**, el sillón 2
chalk, la tiza 5
to change, cambiar
chapter, el capítulo 67
character, el genio
Charles, Carlos 67
cheap, barato -a; cursi (*adj.*) 34
cheat, embustero, -a (*adj. or noun*) 69
cheek, la mejilla 2
chestnut-colored, castaño, -a (*adj.*) 31
chief, principal (*adj.*) 19
chief, el jefe 67
children, los niños 9
to chill, enfriar 58
to choose, elegir (i) 75
circuit, la carrera 38
city, la ciudad 1; 23
class, la clase 41
class (sort), la especie 41
clean, limpio, -a (*adj.*) 15
to clean, limpiar 8; 58
to be clear, constar (*impersonal*) 76
to cleave, rajar 51
clerk, el dependiente 43; el empleado 25
clever, avisado, -a (*adj.*) 72; hábil (*adj.*) 60
clock, el reloj 12
to close, cerrar (ie) 35
cloth, el paño 41
coach, el coche 38
(dress) coat, el frac 1
coffee, el café; (*pl.*) los cafés 17; 34
cold, el frío 27
cold, frío, -a (*adj.*) 14; resfriado (*sickness*) 74
collar, el cuello 29
to comb oneself, peinarse 48
to come, venir 51; 74
you (*polite*) come, viene 57
come! ¡vamos a ver! (*interjec.*) 69
to come across (to find), encontrar (ue) 31; dar con 72
to come close, arrimarse 63

to come to, acudir a 11
comet, el cometa 33
common, ordinario, -a 64
to compete, competir (i) 36
complete, completo, -a (*adj.*) 39
to confess, confesar (ie) 35
confidence, la confianza
to congratulate oneself, felicitarse 48
to conjugate, conjugar 16
to conquer, vencer 58
consequently, por consiguiente (*adv.*) 13
to consider, considerar; juzgar 32
considering, dado que (*conj.*) 53
to consist of, consistir en 56
to be contained in, caber 70
contented, contento, -a (*adj.*) 7
to continue, continuar 58; seguir (i) 57
to convince, convencer 58; to convince oneself, to be convinced, convencerse 48
to cook, cocer (ue) 58; cocinar 8; guisar 1
to copy, copiar 66
corner (*of a street*), la esquina; (*inside corner*) el rincón 19
to cost, costar (ue) 39
couch, el canapé; (*pl.*) los canapés 34
could; if I could only . . . ! ¡Quién supiera . . . ! 54
to count, contar (ue) 35
country, el campo; in the country, en el campo 70; country estate, la hacienda 64; (nation), el país 61, B11
country (*nation*), país 61, B11
course (*of a meal*), el plato 18
cousin, primo, -a 6
Cousiño, Cousiño (*surname*) 2
to cover, cubrir 69; (*irreg. past part.*), cubierto 65
cowardice, act of cowardice, la cobardía 50
to creak, crujir 51
cruel, cruel (*adj.*) 71
to cry, llorar 2; 27
cup, la taza; teacup, taza para te; cup of tea, taza de te 64

to curse, maldecir 74; (*past parts.*) maldito, maldecido
custom-house, la aduana 71
customs, la aduana 71
to cut, cortar
cylinder, cilindro 1

D

dance, el baile 73
day, el día 33
day before yesterday, anteayer (*adv.*) 60
dead, muerto, -a (*past part. of* morir) 65
dear (expensive; *also* beloved), caro, -a (*adj.*) 54; querido (beloved) 72
dear . . . ! . . . de mi alma! (*interjec.*) 69
debt, la deuda 71
December, el diciembre 60
to decide (oneself), decidirse (por) 48; (*with verb*), —— a
I declare! ¡toma! 69
to deduce, deducir 65
to be delinquent, delinquir 51
dentist, el dentista 33
to depart, partir 47
to deprive of, quitar 47
to deserve, merecer (*see* conocer)
to descend, bajar 31
to desire, desear 15
the deuce! ¡diablo! (*interjec.*) 69; ¡mil diablos! 69
devil, el diablo 69
did you? (*see* aren't you? *above*)
to die, morir (ue) 35; (*irreg. past part.*), muerto 65
difficult, difícil (*adj.*) 10
diligent, aplicado, -a (*adj.*) 41; diligente (*adj.*) 7
to diminish, menguar (*see* averiguar)
dinner, la comida 8
dirty, sucio, -a (*adj.*) 15
discoverer, descubridor, -a (*adj. or noun*) 2
disgust, el asco; it disgusts me, asco me da 72
dish (course), el plato 18

to dismiss, despedir (i) 36
to distinguish, distinguir 51
to dive, zambullirse; see bullir 51
to divide, dividir 67
to do, hacer, 74; I shall do, you will do, etc., haré, harás, etc. 42
doctor, el médico 47
does, (he, she, it), hace 38
dog, el perro 1
dollar, el dólar 4; el peso, (in South America) 20; el duro, (in Spain) 1
door, la puerta 13
doubt, la duda 70
to doubt, dudar 43
draft (bank draft), el giro 1
to draw out, sacar 51
to dress, vestir (i) 36; to dress oneself, vestirse
to drink, beber 10; tomar 7
to drive (a carriage, an auto), conducir, guiar, manejar 43
during, durante (prep.) 43
duty, el deber 32
to dwell, alojar 51
to dye, teñir (i) 51

E

each, cada (indecl. adj.)
each one, cada uno, -a (pro.)
each other, (el) uno ... (el) otro 48; mutuamente (adv.) 48
eagle, (la) águila 19 (see agua above)
early, temprano (adv.) 45
to earn, ganar 26
easy, fácil (adj.) 5
to eat, comer 10
to efface, borrar 75
egg, el huevo 17
either, tampoco (adv.) 10
to elect, elegir (i) 75
electrical, eléctrico, -a (adj.) 30
elegant, garboso, -a (adj.) 1
Elizabeth, Isabel 20
to embellish, ennoblecer 73
eminent, eximio, -a (adj.) 73
to employ, emplear 76
employee, empleado, -a (adj.) 25
empty, vacío, -a (adj.) 15

to empty, vaciar 58
at the end of (a month), a fines de (prep.); a últimos de (prep.) 60
enemy, enemigo, -a (adj. or noun) 16
engineer, ingeniero 59
England, (la) Inglaterra 15
English, inglés, -a (adj.) 14
to ennoble, ennoblecer 73
enormous, enorme (adj.) 33
enough, bastante (adj. or adv.) 14
to enter, entrar (en) (intrans. verb) (App. B)
enthusiasm, el entusiasmo 41
equally, igualmente
to erase, borrar 75
to erect, erguir (ye or i) (App. of irreg. verbs)
to err, errar (ye) 39
to escape, escaparse 48
European, europeo, -a (adj.) 64
even, aun (adv. of comparison)
every, cada (indecl. adj.); todos los ... ; everyone, cada uno, -a 14
everybody, todo el mundo 54
to be evident, constar; it is evident, consta 76; se ve
examination, el examen 39
to examine, examinar 41
excellent, excelente (adj.) 64; rico, -a (adj.) 14; sobresaliente (adj.) 39
except, excepto (prep.) 73
exercise, el ejercicio 15
to be exhausted, no poder más 72
to exist, existir 24
expensive, caro, -a (adj.) 54
extremely, (suffix) -ísimo, -a 76
eye, el ojo 59

F

face, la cara 8
to face the street, dar a la calle 72
fair, dulce (adj.) 61
to fall, caer 68
   to fall into the trap, dar en la trampa 72
famous, eximio, -a (adj.) 73

to fancy, antojarse; **he fancies**, se le imagina; se le antoja 49; 76
far, lejos *(adv.)* 48
farthing, el maravedí; *(pl.)* maravedíes, maravedís, maravedises 34
fast, to be fast *(of a watch)*, avanzar 60
father, el padre; father, "dad," papá; *(plural)* papás 34; dear father, papacito 77
favor, el favor *(App. H)*
favorable result, el éxito 39
fear, el miedo 27
to fear, temer 10
February, el febrero 60
to feel, sentir (ie) 35
to feel like, tener ganas de; estar por 56
Fernández, Fernández *(surname)*
to fetch, buscar 12
few, pocos, -as *(adj. or pro.)* 23
field, el campo 71
fifth, quinto, -a 67
finally, al fin *(adv.)* 68
to find, encontrar (ue) 31; hallar 4
finger, el dedo 31
to finish, acabar *(App. B)*; terminar 60, BB15
first, primero, -a *(adj. or pro.)* 19
fish, el pescado *(out of water)*; *(see also* el pez, *in water, not caught)* 41
to flee, huir 68
floor *(of a room)*, el suelo 13; *(of a house)*, el piso; **ground floor** *(of two-story house)* el piso bajo *or* los bajos; **upper floor** *(of two-story house)* el piso alto *or* los altos; **main floor, second floor** *(of house of several stories)*, el piso principal 13; 19
fluctuation, el vaivén 2
fluent (fluid *as adj.*), flúido, -a 71
fly, la mosca 24
fog, la neblina; **it is foggy**, hay neblina 28
following, siguiente *(adj.)* 49
fondness, la afición 75
food, el alimento 76

foolish, tonto, -a *(adj. or noun)* 76
foot, el pie 19
for *(Sp. present for Eng. perfect)*, desde hace . . ; *(Sp. imp. for Eng. pluperf. . .)* 64
for, para *(prep.)* 5; por 4
for, pues *(conj.)* 48
For Heaven's sake! ¡por Dios!
forbid, prohibir 55
force, la fuerza *or* las fuerzas
foreign *(that of another)*, ajeno, -a *(adj.)* 63
to forget, olvidarse (de); **I forget**, se me olvida *(impersonal cst.)* 49
fork, el tenedor 18
fourth, (quarter, *in telling time*), el cuarto 60
fox, la zorra 1
fraction, el quebrado 67
France, (la) Francia 15
French, francés, -a *(adj.)* 14
frequently, a menudo *(adv.)* 48
fresh, fresco, -a *(adj.)* 15
Friday, el viernes 34
friend, amigo, -a 5
from, de *(prep.)* 5
to fry, freír; *(irreg. past part.)*, frito, 68
to fulfil, cumplir (con) 32
full, lleno, -a *(adj.)* 15
to make fun of, reírse de 48

G

Gabriel, Gabriel 12
to gain, ganar 26
garret; **small garret**, buhardilla *(from* buharda, **garret window**) 77
garrulous, hablador, -a *(adj.)* 33
gave; **(they) gave, you** *(polite)* **gave**, dieron; **(he, she, it) gave**, dió 36
Gee whiz! ¡canastos! 69
general, el general 1
generally, generalmente *(adv.)* 14; por lo común *(adv.)* 46
genius, el genio

gentle, dulce (*adj.*) 61
gentleman, el señor 13
George, Jorge 59
Germany, Alemania 15
German, alemán, -a (*adj.*) 2
to get up, levantarse 49
girl, la moza; la muchacha 6; 8
to give, dar 72; (they) give, dan; (he, she, it) gives, da 38
to give (over), entregar 51
glad, contento, -a 7
glass, el vaso (*drinking glass*) 15
Gloria, Gloria (*girl's name*) 71
glory, la gloria 71
to gnaw, roer; *see* leer 58
to go, ir 56; 70; andar 57; 68; dirigirse 48; pasar 25
to go down, bajar 31
to go into, entrar en (*intransitive*) (*App. B*)
to go off, away, irse 49; marcharse 54
to go out, salir 11
to go over (to traverse), recorrer 56
to go with, acompañar 42
to go to bed, acostarse (ue) 35
God, el Dios 27
Gómez, Gómez (*surname*) 64, B3
González, González (*surname*) 2
good, bueno, -a (*adj.*) 10
to be good for, servir (i) 61
good-by, hasta luego, hasta lueguito (*adv.*) 77
Good gracious, ¡canastos! (*interjec.*) 69; ¡Jesús, José, y María! 69
Good heavens! ¡Dios mío! (*interjec.*) 69
graceful, garboso, -a (*adj.*) 1
Gracious! ¡Jesús, José, y María! 69
grains, la mies; (*pl.*) las mieses 17
grandfather, el abuelo 71
grandmother, la abuela 71
to grasp, agarrar; asir 76, B5
a great deal, mucho (*adv.*) 9
it grieves (hurts), duele 31
ground, el suelo 13

ground floor, el entresuelo (*of a building of several stories*) 19
to grunt, gruñir 51
guide, el (*or*) la guía 33
Gutiérrez, Gutiérrez (*surname*)

H

hair, a hair, un cabello; hair (*collective*) los cabellos 31
half, medio, -a (*adj.*) 60; la mitad (*noun*) 67
hall (lecture hall), (la) aula 71
to halt, detenerse 74
ham, el jamón 19
hand, la mano 33
to hand over, entregar 51
to happen, acontecer 72; pasar 55; suceder 55; venir a (*with verb*) 56
happily, felizmente (*adv.*) 57
happy, contento, -a (*adj.*); feliz 7
has, (he she, it; you *polite*), tiene 11
haste, la prisa 72
to hasten, acudir 11
hat, el sombrero 14
to have, haber (*auxiliary for perfect tenses*); tener (to possess) 27; 28; 29; 56; 70; 74
have, (they; you *polite*), tienen 11
to have breakfast, desayunarse 49
head, la cabeza, 74; (chief), el jefe 67
health, la salud 6
health; to be in good health, estar bueno de salud 43
to hear, entender (ie) 35; oír 57; 68
heat, el calor 27
heaven, el cielo 13
Good heavens! ¡Válgame Dios! 69
Helen, Elena 12
to help, ayudar 67
help, el remedio; there is no help for it, no hay remedio 74; can't help (doing), no poder menos de 68
Henry, Enrique 12
her, to her, ella (*disj. pro.*) 42; le (*conj. pro.*); se (*with a fol-*

lowing direct obj. pro.); su (*pos. adj.*) 17; 21
herding, ganadero, -a (*adj.*) 59
here, aquí (*adv.*) 11
hers, suyo, -a (*adj. or. pro.*) 40
herself, to herself (*refl. pro.*), se 38; sí (*disj. pro.*) 42; 48
hi! ¡ea! 69
high school, el liceo 45
him, to him, él (*disj. pro.*) 42; le (*conj. pro.*); se (*followed by a direct obj. pro.*) 38; **(to) himself**, sí, (*refl. pro.*) 38; 42; 48
to hinder, impedir (i) 36
his, su(s) (*pos. adj.*) 17; suyo, -a (*pos. adj. or pro.*) 40; el suyo (*pos. pro.*) 40
hoarse, ronco, -a (*adj.*) 33
hold, tener a 65
holy, santo, -a (*adj.*) 22
to hope, esperar
horse, el caballo 38
horseman, el jinete
hot, caliente 14
hour, la hora 60
house, la casa 10; (*big, ill-proportioned house*), el caserón; (*ugly old house*), la casucha 77
 at the house of, at home, en casa (de) (*adv. or prep.*) 38
how, como (*conj. adv.*) 23
how? (*int. conj.*) ¿cómo? 18
how, lo (*as in:* "... how good they are ...") 29, 2
however, por (*adj. or adv.*) que (*subjunct.*) 53
how many, cuantos, -as 23; **how many?** ¿cuántos, -as? 18
how much, cuanto, -a 23; **how much?** ¿cuánto, -a? 18
humorous, burlón, -a 33
hunger, (la) hambre 27
hungry, to be hungry, tener hambre 27
hurrah for ... ! ¡viva ... ! 54
hurricane, el huracán 2
to be in a hurry, tener prisa 72
it hurts, duele 31; **this foot hurts me**, me duele este pie 31

husband, el esposo
hypothesis, la hipótesis 34

I

I, yo (*pers. pro.*) 13
ice, el hielo 14
ice cream, el helado 39
idle, perezoso, -a (*adj.*) 7
if, si (*conj.*) 45
ignoble, innoble (*adj.*) 73
ill, enfermo, -a 31; malo, -a (*with estar*) 15
to imagine, figurarse; imaginarse 49
immediately, en seguida (*adv.*) 43; pronto (*adv.*) 52
it is important, importa 56
impossible, imposible (*adj.*) 43
to imprint, imprimir (*irreg. past part.*) impreso 65
in, en (*prep.*) 4
in case, en caso (de) que (*conj.*) 53
to be inclined to, estar por 56
Indian, indio, -a 64
(Indian) corn, maíz 3; 72
indifferent, indiferente 41
industrious, aplicado, -a (*adj.*) 41; diligente (*adj.*) 7
industry, la industria 59
inexpensive, barato, -a 24
to inform, hacer saber 57, AA15
inhabitant, el habitante 22
ink, la tinta 6
in order that, a fin (de) que (*conj.*) 53; para que
in order to, para (*conj.*) 5
to insist (on), insistir (en) 56
instead of, en vez de (*prep.*) 45
instinct, el instinto 64
intelligent, inteligente (*adj.*); **very intelligent**, inteligentísimo, -a 76
to intend, pensar (ie) 56
interesting, interesante (*adj.*) 38
to introduce, presentar 42
iodine, el yodo 71
Irish, irlandés, -a (*adj. or noun*) 75
iron, el hierro 37

is, (he, she, it), es 6; **it is** (*in expressions of weather*) hace 60
island, la isla 75
Israelite, israelita (*adj. or noun*) 75
is to, (he, she, it), ha de 29
its, su(s) (*pos. adj.*) 17

J

jacket, la chaqueta 29
jaguar, el jaguar 1
Jane, Juana; **little Jane,** Juanita 77
January, el enero 60
Jesus, Jesús 69
John, Juan 12
joined, anexo, -a; anejo, -a (*adj.*)
Joseph, José 69
judge, el juez; (*pl.*) jueces 65
to judge, juzgar 32
judgment, el juicio 71
July, el julio 60
to jump, brincar 51
June, el junio 60.
to have just, acabar de ... (*App. B*)

K

kerosene, el petróleo 30
key, la llave 70
kilometer, el kilómetro 73
kind, amable (*adj.*) 72
kind, la especie 41.
to kindle, encender (ie) 35
kindness, la bondad (*App. H*)
king, el rey 34
kitchen utensils, la vajilla (*collective*) 16
knife, el cuchillo 18
to know, conocer 58; **to know how,** saber 46; 70

L

to be lacking, faltar 60
lady, la señora 13
large, grande (*adj.*) 6; 22
last, pasado (*past part. as adj., as* el mes pasado, **last month**) 60; (*of a series*) postrero, -a (*adj.*) 19

late, tarde (*adv.*) 35
Latin, latino, -a (*adj.*) 61; latín, (*the language*)
to laugh, reír 68
laugh, (they; you, *polite*) ríen 48
to laugh at, reírse de 48
law, el derecho (*abstract noun only*) 47; la ley 34
lawyer, el abogado 47
lazy, flojo, -a (*adj.*) 31; háragán, -a (*adj.*) 33; perezoso, -a (*adj.*) 7
to lead, conducir 43
leader, el jefe 67
leaf, la hoja 39
lean, flaco, -a (*adj.*) 8
to learn, aprender 56
at least, por lo menos (*adv.*) 72
to leave, partir (*intransitive*) 47
to leave off (*doing a thing*), dejar de ... 50; **he left off writing,** dejó de escribir 50
left, izquierdo, -a (*adj.*) 31
leisurely, despacio, -a (*adj.*) 23
to lend, prestar 45
less, menos (*adv.*) 23
lesson, la lección 6
to let, dejar 62; **to let know,** hacer saber
let's see! ¡vamos a ver! (*interjec.*) 69
letter, la carta 40
to lie (*tell a falsehood*), mentir (ie) 35
to lie (*to lie down*), yacer 76
to lift, levantar 49
light, la luz 30
light (blond), rubio, -a (*adj.*) 14
light (swift), ligero, -a 38
to light, encender (ie) 35
to like (*a person*), querer (ie) a 35; (*a thing*), gustar (*impersonal ost.*) (*App. B*)
I should like, quisiera 44; **I like it,** me agrada; me alegra; me gusta (*App. B*)
linguistic, lingüístico, -a 71
liquid, flúido, -a (*adj.*) 71
listen! ¡oiga! ¡oye!; **listen here!** ¡mire! 69

little (*in size*), chico, -a (*adj.*) 33; pequeño, -a 5
little (*in amount*), poco, -a (*adj.*) 23
little, but little, poco (*adv.*); little, poco de (*partitive adv.*) 23
little girl, la niñita 77
to live, vivir 11
loaf, el pan 17
to loaf, holgarse (ue) 48
to lock, cerrar (ie) 35
to lock up, encerrar (ie) 35
to lodge, alojar 51
long, largo, -a (*adj.*) 33
no longer, no ... más (*adv.*) 41; ya no 13
to look at, mirar 50
to look for, buscar 12
Look out that ... ! ¡Cuidado que ... ! 68
looking-glass, el espejo 48
to lose, perder (ie) 35
Louis, Luis; little Louis, Luisito 67; 77
to love, amar 16; querer a (ie) 35
lukewarm, tibio, -a (*adj.*) 15
to lunch, almorzar (ue) 35

M

madam, señora 13
made, (he, she, it; you *polite*), hacía 64; hizo (*preterite*) 54
Madrid (inhabitant of), madrileño, -a (*adj. or noun*) 25
maize, maíz 3; 71
to make, hacer 74
makes, (he, she, it; you *polite*), hace 38
to make cold, enfriar 58
to make oneself, hacerse 59; 74
to make up one's mind, decidirse por; (*with verb*), ———— a 48
to make one's way toward, to go, dirigirse 48
was making, (he, she, it; you *polite*) hacía 64
mamma, la mamá; (*pl.*) las mamás 34
man, el hombre 9

to manage, echar de 56
manner, el aire 71
to manufacture, fabricar 49; to be manufactured, fabricarse 49
many, muchos, -as (*adj.*), 10
March, el marzo 60
mark (*in school*), la nota 39
Mary, María 12
mathematics, las matemáticas 73
it matters, importa 56
May, el mayo 60
me, to me, mí (*disj. pro.*) 42; 48; me (*conj. pro.*) 21; 38; with me, conmigo 42
meal, la comida 8
to mean (to wish to say), querer decir 72
means, la medida 1
measure, la medida 1
meat, la carne 17
medicine, la medicina 47
to meet, conocer 58; encontrar (ue) 31
to melt, derretir (i) 36
mere truth, la pura verdad 56
middle, in the middle of (*a month*), a mediados de 60
might, with all one's might, a más no poder 72
milk, la leche 17
mine, el mío (*pos. pro.*) 40
mint, la moneda 13
mirror, el espejo 48
miss, doña (*with first name*) 20; la señorita (*used with surname*) 13
mist, la neblina; it is misty, hay neblina 28
Mrs., Mistress, doña (*with first name*) 20; señora (*used with surname*) 13·
mistake, la falta
mistaken, (to be), equivocarse 52
mister, Mr., master, don (*with first name*) 20; señor (*used with surname*) 13
modern, moderno, -a (*adj.*) 25
moment, el momento 40
money, el dinero 19
month, el mes 60

Monday, el lunes 34
more, más (*adv.*) 14; **the more ... the more**, cuanto más ... (tanto) más 23; **no more, no longer**, no ... más (*adv.*) 41
morning, la mañana 11
mortal, mortal (*adj.*) 61
most, ísimo, -a (*suffix*) 76
mother, la madre 6
mountain, la montaña 25
much, mucho (*adv.*) 10
much, mucho, -a (*adj.*) 10
must, deber 35
mutually, mutuamente (*adv.*) 48
my, mi(s) (*pos. adj.*) 17; mío, -a (*pos. adj. or pro.*) 40

N

narrow, angosto, -a (*adj.*) 41
nation, la nación 12
near, cerca de (*prep.*) 30; próximo, -a (*adj.*) 60
necessary, necesario, -a (*adj.*); preciso 43
it is necessary, es necesario 43; es menester 51
to need, necesitar 56
neither, ni; **neither ... nor**, ni ... ni (*conj.*) 7; 41
nephew, el sobrino 61
never, nunca (*adv.*); jamás (*adv.*) 41
nevertheless, sin embargo (*adv.*) 38
new, nuevo, -a (*adj.*) 57
newly, nuevamente (*adv.*) 57
news, las noticias 40
newspaper, el diario 70
news stand, el kiosco (quiosco) 73
New York, Nueva York 59, B5
next, en seguida (*adv.*) 43
next, próximo, -a (*adj.*) 60; **next week**, la semana que viene 60
nice, amable (*adj.*) 72
niece, la sobrina 61
no (none), ninguno, -a (*adj. or pro.*) 19; (*after noun*) alguno 19; 41
no, no (*adj.*) 8; 41
nobody, nadie (*pro.*) 41

no one, ninguno, -a (*adj. or pro.*) 19
nor, ni (*conj.*) 7
North America, América del Norte, Norte América 68
not, no (*adv.*) 8; 41; **not at all!** ¡ca! (*interjec.*); nada (*adv.*; *interjec.*) 41; **not by a good deal**, ni por mucho (*adv.*; *interjec.*) 25
note (*as*, "to make a note of something"), la apuntación 39
notebook, el cuaderno 39
nothing, nada (*pro.*) 41
to notice carefully, fijarse en 56
November, el noviembre 60
now, ahora (*adv.*) 16; ya (*adv.*) 13
to obscure, ennegrecer 73
occasional, suelto, -a (*past part. as adj. from* solver) 65
to occupy oneself with, preocuparse de 48
October, el octubre 60
of, de (*prep.*) 5; (*in expressions of time*); faltan cinco minutos para las ocho, **it is five minutes of eight** 60
often, a menudo (*adv.*) 48
oil (*as*, olive oil), el aceite 71
old (out-of-date), añejo, -a (*adj.*) 2
older, mayor (*adj.*) 23; 33
on, en (*prep.*) 4; adelante (*adv.*) 47
on (*plus present part.*), al (*plus infin.*) 50
on account of, por (*prep.*) 4
on (put on, *as:* "he has his hat on") puesto, -a 59
one, un, una (*indef. art.*) 9
one another, (el) uno ... (el) otro; mutuamente; **the one ... the other**, (el) uno ... (el) otro 48
onion, la cebolla 39, BB5
only, único, -a (*adj.*) 54; sólo (*adv.*) 42; no ... más que (*adv.*) 23; **not only ... but also**, no sólo (*or* solamente) ... sino que 50

to open, abrir 65
opened, abierto (*irreg. past part.*) 65
opinion, el juicio 71
to oppose, oponerse (a) 56
to oppress, oprimir 65; (*past parts.*) oprimido, opreso
or, o (*conj.*) 7; u = o (*before o- or* **ho-**) 64
orange, la naranja 67, BB10
orange blossom, el azahar 1
to order, mandar 44
ordinary, ordinario, -a 64
other (another), otro -a (*adj. or pro.*) 13
ought, deber 35
ought to . . . , hay que . . . 29
our(s), nuestro, -a (*adj.*); (el) nuestro (*pro.*) 40
outcome, el éxito 39
to overcome, vencer 58
to owe, deber 35
own, propio, -a (*adj.*) 52
ox, el buey 2

P

page, la hoja 39; la página (*as of a book*) 58
to pain, doler (ue) 74
paper (*in general, not a newspaper*), el papel; **blotting paper,** el papel secante 70
Paraguay, el Paraguay 61
Paris, París 24, BB8
parrot, el loro 2
part, la parte 67
to pass, pasar 25
to be passed (*in a class on an examination*) recibir 39; aprobar
past, pasado, -a (*past part. as adj.*) 60
path, el sendero 25
to pay, pagar 51
to pay (attention), prestar (atención) 45
peace, la paz 57
pen, la pluma; **fountain pen,** plumafuente, 5; 70
pencil, el lápiz 5
penknife, el cortaplumas 34

pepper, la pimienta 24
perfect, completo, -a (*adj.*) 39
to permit, dejar 62; permitir 55
person, la persona 59
Peru, el Perú 61
pharmaceutical, farmacéutico, -a (*adj.*) 71
philosopher, el filósofo 73
to philosophize, filosofar 57
piano, el piano 6
picturesque, pintoresco, -a (*adj.*) 38
pity, la lástima; **it is a pity,** es lástima 46
planet, el planeta 33
plate, el plato 18
to play, jugar (ue) 35; (*a musical instrument*) tañer, tocar 6; 16; 58
to please, alegrar; **it pleases me, I like,** me alegra; gustar, me gusta, **I like** (*App. B*); placer 76; agradar; me agrada, **it pleases me, I like** (*App. B*)
to be pleased with, complacerse (en) 76
please, tenga V. la bondad de . . . ; hágame V. el favor de . . . ; sírvase V. (*App. H*)
please (yes, please), si me hace el favor (*App. H*)
plus, más 67
pocket, el bolsillo 40
poem, la poesía 54, B11; el poema 33
poetry, la poesía, 54, B11
to point out, enseñar 24
polecat, la zorrilla 77
to polish, bruñir 51
poor, pobre (*adj.*); ¡pobre de él! **poor fellow!** 14; 29
possible, posible (*adj.*) 43
practice, el ejercicio 15
to pray, rezar 51
to prefer, preferir (ie) 55
to be preoccupied with, preocuparse de 48
to prepare, preparar 8
to present, presentar 42
to be present, asistir 64

president, el presidente, la presidenta 33
pretty, bonito, -a 33
to prevent, impedir (i) 36
price, el precio 14
priest, el cura 1
to print, imprimir; *(irreg. past part.),* impreso 65
probably, probablemente *(adv.)* 32
professor, el profesor, la profesora 39
program, el programa 33
provided that, siempre que *(conj.)* 53
prudent, avisado, -a *(adj.)* 72
to pull at, tirar de *(App. B)*
to pull out, sacar 51
pupil, alumno, -a 5
to purchase, comprar 8
pure, puro, -a *(adj.)* 56
to put, meter 40; poner; **to put on** *(clothes),* ponerse 49
to put to bed, acostar (ue) 35
to put on (shoes), calzarse 49

Q

quantity, la cantidad 65
question, la pregunta 52
quickly, aprisa *(adv.)* 57; pronto *(adv.)* 52
quiet, callado, -a *(adj.);* **very quiet,** calladito 77; tranquilo, -a *(adj.)* 49
quotient, el cuociente 71

R

race, la carrera 38
rain, la lluvia; **it is rainy,** hay lluvia 60
to rain, llover (ue) 35
to raise, alzar 58
rapid, ligero, -a *(adj.)* 38
rapidly, rápidamente *(adv.)* 38
rare, raro, -a *(adj.)* 41
to reach, llegar (a) *(intrans.)* 32; 51
to read, leer 58
ready, listo, -a *(adj.)* 32

real, verdadero, -a *(adj.)* 58
really, verdaderamente 58, BB6; ¡va! *(interjec.)* really! 73
reason, la razón 74; *(judgment)* el juicio 71; **there is no reason for,** no hay por qué
to receive, recibir 39
to recount, contar (ue) 35
red, rojo, -a *(adj.)* 11
to reduce, reducir 58
to refrain from, guardarse de 56
to refuse, negarse (ie) (a) 56; oponerse (a) 56
to rejoice, alegrarse (de) *(App. B);* 55
to relate, contar (ue) 35
reliable, cierto, -a 33
to remain, quedar (se) 74
remedy, el remedio 74
to remember, acordarse (ue) de 48
to remind oneself of, acordarse (ue) de 48
to repeat, repetir (i) 36
to reply, contestar 36
repulsive old man, el vejote 77
to request, rogar (ue) 51
respected, respectado -a *(past. part. as adj.)* 64
to rest, descansar 56
to return, volver (ue) 35
returned, vuelto *(irreg. past part.)* 65
rich, rico, -a 14
right, derecho, -a *(adj.); as,* "right hand") 31
to be right, tener razón 74
road, el camino
to rob, robar 47
roguish, socarrón, -a *(adj.)* 33
room *(of a house),* el cuarto 49; la pieza 12
to have room for, caber 70
round, redondo, -a *(adj.)* 33
rose, la rosa 73
ruby, el rubí 34
to ruin, perder (ie) *(person as object)* 56, A18
to run, correr 42
to run away, salvarse 48
to run off, escaparse 48

S

said, (they, you *polite*), dijeron 8, BB14; **(he, she, it),** dijo 3; 24; **(we),** dijimos
saint, santo (*adj. or noun*) 22
sake; For Heaven's sake, ¡por Dios! 27
same, mismo, -a (*adj. before noun*) 24
sardine, la sardina 41
satisfactory, satisfactorio, -a (*adj.*) 22
satisfied, satisfecho, -a (*past part. as adj.*) 10
to be satisfied with, contentarse con 56
Saturday, el sábado 34
to save oneself, salvarse 48
saw, (he, she, it; you *polite*), vió 57
to say, decir 40; 74
say, (they; you *polite*), dicen 24
says, (he, she, it; you *polite*), dice 24
to scatter, esparcir 58
school, la escuela 23
Scotch, escocés, -a (*adj. or noun*) 33
to seat, sentar (ie); **to seat oneself, to sit down,** sentarse (ie) 35
to see, ver 29; 72; **we'll see about it,** allá veremos; **see here!** ¡mire! ¡oiga! ¡oye! 69; 74, B16
to seek, buscar 12
it seems, parece 30
to seize, asir 76; coger 51
-self, mismo (*intensive adj. after noun*) 24
to sell, vender 10
to send, enviar 58; mandar 44
sense, el juicio 71
sentinel, la centinela 33
September, el se(p)tiembre 60
Serafina, Serafina (*girl's name*) 77
  little Serafina, Finita 77
servant, el mozo 6
to serve, servir (i) 36
set of shelves, el estante 70
Seville (native of), sevillano, -a (*adj. or noun*) 25

share (*of stock*), acción 71, A27
to shave oneself, afeitarse 48
she, ella 13
shirt, la camisa 29
shoe, el zapato 29
shore, la playa 43
short, corto, -a 61
should, you should, hay que 29; **I should say so!** ¡Ya lo creo! 69, B14
shoulder, el hombro 40
to shout, gritar 54
to show, enseñar 24
to shut, cerrar (ie) 35
to shut in, encerrar (ie) 35
sick, enfermo, -a (*adj.*) 31 malo, -a (*adj.*) (*with* **estar**) 15
side, el lado 42
sight, la vista 63; **by sight,** de vista
silk, la seda 41
since, desde que (*conj.*); desde (*prep.*) 64
to sing, cantar 47
sir, señor 13
to sit down, sentarse (ie) 35
skilful, hábil (*adj.*) 60
skunk, la zorrilla 77
sky, el cielo 13
slate, la pizarra 5
sleep, el sueño 27; **to sleep,** dormir (ue) 35; **to be sleepy,** tener sueño 27
slow, despacio, -a (*adj.*) 23; **to be slow** (*of a watch*), atrasar 60
slowly, despacio (*adv.*) 23
to be slow in, tardar en 56
sly, socarrón, -a (*adj.*) 33
small, chico, -a (*adj.*) 33; pequeño, -a 5
to smell, oler (hue) 39
to smile, sonreír 68
snow, la nieve 33
to snow, nevar (ie) 35
so, and so (*conj. adv.*), así 3
"so long," hasta luego (*adv.*) 77
and so forth, et cetera, etcétera 49
so many, tantos, -as (*adj.*) 25
so much, tanto, -a (*adj.*) 25
so much, tanto (*adv.*) 25
so that, así que (*conj.*) 47

so that, de manera (de *or*) que (*conj.*) 50; 53; de modo (de *or*) que (*conj.*) 53
sock, el calcetín 16
sofa, el sofá 45
soiled, sucio, -a (*adj.*) 15
soldier, el soldado 14
to solve, solver (ue); (*irreg. past part.*) suelto 65
some, alguno, -a (*adj. or pro.*) 19; 41
some, unos, unas (*adj. or pro.*) 9
some ... others, (los) unos ... (los) otros 48; tales ... tales 59
sometimes, a veces (*adv.*) 44
soon, pronto (*adv.*) 52
to be sorry, sentir (ie) 35
sore, enfermo 31
sort, la clase; la especie 41
soul, (la) alma 19
Spain, la España 15
Spanish, español, -a (*adj. or pro.*) 14
to speak, hablar 4
speech, la palabra 16
to spend, gastar 74
in spite of the fact that, a pesar de que 53
to split, rajar 51
spoon, la cuchara 18; **small spoon, teaspoon,** la cucharita 18
spouse, esposo, -a
spring, la primavera 60
squall, el chubasco 2
square, cuadrado, -a (*adj.*) 33
to stain, teñir (i) 51
statesman, el estadista 16
to stay, quedar (se) 15
to steal, robar 47
steel, el acero 37
still (*as,* "He is still here"), todavía 34; aún 3
still (*as,* "That is still larger"), aun (*adv. of degree*)
stock raising, ganadero, -a (*adj.*) 59
stocking, la media 16
stone, la piedra 68
to stop, detenerse 74
stopped; he stopped writing, dejó de escribir 50
story (*narrative*), el cuento 19
story (*of a house*), el piso 13
stout, gordo, -a (*adj.*) 54
straight, derecho, -a 31
strange, ajeno, -a (*adj.*) 63
straw, la paja 33
street, la calle 12
street car, el tranvía 31
strength, la fuerza; las fuerzas
strike, to strike two (o'clock), dar las dos 72
strong, fuerte (*adj.*)
to struggle (for), luchar (por) 56
student, alumno, -a (*in high school*); 5; el estudiante (*in college*) 30
to study, estudiar 13
stupid, estúpido, -a (*adj.*) 69
such, tal; **such a,** (un) tal 59
sufficient, suficiente (*adj.*) 14
sugar, el azúcar 17
suit, el traje 49
it suits, convenir (*3rd sing. as impersonal*) 74
summer, el verano 60
sumptuous, rico, -a (*adj.*) 14; suntuoso, -a (*adj.*) 73
sun, el sol; **it is sunny,** hay sol 28
Sunday, el domingo 34
to suppress, suprimir; (*past part.*) suprimido *and* supreso 65
sure, seguro, -a (*adj.*) 49; cierto, -a 33
surely, seguramente (*adv.*) 68
sweet, dulce (*adj.*) 61
swift, ligero, -a (*adj.*) 38
swiftly, rápidamente (*adv.*) 38
to swim, nadar 64
swollen, hinchado, -a (*adj.*) 2

T

to take, coger 51
table, la mesa 7
tailor, el sastre 14
to take, tomar 7
to take (*a street car*), agarrar 76, B5
to take care, tener cuidado 68

to take leave (*refl.*), despedirse (i) 52
to take place, acontecer 72
to take a walk, pasearse 66
to take away, quitar 47
to talk, hablar 4
talkative, hablador, -a (*adj.*) 33
taste, el gusto 49
to taste of, saber a; it tastes of onions, sabe a cebollas 64
tea, el te; (*pl.*) tes 17
to teach, enseñar 24
teacher (*primary school*), el maestro, la maestra 63; (*high school, college*), el profesor, la profesora 39
teaspoon, la cucharita 18
telegram, el telegrama 33
to telegraph, telegrafiar 58
to tell, decir 40; 74; I shall tell, you will tell, *etc.*, diré, dirás, *etc.* 42
temper, el genio
tepid, tibio, -a (*adj.*) 15
than, que; de; de (el, *etc.*, lo) que (*conj.*) 5; 23
to thank, agradecer 69; dar las gracias 72
thanks, gracias (*adv.*) 72
that, aquel, -lla; ese, -a (*adj.*) 30
that, aquél, -lla; ése, -a (*pro.*) 30
that, que (*rel. pro.*) 10; 24
that, que (*conj.*) (*expletive*, see 69) 30, 3
the, el, la; los, las 9
their(s), su(s); suyo, -a (s) (*pos. adj. or pro.*) 17; 40
them, ellos, ellas (*pers. pro.*) 42
themselves, sí (*disj. pro.*) 48
then, en seguida (*adv.*) 43; entonces (*adv.*) 43
there, ahí (*adv.*); allí 11; 30
there is, there are, hay 28
these, estos, -as (*demonstr. adj.*) 30
these, éstos, -as (*demonstr.* pro.) 30
they, ellos, -as (*pers. pro.*) 13
thin, flaco, -a (*adj.*) 8
thine, tuyo, -a (*pos. adj.*) 17
thing, la cosa 10
to think, pensar (ie); to think of 9

(*to put one's attention on*), pensar en; to think of (*to have an opinion of*), pensar de 56; 64
think; I think so, creer; lo creo, creo que sí 23; I think (it seems to me), me parece 30
third, tercero, -a (*adj. or pro.*) 19
thirst, la sed 17
thirsty, to be thirsty, tener sed 17
this, este, -a (*demonstr. adj.*) 30
this, éste, -a (*demonstr. pro.*) 30
those, esos, -as; aquellos, -as 30 (*as pro., use accent*)
thought, el pensamiento 64
thou, tú (*pers. pro.*) 13
through, por (*prep.*) 4
to throw, tirar 68
thunder, el trueno 33
to thunder, tronar (ue) 35
Thursday, el jueves 34
thy, tu(s) (*pos. adj.*); (el) tuyo (*adj. or pro.*) 17
time (*as*, "What time is it?"), la hora 60
time (*in general*), el tiempo 35; on time, a tiempo 46; it is time for (to), es tiempo de (que) 43
time (*in series*) la vez 12; at times, a veces (*adv.*) 44; from time to time, de vez en cuando 68
to have a good time, holgarse (ue) 48
tinned, en lata (*adj.*) 41
to tire, aburrir 11
tired, cansado, -a (*with* estar) 15
tiring, cansado, -a (*with* ser) 14
to have as title, intitularse 54
to, a 5; (*after verb of motion, as conj.*, in order to) 50, 2(b)
today, hoy (*adv.*) 4
together, juntos, -as (*adj.*) 45
told, (he, she, it), dijo 3, 24
told, (they), dijeron 8, BB14
tomorrow, mañana (*adv.*) 11
tonight, esta noche (*adv.*) 46
too, demasiado (*adv. of degree*) 46
tooth, el diente 8
to touch, tocar 6
towards, hacia (*prep.*) 42

traitor, traidor, -a *(adj. or noun)* 33
tranquil, tranquilo, -a *(adj.)* 49
trap, la trampa 72
to travel, viajar 43
to traverse, recorrer 56
treacherous, traidor, -a *(adj.)* 33
treacherously, traidoramente *(adv.)* 57
Treasury Street, Calle de la Moneda 13
to treat, tratar 56
tree, el árbol 64
to tremble (with), temblar (ie) (de) 35
trip *(around a city)*, la carrera 38
trolley car, el tranvía *(word used in Spain)* 31; el carro *(word used in South America)*
true, verdadero, -a *(adj.)* 58
truly, verdaderamente *(adv.)* 58
truth, la verdad 6
to try to, tratar de 56
Tuesday, el martes 34
Turk, turco, -a *(adj. or noun)* 33
Turkish, turco, -a *(adj.)* 33
to turn, volver (ue); revolver (ue) 35
twenty, veinte *(numeral adj.)* 20
two, dos *(num. adj.)* 2

U

uncle, el tío 6
under, bajo *(prep.)* 24; debajo de
to understand, entender (ie) 35
to undress, desnudar; **to undress oneself,** desnudarse 49
unhappy, infeliz *(adj.)* 29
United States, (los) Estados Unidos 15
unless, a menos que *(conj.)* 53; no sea que *(conj.)* 53
unlucky, infeliz *(adj.)* 29
until, hasta que *(conj.)* 53
unusual, raro, -a *(adj.)* 41
us, nosotros, -as *(disj. pro.)* 42
to use, emplear 76; usar 34
to be used to *(plus verb)*, soler (ue) 76
useful, útil *(adj.)* 60

V

vacation, las vacaciones 43
value, el valor 33
to vary, variar 58
verb, el verbo 16
very, muy *(adv.)* 10; mismo, -a *(adj. after noun)* 24; -ísimo, -a *(adj. or adv. suffix)* 76; tan *(adv.)* 69; re-, te-, que-, *(prefixes, used alone or together)* 76
very little, poquísimo, -a *(adj. or adv.)* 76, A14
very near, cerquísima *(adv.)* 76
very sunny, it is very sunny, hay mucho sol 28; 60
view, la vista 63
village, la aldea 73
Viña del Mar, Viña del Mar, *(lit., Vineyard of the Sea, name of a beach near Valparaiso, in Chile)* 43
virtue, la virtud 6
to visit, visitar 42
voice, la voz 33
volume, el tomo 67

W

to wait for, esperar
waiter, el mozo 6
to wake up *(transitive)* despertar (ie); *(intransitive)* despertarse (ie) 49
to walk, marchar 54; pasearse 66
wall, la pared
to wander, errar (ye) 39
to want, desear 15
war, la guerra 1
to be very warm, tener mucho calor *(of persons)* 27; **it is warm** *(of weather)*, hace calor 60
to wash, lavar 16
watch, el reloj 12
way, el camino; **in no way,** de ninguna manera *(adv.)* 41
water, (la) agua; *(written and pronounced* el agua) 2; 58
we, nosotros, -as *(pers. pro.)* 13
to wear, usar 34

to weary, aburrir 11
weather, el tiempo 35
to weave, tejer 51
Wednesday, el miércoles 34
week, la semana 34
to weep, llorar 2; 27
weight, el peso 20
well, bien (*adv.*) 10, B7; 23
well, pues (*conj. adv.*) 48
well! ¡va! (*interjec.*) 73; ¡toma! 69
west, occidente; el oeste 1
what, cual (*rel. adj.*) 24
what, qué (*with inf.*); lo que (*with finite verb*) 56
what? ¿cuál? (*int. adj.*) ¿cuál? (*int. pro.*) ¿qué? 18; **What day of the month is it?** ¿A cuántos estamos del mes? 60
when, cuando (*rel. conj.*); luego que (*conj.*) 18; 53
when? ¿cuándo? (*int. conj.*) 18
where (*conj.*) donde, en donde 24
where? (*int. conj.*) ¿dónde? ¿en dónde? 21, B4
whether, si (*conj.*) 45
which, que (*rel. pro.*) 24
which? ¿qué? ¿cuál? (*int. adj. or pro.*) 18
while, el rato 74
while, mientras (*conj.*); mientras que (*conj.*) 64
white, blanco, -a 6
who, whom, que, quien (*rel. pro.*) 10; 24
who? whom? ¿qué?. ¿quién? (*int. pro.*) 18
who, el cual (*or* que) (*rel. pro.*) 25
whose, cuyo, -a (*pos. adj. or pro.*) 24
whose? ¿cúyo, -a? (*int. adj. or pro.*)
why? ¿por qué? 18
wide, ancho, -a (*adj.*) 41
wife, la esposa
William, Guillermo 69
window, la ventana 13
wind, el viento 28
windy; it is windy, hay viento 28
wine, el vino 17

winter, el invierno 60
to wish, querer (ie) 35; **I wish**, quisiera 44 (= I should like); **(they) wish**, quieren 3
with, con (*prep.*) 5; **with all one's might**, a más no poder 72
within, dentro de (*prep.*) 40
without, sin que (*conj.*) 53
why? ¿por qué? (*conj.*) 18
woe to you! ¡infeliz de usted! 29
woman, la mujer; **insignificant woman**, mujercilla 77
to be wont, soler (ue) 76
wood, la madera 70
word, la palabra 16
work, el trabajo 6
to work, trabajar 4
work day, día hábil 60; día útil 60
world, el mundo 54
worse, peor (*adj. or adv.*) 23
worth, el valor 33; **to be worth**, valer 66
it is worth seeing, es de ver 72
to wrestle, luchar 64
to write, escribir 11
writing desk, el escritorio 70
written, escrito (*irreg. past part. of* escribir) 16; 65

Y

year, el año 20
yellow, amarillo, -a (*adj.*) 41
yes, sí (*adv.*) 11; 30
yesterday, ayer (*adv.*) 11
yet, todavía (*adv.*) 34; aún 3
you, to you (thee), **yourself** (*reflex or pers. pro.*), te 21; 38; 48; ti (*disj. pro.*) 42; 48; tú (*pers. pro.*) 13
you, usted, Ud., Vd., V. (*subject or disj. pro.*) 13; 42
you, vosotros, -as (*int. pl., subject or disj. pro.*) 13; 42
to you, te (*int. pers. pro., sing.*), vosotros, -as (*pl.*); le (*formal pers. pro., sing.*), les (*pl.*); ti, vosotros, -as, Vd., Vds., (*disj.*) 38; 42; 48

young girl, joven 35
younger, menor (*adj.*) 23
young lady, la señorita 13
your, vuestro, -a (*pos. adj.*) 17;
 40; tu(s) (*pos. adj.*); su(s)
 (*pos. adj., polite*) 17
yours, suyo, -a (*pos. adj., polite*);
 el suyo (*pos. pro., polite*) 40;
 tuyo, -a (*pos. adj., int. form*); el
 tuyo (*pos. pro., int. form*) 40
youth (lad), el joven 35

Z

zero, el cero 67

SUBJECT INDEX

(Individual words are to be found in the Vocabulary or Table of Contents.)

Accentuation, III, 1-4; in interrogative words, XVIII, 4; in pronouns, XXX, 2; use of accent mark, LXXV, 1, 2.
Adjectives: gender, V, 2, 3; IX, 3; XXXIII, 1, 2; number, IX, 1, 2; position, VII, 2; XXXIII, 4, 6; comparison, XXIII. Descriptive, VII, 2; limiting, VII, 2. Demonstrative, XXX, 1; interrogative, XVIII; possessive, XVII; XL, 5; (def. art. for pos., XL, 6); prepositional, XXXVII; 5; relative, XXIV, 4.
Adverbs: Comparison, XXIII.
Agent, with the passive, XVI, 3.
Agreement: see Adjectives; Passive; Possessives.
Apocopation, XIX, 1-4; XXII, 6, 7.
Articles: uses of, LIX, LXI; def. art. for pos. adj., XL, 6.
Augmentatives, LXXVII, 1, 3.

Brackets, use of in exercises, p. 8, fn. 2.

Capitals, III, 6.
Cardinals: see Numerals.
Changes in Spelling: see Verbs.
Comparison, XXIII.
Conditions: in the indicative, XLV, 1(a); in the subjunctive, see Subjunctive.
Conjunctions: with indicative, L, 1; with infinitive, L, 2; with subjunctive, LIII, 2.
Conjunctive: see Pronouns.
Consonants: see Pronunciation.
Contraction: of articles with a or de, V, 3; of imperative with pronoun object, LXIII, 3; see also Apocopation.

Dates and Time, LX, 1, 2, 4, 5.
Demonstratives: see Adjectives; Pronouns.
Diminutives, LXXVII, 1, 2.
Diphthongs, II, 6; III, 4; LXI, 2, 3.
Disjunctive: see Pronouns.

Exclamations, LXIX.

Fractions: see Numerals—Ordinals.

Gender: see Adjectives; Nouns; Pronouns.

Idioms, XXVII, 5; XXVIII, 4; XXIX; LX, 6; LXIV, 4; Apps. B and H.
Imperative: forms, LIV, 2; LXII; for position of pronouns with, see Pronouns.
Indicative: see Conditions; Conjunctions; Tenses.
Infinitive: see Verbs.
Interjections, LXIX.
Interrogation: see Verbs.
Interrogatives: see Adjectives; Pronouns.
Intransitive verb, p. 28, fn. 1.

Mood: see Verbs.

Negation: see Verbs.
Neuter, XII, 3; XXXI, 3.
Nouns: gender, V, 1; VI; XXXIII, 1, 3; number, IX, 1, 2; XII, 1; XXXIV. Adjectives as nouns, XXII, 8. Abstract and generic, App. F.
Number: see Adjectives; Nouns, App. A.

SUBJECT INDEX

Numerals: Cardinals, XX; XXII; Ordinals, LXVII; App. G.

Object: direct, use of a with, XII, 2.
Omission: of indef. art. with predicate nominative, XIV, 3; with ciento or mil, XXII, 5; of y in numbers, XXII, 2.
Order, with ser and one predicate adjective, p. 10, fn. 1.
Ordinals: see Numerals.
Orthographic changes: see Verbs.

Parentheses, use of in exercises, p. 8, fn. 2.
Participles: present, XXXVII, 1, 2; LVII, 1; past, XVI, 1; cannot be followed by pro. obj., p. 143, A, 1.
Passive: see Verbs.
Person, App. A.
Personal pronouns: see Conjunctive; Disjunctive; Subject.
Plural: see Adjectives; Nouns; App. A.
Position: see Adjectives; Pronouns.
Possession, VII, 1.
Possessives: see Adjectives; Pronouns.
Prepositional: see Pronouns—disjunctive.
Pronouns: conjunctive, XXI; XXXVIII, 1-6; XLVIII, 1; demonstrative, XXX, 2; XXXI; disjunctive, XLII; XLVIII, 1; interrogative, XVIII; possessive, XL; reciprocal and reflexive, XLVIII; XLIX; relative, XXIV; XXV; subject, XIII. Position of personal pronouns, XXI, 2; XXXVIII; LVII, 4; with imperative, LXIII; cannot be used with past part., p. 143, A, 1; with ser, XXXVIII, 7.
Pronunciation: consonants, I; LXXIII; vowels, II; LXXI.
Punctuation, III, 5.

Radical-changing: see Verbs.

Reciprocal: see Verbs.
Reflexive: see Pronouns; Verbs.
Relatives: see Pronouns.
Repetition, of article or preposition, V, 4.

si or sí used to make statements emphatic, p. 111, fn. 1.
Singular: see Adjectives, Nouns; App. A.
Stress: see Accentuation.
Subjunctive: future, LXXVII, 4; past (imperfect), XLIV; present, XLIII; sequence of tenses, XLIII, 4; XLIV, 3, 4; in adjective clauses, LIV, 3; in adverbial clauses, LIII; in conditional sentences, XLV; with impersonal expressions, XLVI, 1, 2; in main clauses, LIV, 1; in noun clauses, LV; in wishes, LIV, 2. See also Apps. C and D. Radical-changing verbs, LII.
Superlative: see Comparison.
Syllabification: LXXV, 3.

Taking away, dative of, XLVII, 1.
Tenses (indicative): conditional, XXXII, 2, 3, 5; imperfect (past descriptive), XXVI; future, XXXII, 1, 3, 4; LXX; past anterior (secondary pluperfect), XLVII, 2; perfect tenses, XXVIII, 5; present, IV, 3; present (imperfect) for English perfect (pluperfect), LXIV, 1; preterite, VIII, 2, 3; progressive tenses, XXXVII, 3.
Time: see Dates.
Transitive verbs, p. 28, fn. 1.
Triphthongs, II, 6; LXI, 2, 4.

Verbs: first conjugation, IV; VIII; second conjugation, X; third conjugation, XI. Principal parts, LXVI, 1. Interrogation, V, 5; negation, VIII, 4, 5; XLI, 1-3. Omission of pro. subj., IV, 2. Infinitive: after conjunctions, L, 2; as noun, L, 3;

LVII, 2, 3; with prepositions, LVI, 1-3; for subjunctive, XLVI, 2. Imperative, see Imperative; participles, see Participles; passive voice, XVI, 1-4; (see also p. 28, fn. 1); reflexives and reciprocals, XLVIII; XLIX; subjunctive, see Subjunctive. Tenses, see Tenses. Changes in spelling (Orthographic changes), LI; LVIII; App. E; inceptives, LVIII, (b); LXV, 3. Irregular, see Table of Contents; List of Irregular Verbs. Radical-changing, XXXV; XXXVI; XXXIX; LII.

Voice, passive: see Verbs.

very much = **muy**, p. 17, fn. 1.

Vowels: see Pronunciation.

Weather, expressions of LX, 6.

www.ingramcontent.com/pod-product-compliance
Lightning Source LLC
Chambersburg PA
CBHW021358290426
44108CB00010B/289